I0198386

Racial Politics and Urban Planning

Racial Politics

and

Urban Planning

Gary, Indiana
1980-1989

ROBERT A. CATLIN

THE UNIVERSITY PRESS OF KENTUCKY

Copyright © 1993 by The University Press of Kentucky

Scholarly publisher for the Commonwealth,
serving Bellarmine College, Berea College, Centre
College of Kentucky, Eastern Kentucky University,
The Filson Club, Georgetown College, Kentucky
Historical Society, Kentucky State University,
Morehead State University, Murray State University,
Northern Kentucky University, Transylvania University,
University of Kentucky, University of Louisville,
and Western Kentucky University.

Editorial and Sales Offices: Lexington, Kentucky 40508-4008

Library of Congress Cataloging-in-Publication Data

Catlin, Robert A.
    Racial politics and urban planning: Gary, Indiana, 1980-1989 /
Robert A. Catlin.
        p.   cm.
    Includes bibliographical references and index.
    ISBN 0-8131-1798-4 (alk. paper) :
    1. City planning—Indiana—Gary.   2. Gary (Ind.)—Politics and
government.   3. Gary (Ind.)—Race relations.   4. Hatcher, Richard
G., 1933-   . I. Title.
HT168.G37C38   1993
307.1'216'0977299—dc20   92-43016

Contents

Figures and Tables

Figures

Tables

Acknowledgments

Several individuals made significant contributions to this work. Dr. Donald Price, director of the University of Florida Division of Sponsored Research, provided seed money to help prepare the manuscript. The anonymous reviewers were most helpful with their comments. Dr. Joe Feagin made several helpful comments concerning Chapter 6. Taghi Arsharmi and Arlene Colvin of the Bureau of City Planning provided necessary statistical data as well as personal insights. Juanita Pelham and Joan Hartley assisted with manuscript typing.

But the people that I wish to give the greatest amount of credit to are my wife, Ethel, and daughters, Janell and Michelle. Their endless support and patience kept me going when I felt that no one would accept this book. These three individuals embody the "family values" that so many political operatives talk about today but so few practice.

Introduction

On June 22, 1982, I traveled to Gary, Indiana, to interview for the position of chairman of the Department of Minority Studies at Indiana University's branch campus located there. Gary had a population of 150,000, a majority-black population, and since 1967 was headed by Richard Gordon Hatcher, one of the first black mayors of a large U.S. city. My childhood impressions of Gary were developed when I grew up on Chicago's South Side. During the 1950s and early 1960s, my family and I would drive through that city on the Indiana Toll Road on our way to visit relatives in South Bend and Ft. Wayne, and all that I could remember about Gary was the billowing smoke and dust from the U.S. Steel Company's mills and a grimly, depressing downtown. As my plane flew over Chicago's downtown and sparkling lakefront on its approach to O'Hare Airport, I asked myself if I really wanted to leave the warm, sunny Tampa Bay area and the University of South Florida for an old Rust Belt town like Gary. Quickly, I assured myself that no matter how bad Gary might be, there was always the excitement of Chicago, just one hour away by either expressway or the Chicago, South Shore, and South Bend electric commuter railroad.

I was met at the airport by Dr. F.C. Richardson, dean of Indiana University Northwest (as the Gary branch was called) Division of Arts and Sciences, which housed minority studies. Dr. Richardson—who in 1989 would become the first African-American president of the State University of New York, College at Buffalo—told me about the positives and negatives of Gary during our two-hour ride to the campus. Most of the negatives were known already to most social scientists like myself who were concerned with the urban condition: the decline of the steel industry and the loss in the northwest Indiana region, from 70,000 steel industry jobs in 1979 to only 40,000 in 1982; an old decaying physical plant and infrastructure; an "individualistic"[1] political culture that historically focused on the personal gain of politicians at the public's expense; white flight from the central city to the suburbs; and recently, the drastic cuts in federal aid programs that during the 1960s and 1970s had propped up cities like Gary.

Dr. Richardson told me, with a great deal of pain and sorrow, about the bitter resistance by Gary's white ethnics (eastern and southern European ancestry) and business leaders to Hatcher's 1967 mayoral campaign and later to his administration, even at the expense of their own self-interests. He told of the flight of business from downtown Gary to the suburbs—a direct contrast with the practice of businesses and institutions in other cities that experienced a transition from white to black political leadership between 1967 and 1980, such as Newark, Atlanta, and Detroit—and petty acts such as the name changes of adjacent East Gary to Lake Station, of the region's leading newspaper from the *Gary Post-Tribune* to just the *Post-Tribune,* and of Gary National Bank (the region's largest) to Gainer Bank. However, the most mean-spirited and, from a traffic-safety perspective, perhaps the most dangerous act was the refusal of the Indiana Department of Highways to post Gary directional signs on the interstate highways leading to that city, something I could not help but notice as we turned off I-94 and headed toward the campus along Broadway, Gary's main street.

But Dr. Richardson revealed lots of positives about Gary as well. He noted that, although the city was unattractive when viewed from the major thoroughfares, most residential neighborhoods contained neat, well-maintained single-family homes, with the majority being owner-occupied. Because of white flight and the declining economy, housing was cheap; in 1982, a single-family detached dwelling with basement and fenced rear yard cost from $30,000 to $50,000, compared to a range of $60,000 to $80,000 for comparable shelter in Chicago or its suburbs, and one could find housing right on the Lake Michigan beach for only $100,000. The proximity to Chicago meant that Gary residents could travel there not only for recreational, cultural, and entertainment opportunities but to jobs as well. And most important, because of Mayor Hatcher, opportunities were plentiful for blacks with qualifications.

Dr. Richardson's positive notions about Gary were confirmed as we drove around the city. Although there were some deteriorated neighborhoods in the central core, and the commercial strips were ugly and run-down beyond belief, most residential areas were indeed clean and well-maintained, with obvious evidences of care. Lawns were mowed, houses and fences were being painted, and generally, Gary's residential areas appeared to be just like any other typical midwestern suburb in early June engaged in the clean-up/paint-up/fix-up euphoria of late spring. The people, virtually all of whom were black, moved about in a brisk, confident manner in contrast with the sullen, submissive, and defeated blacks in

Tampa and most other southern U.S. cities. I met leaders in city government, including Gail Harris, the planning director who was a young black
woman as well trained and knowledgeable as any other planning director of
a midsize city that I had encountered in my twenty years of professional
experience in that discipline. Slowly but surely, I came to feel not only that
Gary was relatively attractive from an environmental point of view but that
the stereotypes of black-run cities—depressed, dying, lacking in leadership—might prove incorrect when held up to the light of reality.

My interview was successful, and in August of 1982 I moved to Gary to
begin work there. Between 1982 and 1987, I served as an adviser and
consultant to the Hatcher administration, supervising preparation of the
city's revised Comprehensive Plan, the Parks and Recreation Plan, and
specific proposals such as the Fire Station Development Program and the
Year 2000 Airport Development Plan. I served as a member of the Gary
Chamber of Commerce, chaired the Airport Promotion and Development
Commission, and served on the board of directors of Gary Neighborhood
Services. This experience provided me with a valuable firsthand look at the
inner workings of Gary's city government, especially its relationships with
adjacent local governments, state and federal agencies, and the private
sector. During my five years there, I kept notes about these experiences,
knowing that one day I might write an account of my days in Gary.

During the 1980s, a new urban literature emerged that discussed issues
such as the national shift from an industrial to a service economy, the
impacts of Reaganomics on cities and suburbs, and the gradual, continued
deterioration of the central city core. Carl Abbott tested the generalization
that a technical role for planners limits their influence on key land-use
decisions. Abbott noted that by making linkages with elected officials and
influential private-sector participants, Portland, Oregon's planners were
able to break the shackles of technology and play major roles in the
development and implementation of public policy as related to planning
issues.[2]

In his study, *City, State and Market: The Political Economy of Urban
Society,* Michael Peter Smith discussed the shift from an industrial to a
service economy, the flight of capital and jobs from the U.S. to Third World
nations, the impact of "Reaganomics" on central cities, the decline of trade
unionism, and the ineffectiveness of enterprise zones. Smith concluded that
during the late 1980s, grass-roots movements of both lower- and middle-
class residents began to oppose extending business tax breaks that impoverished already strained local services. He felt that this new grass-roots
political mobilization in Sun Belt cities was an encouraging sign that the
popular restructuring of state, capital, labor, and communities might yet
produce new forms of popular resistance to the elite restructuring that
occurred during the 1980s.[3]

H.V. Savitch's analysis of New York City, Paris, and London covered
the period from 1960 to 1980 and discussed each city's transformation from
an economy based on industry to one based on services and information. He
noted that all three are world cities and perhaps have more in common with
other world cities and each other than with smaller cities in their own
nations.[4] In *City Limits,* Paul Peterson stated that cities are similar to
business firms in that both seek to maximize the economic return on the
resources they control. In the case of cities, these resources consist mostly
of land-use controls, and in making decisions about land use, cities are
handicapped by the need to compete economically. Being competitors in a
market economy, cities are driven to make development policies that will
best enhance their economic position. He called for three drastic reforms on
the part of the federal government to counter the market economy thrusts of
cities: (1) the full faith and credit of the federal government should stand
behind all state and local government indebtedness, (2) the federal government should institute a revenue-sharing plan that would attempt to equalize
per capita fiscal resources available to each state and local government, and
(3) minimum standards of service provision should replace existing grant-
in-aid programs requirements. Written in 1981, Peterson's recommendations, controversial then, are all but irrelevant by 1991 as our nation faces a
$300 billion annual budget deficit.[5]

John H. Mollenkopf in *The Contested City* discarded the notion of
markets operating in a neutral manner and instead suggested that, because
of coalition-building among business leaders, local politicians, and members of Congress, national policy relating to taxes, capital expenditures, and
other forms of direct subsidy, have tilted the market process toward suburbs
at the expense of central cities and toward the Sun Belt at the expense of the
Frost Belt.[6] Clarence N. Stone and Heywood T. Sanders's *The Politics of
Urban Development* consists of articles that look at the interaction between
private elites who control investment capital and public elected officials
who control public authority. Stone and Sanders felt that the two sets of
participants must eventually reach an accommodation and that the only real
difference is in how the accommodation is reached.[7]

In *The Politics of Urban Planning,*[8] William C. Johnson discussed the
interplay between the discipline of urban planning (one that is concerned
with the design and function of built environments) and the discipline of
political science. Because of shifts in federal public policy that deprived
urban areas of resources needed for rebuilding the cities and because of the
actions of business elites who favored downtown and suburban development at the expense of central-city neighborhoods, Johnson felt that planners must reexamine their values and build coalition with elected officials,
business leaders, and neighborhood groups in order to maximize planning
effectiveness.

Also, during the early and mid-1980s, urban planning academics published several books indicating how central cities were coping with problems of decay that were exacerbated by the Reagan administration's budget cuts. George Sternlieb in *Patterns of Development*[9] discussed New York City's rebound because of its prominence in service industries in contrast with Houston's decline because of the glut in oil prices. Susan Fainstein's *Restructuring the City*[10] focused on problems and opportunities in New Haven, Detroit, New Orleans, Denver, and San Francisco, offering suggestions for improvements ranging from public-private partnerships to improved representation of working-class peoples. In *Bum Rap on America's Cities*,[11] Richard S. Morris blamed federal policy for not only deemphasizing domestic issues but favoring Sun Belt states at the expense of the Frost Belt. Paul R. Porter and David C. Sweet in *Rebuilding America's Cities: Roads to Recovery*[12] stressed the need to emphasize public-private partnerships and local innovation to make up for loss of federal dollars. And in *Urban Decline and the Future of American Cities,*[13] Katherine C. Bradbury, Anthony Downs, and Kenneth A. Small recommended that federal and state decision-makers remove policy biases against big cities and against the Frost Belt and better understand the regional impacts of policy decisions made for large and midsize cities. In other words, these authors were saying that a negative policy recommendation against a city such as Detroit might hurt the residents of southeast Michigan and northwest Ohio more than Detroiters.

During and after my stay in Gary I read this literature, and in every instance my reaction was "This does not apply to Gary." First of all, except for Mollenkopf, the works mentioned here and others too numerous to mention had a common thread: *that public and private elites will reach an accommodation based on mutual interest.* In Gary, I found instead that petty jealousies, ignorance, and thinly veiled racism, not mutual interest or common sense, were the basis for private-public decision-making. Second, the urban literature of the 1980s dealt mainly with large cities. Abbott's work was a case study of Portland, Oregon. Savitch discussed New York, Paris, and London. Peterson used a case study of New York to make his points. Sternlieb focused on New York and Houston. Fainstein et al. concentrated on Detroit, New Orleans, Denver, and San Francisco, and although New Haven was included in both her work and that of Stone and Sanders, New Haven lies in the shadow of Yale and is certainly no Gary. The closest the literature came to dealing with the type of dynamics I experienced in Gary was Richard Child Hill's "Crisis in the Motor City."[14] and later Joe Darden, June M. and Richard Thomas, and Hill's *Race and Uneven Development,*[15] works that detailed the impact of white racism on land-use and economic development decision-making. However, even Detroit, with its size and scale and the presence of the "Big Three" automakers, cannot be compared with Gary.

As I looked back at my Gary experience it became more and more apparent that this book must be written. By 1990, although the urban affairs literature dealt considerably with black-run cities, the major focus was on mayoral politics written from the perspective of outside academicians working with secondary data.[16] Few works focused on the entity of city government itself, especially the interrelationships with external forces. The few works that were prepared by insiders, such as William Lucy's in 1988,[17] tended to portray mayors as individuals concerned mainly with short-term political ends. This certainly was not my experience with Richard Hatcher or his successor Thomas V. Barnes in Gary.

In 1990, "60 Minutes," "Nightline," and the national print media featured the near bankruptcy of East St. Louis, Illinois, and the trial of Washington, D.C., Mayor Marion Barry on drug possession charges. In both cases the entire picture was not presented: empirical evidence such as white flight, including abandonment by business and industry, along with neglect on the part of county and state government, was not presented in the East St. Louis case with the same intensity as the inference and innuendo of black incompetence. In Marion Barry's case, the sensationalism of adulterous sex and drugs overshadowed the clear evidence of entrapment on the part of the U.S. Prosecutor's Office, which had been investigating Barry for years in an attempt to remove from office this militant former antipoverty program administrator and 1960s civil rights activist.[18] On the other hand, when Bridgeport, Connecticut, a white-led city of 140,000 with a black minority filed for bankruptcy in June 1991, no mention of incompetence on *that* government's part was made by the national print and electronic media. By the close of 1991, I felt that my story about Gary had to be told in order to present a firsthand, truthful perspective of the problems and difficulties faced by black-controlled city administrations imbedded in a hostile white-dominated environment where black leaders must compete at a disadvantage for increasingly scarce resources.

A limitation of case studies in urban policy literature is that too often they only apply to the jurisdiction studied. However, even though there are some factors present that applied—at least in 1980—only to Gary, the phenomena of the majority-black/black-governed city is one that grows with every passing day. In 1970, only seven U.S. cities with populations of 50,000 or more were majority black, but in 1980, this figure grew to 15 and by 1990, 25 cities were in that category. As more and more U.S. cities become majority black in the years ahead, situations unique to Gary will find themselves repeated elsewhere. Therefore, an accounting of the Gary experience in the 1980s will add to the body of knowledge of majority-black cities and, more important, be transferred to other urban centers so that public policy mistakes made in Gary and northwest Indiana may be avoided elsewhere.

This work attempts to shed some light on three myths concerning majority-black cities: (1) that blacks are incompetent in urban governance, (2) that political empowerment is not directly transferable to economic empowerment, and (3) that leaders in the white governmental, business, and institutional communities, being relatively well-educated, will be "fair" once black-run governments display a measure of competence and commitment. My experience in Gary was that, instead, (1) black administrators were, if anything, more competent than their white counterparts, (2) political empowerment not only resulted in gains in the areas of municipal employment and contracts, as shown by Peter Eisenger,[19] but there was some transfer to economic empowerment in terms of entrepreneur gain in the private sector as well, and (3) especially in an environment of scarcity and retrenchment, white leaders were all too quick to resort to blatant racism[20] (however subtly disguised) in order to protect what they perceived to be a short-term advantage even at the expense of real long-term gains (see the Gary Airport Case in this book).

This book is written in a participant-observer style, similar to that of Allan Jacobs's *Making City Planning Work* (Planners Press, 1979). It begins with a brief chapter on the phenomena of majority-black/black-governed cities. Following this is a chapter on Gary's history: the evolution from a "new town" founded by the U.S. Steel Company in 1903 through its period of relative economic success from 1920 through 1960 and eventually its economic decline by 1982.

After a brief chapter detailing some constraints unique to Gary in the 1980s but becoming more commonplace as the number of "Garys" grows during the years to come, Chapter 4 recounts my first impressions of Gary after moving there. Chapters 5, and 6, and 7 focus on detailed case studies involving long-range comprehensive planning, an attempt at governmental consolidation, and development of the city's airport. The book closes with a relatively brief chapter on a comparison of the administrations of Richard Hatcher and Thomas V. Barnes and also discusses prospects for Gary and similar cities in the twenty-first century.

Though I hope academicians will read and review this book, it isn't written for that group alone. This work is prepared for a much broader audience, including public administrators and urban planners, who more and more in the years to come will find themselves working in or with cities like Gary. This book is really written for a broad spectrum of citizens who wish to obtain a perspective on one aspect of the urban condition in addition to the views offered by the popular electronic and print media. For when all is said and done, while the academic community should review this work, it is much more important for the broad spectrum of citizens—black and white, U.S. and foreign nationals, liberals, conservatives, and moderates—to have an inside view of the rapidly evolving phenomena of majority-black cities.

1

The Emergence of the
Majority-Black/Black-Run City

Since the passage of the U.S. Voting Rights Act of 1965, African-Americans have made tremendous progress not only in registering to vote and doing so but in electing black officials as well. In 1965, there were fewer than 400 black elected officials, including 256 at the municipal level and only 41 mayors, all presiding over small all-black communities, the largest being Mound Bayou, Mississippi, with a population of only 4,000. Not only were these cities located in the Deep South or border states, all of which were then openly hostile to the notion of racial equality, but in the early 1960s, the federal government was lukewarm toward civil rights, and the urban federal aid programs of the War on Poverty, Model Cities, and related efforts were just beginning to crystallize. Needless to say, those 41 black mayors, while obviously excellent role models for younger citizens, were without any real power, patronage, and effectiveness as change agents.

Every year after 1965, the number of black elected officals increased, and by 1989 the total was 7,226, including 3,595 at the municipal level. There were 323 mayors (the highest total ever), 31 of whom presided over cities of 50,000 people or more.[1] In 1990, three of America's five largest cities (1990 U.S. Census)—New York City, Philadelphia, and Los Angeles—were headed by black mayors. And, of course, Chicago had two black mayors, Harold Washington, elected in 1983 and reelected in 1987, and Eugene Sawyer, voted into office by the Chicago City Council after Washington's untimely death in November 1987. Unlike the black mayors of small southern towns in the early 1960s, these mayors have strong media presence, control budgets of up to billions of dollars each year, have the power to control at least some hiring and the awarding of contracts,[2] and, at least until the early 1980s, had considerable federal funding to make visible improvements in their cities.

Much has been documented about these black mayors individually and collectively in both the academic literature referred to earlier in the introduction to this book and the popular media, including television, radio, newspapers, magazines, and even videos.[3] However, both the academic and the journalistic communities tend to place all black mayors in one box, giving each the same amount of responsibility, vested authority, and control. In reality, the picture is much different. Responsibility, authority, and control are variables that depend on three independent factors: (1) the percentage of blacks, as well as black registered voters, in the city's total population, (2) the type of municipal government, and (3) external factors such as relationships with the local business and institutional community, state government, federal government, and, in some instances, even international entities. The first two can be described briefly on a national basis in this chapter. The third variable is one that fluctuates widely from city to city and is treated for Gary in Chapters 4, 5, 6, and 7.

The Percentage of Blacks

Regardless of population characteristics, municipal government type, political culture, or external factors, a mayor is always portrayed as the city's leader, its general, its CEO, its boss. The buck stops at the mayor's office. It is the mayor who presides over the city council, cuts ribbons for the opening of new buildings and other capital improvements, and ultimately signs off on city ordinances, proclamations, and comprehensive plans. Given the historic subordination of black citizens in the United States through the mid-1960s, the arrival of black mayors such as Carl Stokes in Cleveland and Richard Hatcher in Gary, both in late 1967, was hailed by liberals nationally and internationally as a sign of the new times. No longer would black citizens have to approach white locally elected officials hat in hand begging for equity, for now they had leaders who were the same color as themselves and who could understand their problems. Academics like Sherrie Arnstein noted that instead of debating appropriate levels of citizen power, blacks could now talk about citizen control.[4] Black parents could point to the new black mayor and tell their young children, "Look, if you work hard enough, anything is possible. You too can rise to the top."

More than twenty years have passed since the emergence of the first black mayors. Initial reviews by scholars are in, and they are largely mixed.[5] The euphoria of the late 1960s and early 1970s has been replaced by sober analysis that indicates that, among other things, a black mayor is limited by the percentage of blacks in the electorate as to how responsive he can be (even symbolically) to the needs of the black community. Bryan Jackson points out that Tom Bradley in Los Angeles was ineffective in curbing police abuses of black citizens and dealing effectively with youth gang violence in that city mainly because, with blacks constituting only 17 percent of the population (a percentage that is slowly decreasing because of more rapid in-migration of Hispanics and Asians), he must govern with a fragile coalition of blacks, white liberals (primarily Jews), and, most important, the white business community, which insists on "stability," including a strong independent police force. In 1991, it was this independent police force that was responsible for the beating of Rodney King, and Mayor Bradley was unable to fire police chief Darryl Gates. Jackson also indicates that Bradley was not effective in raising the percentage of city dollars to blacks in the form of contracts and vendor services or the hiring of professional employees, except for a few token blacks in visible positions.[6] On the other hand, cities with black majorities, including Atlanta, Detroit, and Newark, all had the experience of seeing a new black mayor immediately subordinating their city's law enforcement agencies and, in doing so, making police brutality, which was a prime issue in the 1960s, virtually a thing of the past.[7] Also, as Huey Perry points out, black mayors operating in cities with black majorities have been able to increase black employment and the percentage of contracts awarded to blacks.[8]

One might postulate that given the unfortunate history of racial divisiveness in the United States, it stands to reason that a black mayor may best represent the hopes, dreams, and aspirations of black citizens if the city's population is majority black, thus producing an electorate that is majority or almost majority black. The more cities that are majority black and elect black mayors (almost all eventually do), the more black mayors are able to articulate a policy of equity for black citizens. This is not to put forth the argument of zero sum game, i.e., equity for black citizens means an unfair loss for whites. Even given a black majority, white citizens, including those in Gary, Indiana, can still rely on the influence of the white business and institutional leadership in the city and the region; county, state, and federal governmental limitations on mayoral powers; and, in the final analysis, deference on the part of many blacks as a result of 250 years of slavery and 100 years of legally enforced segregation.

Since the end of World War II, black in-migration to central cities coupled with white flight to the suburbs has produced, first, increasing percentages of black minorities and, finally, black majorities. The first large majority-black city was Washington, D.C., in 1960. In 1970, six additional cities with populations of 50,000 or more followed suit: Newark; Atlanta; East St. Louis; East Orange, New Jersey; Compton, California; and Gary. In 1980, there were eight more large cities with black majorities: Baltimore; New Orleans; Birmingham; Richmond, Virginia; Inglewood, California; Camden, New Jersey; Wilmington, Delaware; and Detroit (see

Table 1. Majority-Black Cities with Populations of 50,000 or More by 1980
(Ranked by Total 1990 Population Size)

City	1990			1980			1970		
	Total Population	Black Population	% Black	Total Population	Black Population	% Black	Total Population	Black Population	% Black
1. Detroit	1,027,974	777,916	75.7	1,203,339	758,939	63.1	1,511,482	660,428	43.7
2. Baltimore	736,014	435,768	59.2	786,775	431,151	54.8	905,759	420,210	46.4
3. Washington, D.C.	606,900	399,604	65.8	638,333	448,906	70.3	736,510	537,712	73.0
4. New Orleans	496,308	307,728	62.0	557,515	308,149	55.3	593,471	267,308	45.0
5. Atlanta, Ga.	394,017	264,262	67.1	425,022	282,911	66.6	496,973	255,051	51.3
6. Newark, N.J.	275,221	160,885	58.5	329,248	191,745	58.2	382,417	207,458	54.3
7. Birmingham, Ala.	265,968	168,277	63.3	284,413	158,224	55.6	300,910	126,388	42.0
8. Richmond, Va.	203,056	112,122	55.2	219,214	112,357	51.3	249,621	104,766	42.0
9. Gary, Ind.	116,646	93,982	80.6	151,953	107,644	70.8	175,415	92,695	52.8
10. Inglewood, Calif.	109,602	56,861	51.9	94,245	54,010	57.3	89,985	10,066	11.2
11. Compton, Calif.	90,454	49,598	54.8	81,285	60,812	74.8	78,611	55,781	71.0
12. Camden, N.J.	87,492	49,362	56.4	84,910	45,008	53.0	102,551	40,132	39.1
13. East Orange, N.J.	73,552	66,157	90.0	77,690	64,626	83.2	75,471	40,099	53.1
14. Wilmington, Del.	71,529	37,446	52.4	70,195	35,858	51.1	80,386	35,072	43.6
15. East St. Louis, Ill.	40,944	40,167	98.1	55,200	52,751	95.6	69,996	48,368	69.1

Source: U.S. Census, 1970, 1980, and 1990.

Table 2. New Majority-Black Cities with Populations of 50,000 or More in 1990
(Ranked by Total Population Size)

	1990			1980		
City	Total Population	Black Population	% Black	Total Population	Black Population	% Black
1. Memphis, Tenn.	610,337	334,737	54.8	646,356	307,402	47.6
2. Jackson, Miss.	196,637	109,620	55.7	202,895	95,357	47.0
3. Savannah, Ga.	137,560	70,580	51.3	141,390	69,241	49.0
4. Macon, Ga.	106,612	55,645	52.2	116,896	52,068	44.5
5. Albany, Ga.	78,122	42,962	55.0	74,059	35,297	47.7
6. Mt. Vernon, N.Y.	67,153	37,138	55.3	66,713	32,297	48.4
7. Irvington TWP, N.J.	61,018	42,760	70.1	61,493	23,397	38.1
8. Pine Bluff, Ark.	57,140	30,583	53.5	56,636	27,766	49.0
9. Monroe, La.	54,909	30,504	55.6	57,597	27,968	48.6
10. Harrisburg, Pa.	52,376	26,502	50.6	53,264	23,215	43.6

Source: Preliminary 1990 U.S. Census PL 1417 Counts.

Note: These cities were not majority-black in 1980.

table 1). The 1990 U.S. Census shows ten additional cities with 50,000 or more residents that are majority black, led by Memphis and Jackson, Mississippi, for a total of 25 majority-black U.S. cities (see table 2). Also, it is important to note that in 1970 there were 152 places with populations of 2,500 or more that had a black majority. In 1980, that figure had increased to 254 places, and by 1990, 275 in this category were majority black. Among places with populations between 1,000 and 2,500, 81 were majority black in 1970, 151 in 1980, and 187 in 1990.

Of the fifteen large cities with black majorities in 1980, all except Wilmington, Delaware, had elected black mayors by 1990. In all except Wilmington, there were majority-black city councils as well. We can then say that with a majority-black population soon comes a black mayoral presence and, eventually, a majority-black city council, therefore creating black governance.

Black governance is by no means monolithic. In addition to the reality that in the United States, citizens are but a creation of the states and derive only those powers awarded to them by benevolent (or not so benevolent) state governments, other factors must be considered in weighing the effectiveness of black mayors. These include but certainly are not limited to type of government and "externalities." Certainly, black mayors in cities *without* the benefit of a majority-black populations and electorates will be impacted more by these factors.

Types of Municipal Governments

Students of municipal government will recall that three types of governmental structures predominate: (1) weak mayor, (2) strong mayor, and
(3) council manager. A fourth type known as the commission[9] was popular
at one time; it, like the strong mayor and council manager, was a product of
the reform-minded Progressive Era of 1900-1915. However, since the end of
World War II, it lost ground and was replaced by either the council manager
or strong mayor form in hundreds of incorporated municipalities, the most
prominent being Memphis, Birmingham, and St. Paul, Minnesota. By
1983, this form of government was present in only 5 percent of all incorporated municipalities in the nation. The council manager was most popular
with 38 percent, while the weak mayor had 33 percent and the strong mayor
only 24 percent.[10]

The weak mayor form of government was the original format for
incorporated municipalities and was the type seen almost exclusively in the
nineteenth century. Fearful of a strong centralized government, nineteenth-
century leaders developed a form that vested power mainly in the city
council, the members of which in most cases were salaried and took this
responsibility on a full-time basis, and in a wide variety of quasi independent boards and commissions. Often, the mayor could not succeed himself
in office, and terms were limited to as little as two years. While the mayor
had executive powers, whatever little professional staff expertise that was
available was retained by the city council. The resulting power vacuum was
filled by political machines and by the use of patronage. These political
machines actually controlled not only the mayor and city council but also
municipal hiring and the awarding of contracts. Totally unaccountable to
the electorate, the political machines, as embodied by "Boss Tweed" of the
infamous Tammany Hall organization in New York City and Frank Hague
in Jersey City, were rife with graft and corruption. Present examples of the
weak mayor form of governance are Chicago, Los Angeles, San Francisco,
Cleveland, and Boston.

The strong mayor form of government came about as a result of the
early twentieth-century Progressive Movement, which was mostly middle-
class and WASP in nature. The Progressives had an announced agenda of
"cleaning up" government by eliminating graft and corruption. Some political scientists now claim that actually the Progressives had a hidden agenda;
to wrest political power from white ethnic immigrants and their descendants
who were converted and enlisted by the political machines.[11] Power was
vested in a mayor who, unlike his predecessors, controlled virtually all staff
expertise and did not have independent boards and commissions to dilute
his power. If these entities were present they were advisory only.

The city council was made up of part-time, largely unpaid servants who
took the job out of a sense of civic responsibility, or as a stepping stone to

higher office. These councils had no staff capacity and could only override a mayoral veto with either a two-thirds majority or a greater than majority vote. Coupled with "at large" elections for the city council, accountability was centered upon the mayor, and both he *and* the city council members had to appeal to a citywide electorate. Therefore, newspaper endorsements and advertising were extremely important. Large campaign war chests were needed to ensure victory, and only the city's business and professional class leadership had resources sufficient enough to make these types of contributions. Examples of the strong mayor form of government are New York City, Tampa, and Gary. In Gary, of the nine city council members, six are elected by district and three are elected at large. All nine members of the Gary City Council are employed in full-time jobs outside city government. In 1982, seven of the nine were black and two were white. By 1990, eight council members were black and one was Hispanic.

The council manager form of government is the most popular nationwide, especially in small and medium-sized cities with populations under 50,000. However, it is found in cities as large as San Diego, California. Like the strong mayor form, the council manager model was a creation of the Progressive Movement. The attempt was to "professionalize" government with the innovation of the city manager. The city council, elected at large, enters into a contract with a professional manager who runs the day-to-day operations of the city. All city staff report to the manager. Staffs are hired on the basis of a merit system, and political patronage is extremely limited. In this model, the mayor is simply the presiding officer of the city council and at best is no more than a first among equals. In many cities the mayor's position simply rotates annually or biannually among members of the city council.

In the weak mayor system of governance, a mayor must have complete support of a majority of the city council in order to govern effectively. Harold Washington, Chicago's late mayor, won the 1983 general election with 52 percent of the vote and took office only to find that among the 50 aldermen who formed Chicago's city council, he had only 21 supporters—17 blacks and 4 whites. Alderman Edward Vrdolyak, leader of the remnants of the old Daley machine, controlled a bloc of 29 aldermen—28 whites ethnics and 1 Puerto Rican. For three years, the "Vrdolyak 29," as characterized by the local media, successfully blocked Washington's choices for appointments to the many quasi-independent boards and commissions, quashed his legislative agenda, interfered with his overtures to the state legislature for funding, and then delivered a volley of shots in the local media, calling Washington and his allies incompetent, dishonest, and foolish. Only after a court-ordered redistricting of ward boundaries and a subsequent special election in 1986 did Washington gain enough council votes to develop a working majority. In the special election of 1986, 2

Table 3. Black Mayors of Cities with Populations Over 50,000 in 1985
(Ranked by Total 1980 Population)

City	Mayor	Total 1980 Population	% Black	Government Type	Black-Majority City Council
1. Chicago	H. Washington	3,000,000	40.0	weak mayor	no
2. Los Angeles	T. Bradley	2,996,763	17.0	weak mayor	no
3. Philadelphia	W. Goode	1,588,220	40.2	weak mayor	no
4. Detroit	C. Young	1,203,339	63.1	strong mayor	yes
5. Washington, D.C.	M. Barry	638,333	70.3	strong mayor	yes
6. New Orleans	E. Morial	557,515	55.3	strong mayor	no
7. Atlanta	A. Young	425,022	66.6	strong mayor	yes
8. Oakland, Calif.	L. Wilson	339,288	46.9	weak mayor	no
9. Newark, N.J.	K. Gibson	329,248	58.2	strong mayor	yes
10. Charlotte, N.C.	H. Gantt	314,447	31.0	strong mayor	no
11. Birmingham, Ala.	R. Arrington	284,413	55.6	strong mayor	no
12. Richmond, Va.	R. West	219,214	51.3	weak mayor	yes
13. Spokane, Wash.	J. Chase	171,300	1.6	council manager	no
14. Flint, Mich.	J. Sharp, Jr.	159,611	41.4	strong mayor	yes
15. Gary, Ind.	**R. Hatcher**	**151,953**	**70.8**	**strong mayor**	**yes**
16. Hartford, Conn.	T. Milner	136,392	33.9	weak mayor	no
17. Pasadena, Calif.	L. Glickman	119,374	20.6	council manager	no
18. Berkeley, Calif.	G. Newport	103,328	20.1	council manager	no
19. Roanoke, Va.	N. Taylor	100,247	22.0	council manager	no
20. Camden, N.J.	M. Primas	84,910	53.0	weak mayor	yes
21. Compton, Calif.	W. Tucker	81,826	74.8	council manager	yes
22. Carson, Calif.	T. Mills	81,221	29.3	council manager	no
23. East Orange, N.J.	T. Cooke, Jr.	77,690	83.2	weak mayor	yes
24. Pontiac, Mich.	W. Holland	76,715	37.2	council manager	no
25. Evanston, Ill.	A. Winfield	73,706	21.4	council manager	no
26. West Palm Beach, Fla.	E. Mack	62,530	28.2	council manager	no
27. East St. Louis, Ill.	C. Officer	55,200	95.6	strong mayor	yes

Source: 1980 U.S. Census.

blacks, 1 Puerto Rican, and 1 Mexican-American, all allies of Washington, replaced Vrdolyak's cronies, giving the two opposing forces 25 votes each.

Now Washington was able to break the tie. Washington's appointments to boards and commissions were seated, his city budget sailed through the city council, and finally Chicago was able to speak with one voice to the state legislature and the governor's office. Buoyed by these victories, Washington was a relatively easy winner in both the Democratic party primary and general election of 1987.[12]

Black (and white) mayors have essentially only the power of persuasion in the council manager form of government. Even if they are able to be elected mayor in their own right, not subject to a one- or two-year rotation, the only means of formulating an effective agenda is to develop linkages and eventually coalitions with a majority of fellow council members. This is difficult enough for a white mayor in this system but virtually impossible for one who happens to be black, according to Eva Mack and James Poole, both of whom served as mayor/council members in West Palm Beach during the 1980s.[13]

The strong mayor form offers the most promising opportunity for a black or a white mayor to influence public policy. With direct control over city staff, boards, and commissions and with little real resistance from a part-time city council that can be controlled by the mayor with the approval of only one-third plus one minority of that group, the mayor is not only powerful but also accountable in full. He cannot blame lack of council support or control over city staff for failings and mistakes.

Table 3 shows the 27 black mayors of cities with populations of over 50,000 in 1985 (the midpoint of my time in Gary). Of that number, 11 governed majority-black cities. Of the 27 cities, 10 had a weak mayor form of government, 8 had the strong mayor form, and 9 were of the council manager type.

It would seem that in Gary the mayor has the optimum setting for influencing and shaping public policy. With a majority-black population and electorate, the mayor can articulate the most vocal position possible for black equity. As a "strong mayor," Gary's elected leader does not have to worry about sharing power with quasi-independent boards and commissions or a full-time salaried city council. Actually, the major of Gary can control the city council with just one-third plus one, or four of the nine members, by the expeditious use of the veto. However, no matter how powerful Gary's mayor might be in terms of governmental structure, this person must contend with a wide array of external forces: adjacent local governments; county, state, and federal governments; and business and institutional elites. How Gary mayors have handled these external pressures is described in the following chapters.

2

The Evolution of Gary

Gary was founded in 1903 by the U.S. Steel Corporation. Needing a site midway between the coal fields of Appalachia and the ore deposits of Minnesota's Iron Range, this corporation picked a barren, unpopulated forty-square-mile site on Lake Michigan about thirty miles from downtown Chicago.[1] At first, land was purchased only for a steel mill, but because of its immense size, requiring at least ten thousand workers, housing was needed within walking distance of streetcars. Therefore, it was necessary to develop a new city as well.[2] In April 1906, plans for the new plant and city were announced, with the municipality being named for Judge Elbert Gary, then U.S. Steel's chairman of the board.[3]

The surveyors laid out the town on the old gridiron or checkerboard pattern, with two intersecting business streets, Broadway and Fifth Avenue (see figure 1).[4] No attention was given to contemporary city planning techniques such as wide diagonal streets radiating from central nodes, the integration of open space with residential land use, and the protection of natural features such as lakes, rivers, and woodlands. The town site was set behind the plant with the latter taking up virtually the entire lakefront.[5] No professional city planners were hired by U.S. Steel to design Gary. Though U.S. Steel officials knew that Gary was going to be a large city, they did not consult experts to determine the best arrangement of streets, land-use types, and parks in areas where workers were to live. Ironically, not only did U.S. Steel secure the best engineers and technical consultants to plan the mill, but they were enthusiastically supporting Daniel Burnham's plan for Chicago at the same time.[6]

To make matters worse, U.S. Steel actually built only half a town. The first subdivision with wide streets, large lots, and complete utilities, including electric, gas, water, telephone, and sewer, was designed for the mill's

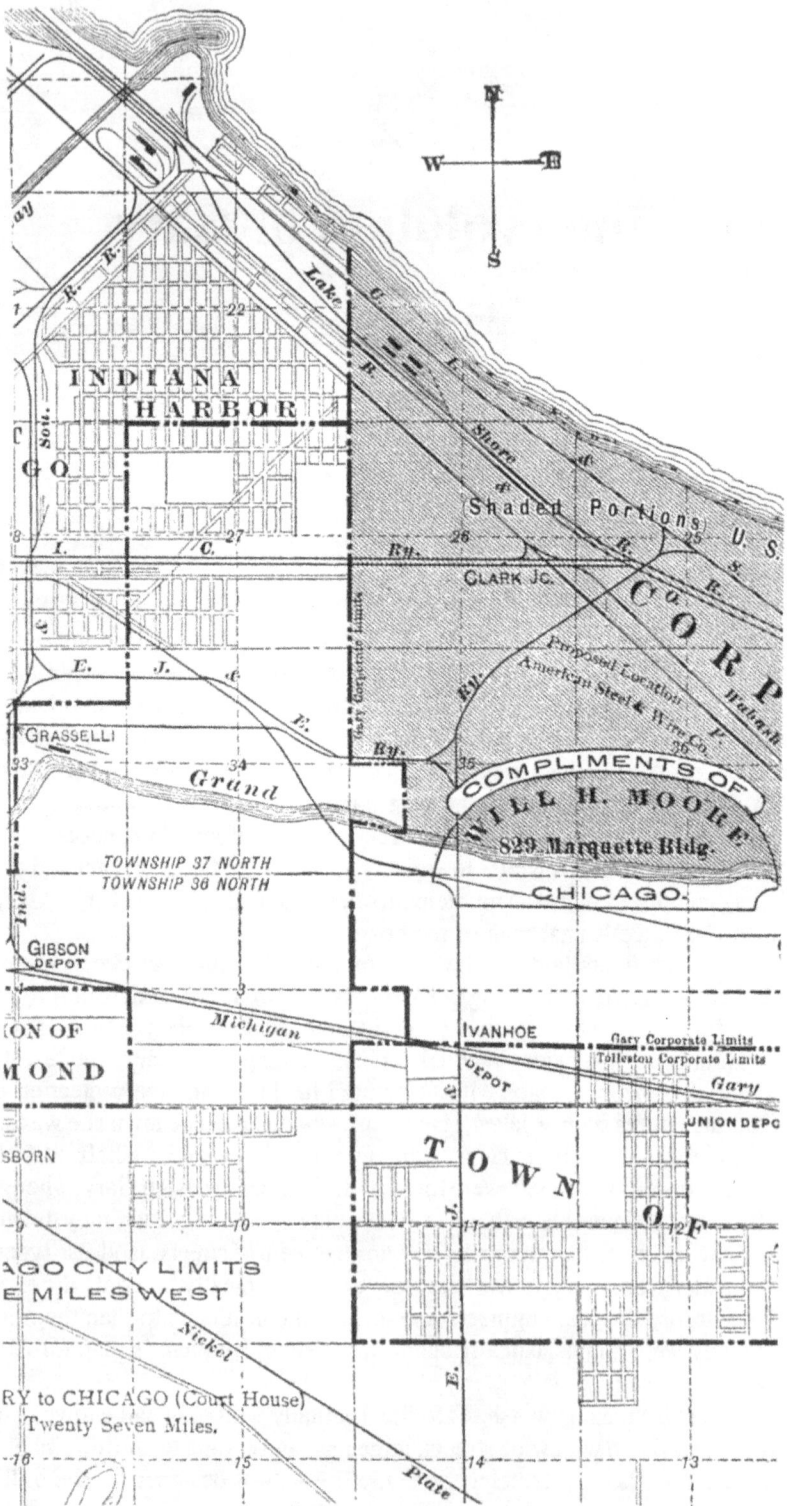

INDIANA

HARBOR

Lake

Shore

&

Shaded Portions U.S.

CLARK JC.

CORP

Proposed Location

American Steel & Wire Co.

Wabash

COMPLIMENTS OF

WILL H. MOORE

829 Marquette Bldg.

CHICAGO.

GRASSELLI

Grand

TOWNSHIP 37 NORTH
TOWNSHIP 36 NORTH

Ind.

GIBSON
DEPOT

ON OF

MOND

Michigan

IVANHOE

Gary Corporate Limits
Tolleston Corporate Limits

Gary

UNION DEPO

SBORN

TOWN

OF

AGO CITY LIMITS
E MILES WEST

Nickel

RY to CHICAGO (Court House)
Twenty Seven Miles.

Plate

Figure 1. The Original Plan for Gary, Indiana, 1906

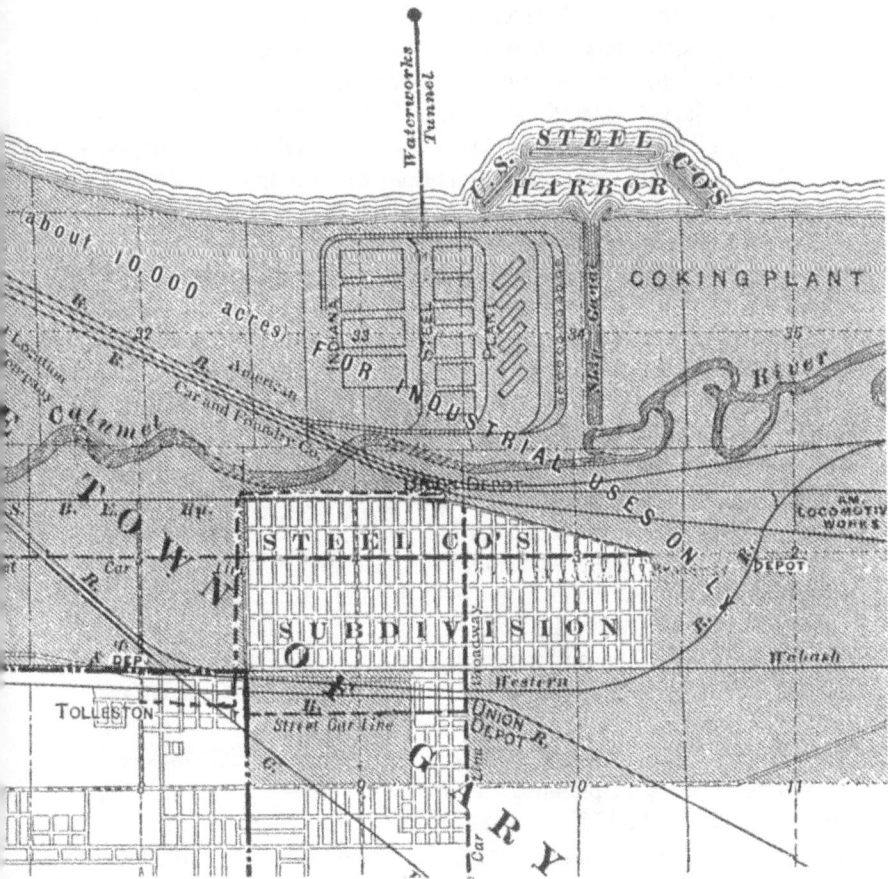

executives, supervisors, and foremen, along with the city's professional class. The portion south of the first subdivision was sold to speculators who created instant housing for unskilled laborers who comprised 90 percent of the work force. Within a few years, this area, crowded and unplanned, with poor or nonexistent public services, turned into a festering slum.[7]

Despite these basic mistakes, Gary grew quickly and spectacularly. From barren dunes and marshland in 1906, the town developed to a population of 16,802 in 1910 and 51,378 by 1920.[8] The city's professional and executive class was made up almost entirely of native-born whites, while the unskilled and semiskilled group was drawn mainly from migrants from southern and eastern Europe.[9] Under the leadership of William A. Wirt, an innovative school system enrolled 4,800 children by 1913 and by that time had established a national reputation for excellence, especially in preparing the children of immigrants to function in American society.[10] In 1909, Judge Gary pledged today's equivalent of $10 million for the establishment of a YMCA, which quickly became the city's cultural center, and U.S. Steel made several smaller donations of land and monies for civic activities within the city of Gary.[11]

After a divisive steel strike in 1919, Gary entered its golden age. The black population, which numbered only 383 in 1910, rose to 5,300 by 1920, 10 percent of the total, because of the "great migration" during World War I. During the 1920s, strong heavy-handed involvement by U.S. Steel in city government continued, including in matters involving city planning. A planning commission was established in 1920, and a consultant firm allied with Daniel Burnham's office was engaged to prepare a land-use plan.[12] This plan, completed in September of that same year, featured large lakefront parks, boulevards, a civic center, and a proposed zoning ordinance.[13] However, it was fought by U.S. Steel, realtors, and the railroads. For example, U.S. Steel opposed a boulevard that would run along Lake Michigan just as Lake Shore Drive does in Chicago because it would have taken up room needed for the expansion of the coke plants, blast furnaces, and storage yards. The mill superintendent stated, "The steel corporation has no apologies to offer for the way the city was first laid out and the accomplishments."[14] By 1923, the plan was dead, and, because of lack of interest, the commission could not secure a quorum to elect officers.[15]

Unburdened with planning, a construction boom began in 1924 not unlike that during the 1970s in Sun Belt cities such as Houston, Tampa, and San Antonio.[16] Not concerned with the instability of the steel industry, entrepreneurs built skyscrapers to tower above the mills to the north and the hovels to the south. These projects and their 1991 equivalent dollar cost included a $25 million Elks Temple, a $20 million Masonic Temple, a $50 million Knights of Columbus Club-Hotel, the $100 million Hotel Gary, a $50 million City Hall and county courthouse, and a $100 million bank and office building.[17] In 1926 alone, over $2 billion in building permits were issued (1991 dollars).[18] Public improvements for utilities and parks totaled a 1991 equivalent of over $300 million between 1925 and 1930. Despite these expenditures, the strong industrial economy enabled Gary to keep its tax rate well below the average of all U.S. municipalities with populations over 25,000.[19] In addition to the steel mills and related industries, Gary became a state convention center.[20] In 1928, eleven major statewide associates brought 12,000 visitors to Gary, with each spending a 1991 equivalent of $140 per day.[21] As a result of all this strong economic activity, Gary's population almost doubled from 55,000 in 1920 to 100,000 in 1930.

Because of the depression, Gary's population grew by only 11,000 during the period of 1930-1940. During and after World War II, while the population rose to 134,000 in 1950 and 178,000 in 1960 without the benefit of major annexations, the drive and enthusiasm present among the business community during the 1920s was clearly lacking. After World War II, the tendency toward suburbanization became dominant, and by the early 1950s real estate loans fell off sharply as banks made their primary investments just outside the city.[22] In Gary, private builders began having difficulty obtaining financing for projects within the city. After World II, virtually no new private construction in downtown was undertaken. While Gary provided 16,000 jobs in retail sales in 1950, that figure declined to only 9,000 by 1965.[23]

Downtown Gary was thriving until the mid-1950s without any substantial competition to its role as the regional center for retail shopping, business transactions, professional services, and entertainment. In 1950, citywide retail sales reached an all-time high, with 14,000 jobs in the downtown area, including 8,000 in the CBD (central business district) alone.[24] This started to change as early as 1955 when the Village Mall opened in suburban Ross Township as northwest Indiana's first auto-oriented shopping center. By 1960, Gary retail sales had dropped considerably, with only 10,000 people employed in this sector, including only 6,000 in the CBD, a 20 percent decline in only five years.[25] The sales to suburban customers trailed off drastically, and 25 percent of Gary's residents' purchases were being made outside the city.[26]

This phenomenon was not just occurring in Gary. By 1960, Chicago, Detroit, Minneapolis, and several other midwestern cities had seen new shopping malls open on their periphery, some of them enclosed. Economists were predicting that while the "office" function would remain downtown, and perhaps even in a strengthened role, retail trade would gradually shift to the suburbs.[27] By 1965, virtually every central city in America with populations over 100,000 had prepared and adopted downtown development plans to counter the effects of suburbanization. Most of these plans, while recommending pedestrian malls with off-street parking to attract shoppers, were based on the development of office complexes and then ancillary uses such as hotels, restaurants, small shops, and convention centers.[28]

Gary, however, was content to rely on the status quo. During the early 1960s, the mills were booming, and every weekend, highly paid steel-workers would come down Broadway to pay cash for a wide variety of merchandise.[29] The 1964 plan made no mention of the shift in downtown's focus from retail shopping to offices and there wasn't even a special CBD land-use plan as part of that proposal.[30] Although cities such as Minne-apolis; St. Paul; Hartford and New Haven, Connecticut; Fresno, California; and Providence, Rhode Island, had prepared comprehensive downtown development schemes in the 1950s and by the early 1960s were using urban renewal to implement them, Gary's response to downtown problems was the halfhearted Gateway project started in 1962.[31]

Urban renewal began with the U.S. Housing Act of 1949. No sooner did this legislation pass than dozens of cities that had been waiting eagerly with plans prepared for these grants were ready to start project activities. By 1955, after some seventy cities had shared over $500 million in federal assistance under this program, Gary finally established an urban renewal agency.[32] By state law, a five-member board was created, two of whose members were appointed by the mayor, two by the city council, and one by Lake County. Two projects were initiated between 1956 and 1962: the first was a small residential redevelopment project known as Pulaski and the second, an attempt at downtown redevelopment, was called Gateway. The Gateway project, consisting of 2.4 acres of the approximately 150 net acres of downtown land and acquired during the period of 1963-1966, was sold to private developers at a net loss of $400,000 to the redevelopment agency. The site was divided into two parcels. One was used to construct a Holiday Inn. Construction started in 1966. The hotel was opened in 1969 and ran at a deficit until it went bankrupt and closed in 1975.[33] The other site was sold to a tire company, which opened a store in 1971. It was demolished in 1982 for the Genesis Convention Center complex, which will be discussed later in this book.

Until the mid-1960s, there was a waiting list for professional office space in Gary's most prestigious office building (which constituted about 30 percent of Gary's office space). By 1968, the waiting list had disap-peared, and by 1972, one-fifth of the building was unoccupied.[34] While similar scenarios were being played out in most other industrial cities across the nation during this time, Gary's decline was much more pronounced. For example, by the 1960s, new urban housing in central cities nationally was being built at the rate of 1 percent of the total stock per year, but the rate for Gary was 0.5 percent.[35] By 1967, half of Gary's housing was over thirty years old, and a Public Health survey concluded that the city had a significant rat problem, which could be expected to worsen. In 1951, when white ethnics led by Peter Mandich took over the local Democratic Party and, shortly afterward, City Hall as well, a bitter conflict between city government and the local business elite developed setting the stage for Hatcher's later election.[36]

The Election of Richard Gordon Hatcher

Richard Gordon Hatcher was born in 1933 in Michigan City, Indiana, twenty miles east of Gary. One of thirteen children, Hatcher fought his way out of poverty to earn a degree from Indiana University and then, in 1959, a law degree from Valparaiso University. His first job was in the Lake County prosecutor's office, and he opened a private law practice on the side. Immediately upon passing the Indiana bar exam, also in 1959, Hatcher became deeply involved in civil rights. He fought Gary's Methodist Hospital's Jim Crow patient assignment policy, led a Gary delegation to the 1963 Civil Rights March on Washington, took on cases of alleged police brutality, and led the fight for the establishment of a local ordinance for open housing. So successful was Hatcher in bringing public attention to these issues that, in 1963, he was elected as an "at large" city councilman.

During his early years on the city council, he established a reputation for incorruptibility, independence from Gary's political machine, which threw crumbs to blacks in exchange for their votes, and militancy on civil rights issues. In 1965, under Hatcher's leadership, the city passed an omnibus civil rights ordinance, which included a provision for open occupancy. Even though this ordinance contained virtually no enforcement powers, its passage catapulted Hatcher to the top of Gary's black political spectrum.

In 1967, Hatcher chose to run for mayor. The city's population was by now divided evenly between blacks and whites, with whites having a slight edge in voter registration. As Democrats outnumbered Republicans nine to one, victory in the Democratic party primary would be tantamount to election. Hatcher's strategy was to capture 10 to 15 percent of the white vote, mainly liberal, middle-class, largely Jewish residents in the Miller neighborhood. This would be coupled with an attempt to gain at least 80 percent of the black vote, which would mean wresting it away from the corrupt old-line machine. Hatcher would have to run against A. Martin Katz, the incumbent mayor, a moderate Jewish lawyer who had luke-warmly supported the civil rights ordinance, and Bernard Konrady, a local Slovak businessman who would run a right-wing "law and order" campaign. The local newspaper, the *Gary Post-Tribune*, run by conservative, business-oriented whites who strongly supported the status quo, virtually ignored Hatcher during the early weeks of the campaign in February and March. But as the winter snows melted, Hatcher's campaign heated up. The machine not only attempted to spread lies, rumors, and innuendo about Hatcher, insinuating that he was a radical and a communist, but they instituted a campaign of violence against his supporters as well. Hatcher's supporters retaliated by beating up the white machine's "gorillas," and the violence stopped. The black community was organized on a block-by-block basis by Hatcher supporters. Hatcher stickers began to be displayed in the windows of black homes and on automobiles. With the white vote split between Katz and Konrady, Hatcher won the primary in May 1967 with 40 percent of the total vote. Seventy-five percent of blacks voted for Hatcher, as did only 5 percent of all whites.

After the primary, Hatcher's campaign organization prepared to dissolve itself. John Krupa, chairman of the Lake County Democratic Party announced his full support for Hatcher on May 19, 1967, just days after the primary. But white racism presented another reality. There had been racial conflict between black and white workers ever since World War I, when large numbers of blacks began to migrate to Gary. In 1964, George Wallace ran for president in the Indiana Democratic primary and obtained 67 and 77 percent of the vote in the two main white sections of the city, Miller/Aetna and Glen Park. The Democratic machine felt they could call upon this reverse army of hatred if they chose not to fully support Hatcher in the November general election.

In late May of 1967, John Krupa met with Hatcher. Krupa first demanded that Hatcher purge his campaign organization of its white and black "radical elements." Hatcher asked Krupa, "What radicals?" After sparring around on this point for a few moments, Hatcher recalls: "Krupa said he wanted to name the police chief and controller and several key officers, and I told him, 'look, too many people have worked too hard on this and I'm not going to abdicate my responsibilities or sell them out. I'm going to name my own police chief and controller.'"[37]

After that meeting, Krupa, realizing that he and the Lake County Democratic machine could not control Hatcher, denounced him as a "Kremlin agent." Recognizing that if Hatcher won and named all of his key administrators the machine would lose all power over municipal jobs and contracts, Krupa and other machine officials began publicly to support Joseph Radigan, a local furniture store owner and the Republican party nominee. Hatcher, seeing that the general election would be a real battle, registered 5,000 additional voters. Krupa, who was also secretary of the Lake County Election Board, challenged 5,300 black voters, removed them from the voting rolls, and prepared to register 15,000 nonexistent white voters. However, one of the white registrars, Marian Tokarski, was unwilling to participate in this fraud and presented Hatcher with an affidavit detailing Krupa's scheme. With this evidence, Hatcher requested U.S. Justice Department intervention and filed suit in federal court. The Justice Department provided details of 1,100 new false registrations in white sections of the city. With this evidence, the federal court issued a strong restraining order, and the machine backed off. On election day, even with almost the entire Indiana State Police Force inside the city and thousands of National Guardsmen outside on alert, the machine attempted to steal the election by seeing to it that voting machines in black precincts were "out of order." Hatcher prepared for this by having on hand over a dozen voting machine mechanics from Chicago ready to fix the machines. Coordinating this effort, along with providing sufficient poll watches to prevent the flagrant undercounting of ballots, was evidence of the strong organizational effectiveness developed by Hatcher in a relatively short period of time. And white Gary policemen who stood in front of polling places in black precincts were run away by armed gangsters from Chicago covertly hired by Hatcher supporters who were prepared for this "dirty trick."[38]

On November 5, 1967, a massive voter turnout took place for this election: 72 percent of registered whites and 76 percent of registered blacks. Hatcher won the election by a vote of 40,000 to 38,000. Only 10 percent of whites but 96 percent of blacks voted for Hatcher. In the weeks after the elections, the Katz administration refused to provide for a transition of power, and when Hatcher took office on January 2, 1968, the doors of city hall were chained shut.[39]

To show that racism dies hard, sixteen years later the exact same primary and general election scenario was repeated in nearby Chicago when Harold Washington was finally elected mayor. Nothing was learned from the Gary experience.[40]

When Hatcher was elected in 1967, as the result of ethnic white divisiveness coupled with an outpouring of black pride, the split between city government and the business community widened, and Gary's physical decline accelerated.[41] The 1970 U.S. Census showed a population decrease for the first time, 175,000 compared to 178,000 in 1960. In 1970, Gary's housing stock of 54,000 units included only 3,000 dwellings built after 1950, almost all of which were federally subsidized. On the other hand, 13,500, or almost 25 percent, had been constructed before World War II.[42]

When Mayor Hatcher took office on January 2, 1968, he inherited an urban renewal agency that, in the nineteen-year history of federally assisted urban development, had formulated only one residential project and completed land assembly for 2 percent of the downtown area. Despite the fact that retail sales downtown had fallen steadily since the opening of the suburban mall referred to earlier, no plans for downtown revitalization were approved by the plan commission, city council, or redevelopment commission between 1955 and 1968. There had been no new construction of any kind downtown since the 1920s except for two small office buildings located off the major Broadway spine, and, to make matters worse, Mayor Hatcher faced an openly hostile business community that had thrown their entire weight behind his opponents in both the primary and general elections.

Mayor Hatcher was elected to office mainly with the support of working-class blacks. As the Gary business community was opposed to his candidacy from the start of his campaign, it made little political sense for Hatcher to push for downtown redevelopment at that time. Even if these businessmen had been favorable to full-scale CBD revitalization, it could have been political suicide for him to do so because, in 1968, black citizens in Gary and across the nation were claiming that urban renewal was really "Negro removal," as the early projects indeed cleared large tracts of black-occupied slums to be replaced by upper- and middle-income housing units occupied mostly by whites. By 1968, even though removal of low-income families and their subsequent replacement by middle-income types had largely ceased as residential reuse projects had been replaced by commercial revitalization schemes in the CBD, the negative experiences of blacks with urban renewal were still very recent, not easily forgotten, and generally believed to be one of the underlying causes of the urban riots of 1965-1968.[43] Therefore, the Hatcher administration felt that it was best at that time to put aside any serious thoughts about downtown revitalization.

Between 1968 and 1977, urban renewal, along with the Model Cities program, the "War on Poverty," and other federal aid efforts, was channeled into the Midtown and Small Farms areas, both part of the historic center of Gary's black community. With promises that all new construction would be for present neighborhood residents, almost 2,900 housing units were demolished, and by 1977, only 476 new ones were built on the renewal sites, including 220 units of public housing. During 1972 alone, over $18 million was expended, with 40 percent spent for "make work" youth programs. Only 38 percent was spent for housing and 5 percent for economic development, which consisted mainly of counseling services for small minority-owned businesses.[44] The only downtown development was sponsored by the Gary Downtown Improvement Association, created by businessmen under state enabling legislation just before Mayor Hatcher was elected. This group prepared elaborate plans and brochures based on recapturing the local market and convincing well-off whites who had left the city to return. However, the only thing built was a three-hundred-car parking garage that opened in 1973.[45]

In 1971, Mayor Hatcher was opposed by Dr. Andrew Williams, Jr., a prominent black physician who was then the Lake County coroner. Williams conducted a vigorous campaign, even publishing a small book in which he attacked the mayor for failing to work with the business community, tearing down almost 3,000 units of low-income housing without replacement, using federal funds extravagantly, and participating in machine politics.[46] Williams was covertly backed by downtown businessmen who welcomed his moderate approach, but Mayor Hatcher defeated him, winning over 60 percent of all votes cast. After Williams's defeat, downtown businessmen responded by announcing plans for two huge enclosed shopping malls totaling over 1 million square feet. Both were to be located in suburban Merrillville, fifteen miles from downtown Gary. By 1978, the three anchor department stores and over one hundred retail establishments in downtown had either closed altogether or moved to the new malls and nearby strip centers, taking their tax dollars with them. Black residents were embittered by this action as there was no public bus service between Gary and the shopping malls in Merrillville. Other enterprises followed the retail stores from downtown to the suburbs. Both major banks constructed new headquarters facilities there. A new hospital opened, soon to be followed by almost 90 percent of Gary's white and Asian physicians. The 300-room downtown Holiday Inn closed and essentially reopened in Merrillville, this time as a 400-room resort facility complete with a "Holidome" and a 3,000-seat concert hall. It is estimated that between 1970 and 1980, almost $600 million was spent on this construction, all by the private sector.[47] So successful were these developments that by the early 1980s black shoppers from Gary accounted for almost one-quarter of all sales there, and at the Holiday Inn concert hall, almost half of all performances featured black music, attracting residents from both Gary and Chicago. Meanwhile, the number of business establishments in downtown Gary fell from over 500 in 1960 to less than 40 by 1979. Corresponding numbers of employees in retail trade downtown fell from 10,000 to only 300. Even the city's major hospital attempted to move in the late 1970s, but Hatcher was able to apply pressure on the U.S. Department of Health, Education, and Welfare and Department of Housing and Urban Development to block federal grants for such an action. In 1979, Methodist Hospital entered into a consent decree with the city, pledging not only to keep their Gary facility open but to match dollar for dollar new construction in the suburbs with new construction and for modernization of their original facility.[48]

NIS and Downtown Rebuilding

In 1978, the Hatcher administration turned its attention toward downtown, which by now had been all but deserted by private business. As most of downtown's merchants and bankers had already left for Merrillville, the thought of "Negro removal" was as passé as the word Negro itself. The Model Cities program, with its liberal provisions for employment and social

services, was folded with urban renewal and several related programs into
the community development block grant, which stressed physical and
economic development at the expense of social programs. In an innovative
approach to downtown rebuilding, Gary, along with St. Paul, Minnesota,
and Dayton, Ohio, applied for and was selected by the Department of
Housing and Urban Development (HUD) to be included in a program
known as the Negotiated Investment Strategy (NIS).[49] The main purpose of
NIS was to combine and coordinate various federal assistance programs and
focus their application to a specific area, in this case, downtown. Actually,
NIS was nothing really new; the approach goes back at least as far as the
General Neighborhood Redevelopment Program of the 1950s, the Community Redevelopment Program of the early 1960s, and even the Model
Cities program. NIS was concerned not only with federal aid program
coordination but with active involvement of the private sector as well.
Gary's NIS program was prepared by the planning staff in 1978 and
approved by HUD and other federal agencies in 1979. The area of imple-
mentation included an 18-block, 90-acre zone that, while much more
comprehensive than the old Gateway project, still left out most of the old
Broadway retail corridor and almost 40 percent of the total downtown. Out
of the NIS came several projects: the Genesis Convention Center, the
Sheraton Hotel, the U.S. Steel Office Building, the Adam Benjamin Metro
Center, the Genesis Towers, the Parks and Recreation Administration
Building, and the Fifth Avenue Houses.

The Genesis Convention Center.   Usually, a convention center is the last
major project in downtown revitalization. First should be new office buildings, which establish a strong daytime white-collar population, then, ancillary facilities such as hotels, restaurants, and boutiques, and finally, a
convention center complex. Gary's planners were keenly aware of this, but
with no major private sector construction downtown since the 1920s and
local business departure to Merrillville, the administration's view was that a
development of this type could stimulate private construction of the ancillary facilities needed to make a convention center work. So in 1979, plans
were drawn up for a 250,000-square-foot center containing a main hall that
could seat 7,500 for athletic events and 8,500 for concerts. The center also
would contain meeting rooms and a 400-car parking garage. The cost of $16
million was paid for mainly by the Community Development Block Grant
Program and monies from the Economic Development Administration
(EDA), with no bonded indebtedness to Gary taxpayers.

    The center opened in December 1981 and by 1991 experienced limited
success. Because of cost overruns, there was no money to install kitchen
facilities, making banquets very difficult to host. Even minor items such as
public telephones and rest room directional signs were omitted because of

lack of funds. The main hall, while excellent for athletics, does not work well as a concert facility because of poor acoustics, and the center has to compete with the luxurious Holiday Inn Complex in Merrillville (known by 1991 as the Radisson Star Theatre) even for black-oriented performances. Although several successful events have been held there, including NBA basketball games, rodeos, and a national church convention, the Genesis Center remains idle much of the time and had an annual deficit of over $1 million by 1987. No group from outside Gary had by December 1991 sponsored an event there, even though the Genesis is the only large convention center in northwest Indiana. Reasons given for this are Gary's high crime rate and continued divisiveness over the transition from a white-led to a black-led government. Regardless, this center cannot even begin to work until first-rate hotels and restaurants are constructed nearby, the perception of danger is somehow removed, and the center itself is upgraded to add basic facilities such as a full kitchen and improved acoustics, along with luxury items such as plush carpeting and seating of the quality found at the Merrillville Holiday Inn Complex referred to earlier.

The Sheraton Hotel. The old Holiday Inn closed in 1975 and was boarded up. The NIS plan called for its acquisition, rehabilitation, and sale. By the use of the Economic Development Administration, Urban Development Action Grants, and Community Development Block Grants, the hotel was purchased and rehabilitated at a cost of $2.5 million. It was sold to a private Gary group with a loan guaranteed by the city and reopened in January 1981, with the private group leasing the facility to the Sheraton Hotel chain. Although the hotel's utility bills were paid by the city, the hotel closed in September 1985 because of low occupancy, and title reverted back to Gary. Although the mayor's critics charged that its failure was caused by mismanagement and lack of foresight by the group that purchased the hotel, there is probably a better explanation.

The Sheraton failed for exactly the same reason that the old Holiday Inn did. Downtown hotels draw their trade primarily from clientele arriving for business purposes. As there are only 2,000 workers and visitors in downtown Gary on a given day, most of them government employees, and not a single regional business headquarters, the market for a hotel is seriously constrained. As the hotel opened almost one year before the convention center, it couldn't even count on the sparse number of events held there to initiate a rapid cash flow. Until there is substantial office construction downtown, creating from 5,000 to 10,000 jobs, it will be very difficult to attract and maintain a first-rate 300-room hotel facility.

The U.S. Steel Office Building. Gary planners felt that if U.S. Steel could be persuaded to move their offices from decaying structures at the

mill site to downtown, only a few blocks away, this would provide an
incentive for other investors to build similar complexes nearby and provide
the environment necessary to make the convention center and Sheraton
Hotel work. U.S. Steel was interested, and a three-acre site at the Fifth
Avenue and Broadway intersection was acquired and cleared by 1980 by the
city's redevelopment agency. However, U.S. Steel demanded a $10 million
tax break in addition to a 100 percent land write-down before agreeing to
build the office tower.[50] The city administration refused, U.S. Steel withdrew their offer, and, as of 1991, the site was still vacant. In 1982,
landscaping was installed, and it functioned as a park. In January 1987, it
was sold to a Gary physician for only $4,800, even though the city had spent
over $200,000 to acquire it, demolish old buildings, and landscape the
grounds. The physician planned a modest two-story medical center on what
is the main intersection in this city of 145,000 residents. As of December
1991, that building was not under construction.

The Adam Benjamin Metro Center.   In 1981, Congressman Adam Benjamin, Jr., was able to obtain almost $65 million from the Urban Mass
Transit Administration to upgrade the South Shore Commuter Railroad that
runs between Chicago and South Bend, with a major stop in downtown
Gary. Though most of these funds were used to purchase new railway cars
and upgrade the tracks and electric power systems, almost $10 million was
allocated to build a multimodal transportation center just north of the
convention center/city hall complex. The center, which opened in October
1985, contains not only the South Shore railroad station but also a terminal
for both the interstate and the local bus company as well as their offices.
Also available is about ten thousand square feet of leasable commercial
space, which by 1988 was about 50 percent rented. This facility seems to be
working quite well as late as 1990, with the parking lot and adjacent garages
filled to capacity during weekdays.

The Genesis Towers.   The old Hotel Gary on Broadway was built in 1926
at a cost of $2.5 million and was Gary's top lodging facility for over forty
years. Blacks could not even rent rooms there until the 1940s. By the late
1960s, low occupancy had become a problem, and the hotel finally shut
down in 1974 and was boarded up. The NIS program called for its rehabilitation as units for senior citizens. The hotel was restored by Community Development Block Grants, Urban Development Action Grants,
and public housing monies. It reopened in 1981 with 140 units of senior
citizen housing. The Gary Housing Authority also maintains their central
office in this building. This project is an unqualified success, and the stable
resident population has even provided a basis for renovation of an adjacent
drug store and a small office complex.[51]

The Parks and Recreation Administration Building.   Another part of the
NIS program was redevelopment of the block just east to city hall and the
Holiday Inn-Sheraton Hotel. Plans were formulated to clear the block,
relocate almost one hundred residential households, and build a headquarters structure for Gary's Parks and Recreation Board. This structure, which
was planned to contain offices for the parks board and fitness center,
opened in August 1986 and by June 1987 had sold almost 25 percent more
memberships than was forecasted for that time period.

The Fifth Avenue Houses.   Just west of downtown along Fifth Avenue
are hundreds of apartment units in buildings constructed during the 1920s as
upper-middle-income housing for what was then Gary's professional class.
Tastefully designed and well built, these structures were gradually abandoned and boarded up when the surrounding neighborhood underwent
racial change from white to black in the late 1960s and early 1970s. NIS
plans called for their rehabilitation and leasing as Section 8 housing. The
rehabilitation work was completed in 1983, and over six hundred units were
placed in operation under this program. While the rehabilitation was well
done and the management is in capable hands, the noise from eighteen-
wheel diesel trucks on Fifth Avenue now creates a poor environment that
encouraged upwardly mobile residents to move out as soon as possible. By
1990, these buildings were beginning once again to show signs of deterioration.

The "High" Years of the Hatcher Administration

During the period from 1971 to 1980, despite the opposition and eventual
exodus of the white business community, Hatcher enjoyed extremely strong
support among the black masses. He was able to attract almost $300 million
in federal funds between 1968 and 1980 for a variety of projects, including
job training and employment, social services, educational assistance, urban
renewal, and assisted housing. He built the first public housing in Gary
since the Korean War, and by 1982, almost 3,400 federally assisted dwellings had been constructed under his administration. In the first twelve years
of his administration (1968-1980), the Gary city work force added over
1,100 black employees, including over 150 professionals. With the steel
industry at peak levels, unemployment in Gary never rose above 8 percent
during the recession of 1973-1975. During the early, heady days of the
Hatcher administration, expectations were not only raised but many were
actually met. This resulted in his reelection in 1975 and 1979, both times by
margins of over 60 percent. When I arrived in Gary in June 1982 for my job
interview with Indiana University, Mayor Hatcher and his administration
were very much in control despite the recession and a reduction of U.S.
Steel's work force from 25,000 to only 7,000 employees from 1979 to 1982.

3

External Constraints on Planning and Development

The urban literature of the late 1960s and early 1970s warned that as cities became majority black and black governed, whites, along with the cities' business industries and institutions, would flee to the metropolitan area's outskirts, leaving behind a hollow black core strangled by a white noose of new suburban growth loaded with positive tax ratables.[1] Of the U.S. cities with 100,000 or more residents that had black majorities by 1970—Washington, D.C., Atlanta, Newark, and Gary—we do find that, for the first three, while white out-migration continued during the period of 1970-1980 business and industry did not necessarily follow, especially those with corporate headquarters located there. By 1990, black political scientists were debating whether the strategies of Andrew Young in Atlanta and Coleman Young in Detroit, both geared to enhance downtown development, were more beneficial to the black masses than the policies of Harold Washington in Chicago or Kenneth Gibson in Newark, which were oriented more to the development of small business and neighborhood groups.[2]

Upon first glance, even the most casual of observers· realizes that stunning differences exist between Gary on one hand and Atlanta, Newark, Detroit, and Chicago on the other. Gary is a company town with the steel employers headquartered in Pittsburgh and Bethlehem, Pennsylvania, and Dallas, Texas. Atlanta is the undisputed capital of the southeast U.S., with ten Fortune 500 corporate headquarters, dozens of regional Fortune 500 headquarters, and the nation's second busiest airport. Newark, the corporate headquarters of Prudential Insurance Company, has enjoyed the spillover of New York City's information industry since the early 1970s as it is only a twenty-minute subway ride from Newark's downtown to the World Trade Center in lower Manhattan. Detroit is home to not only the "Big Three" automakers but ten other Fortune 500 corporate headquarters. And

Chicago, America's "second city" of three million residents, is home to twenty-six Fortune 500 corporations and historically has been the nation's transportation center.

But Gary does not compare well to other cities its size and of its relative location to major U.S. cities. For example, Stamford, Connecticut, had a 1980 population of only 102,466, considerably fewer than Gary's 151,943 residents at that time. Stamford is located sixty miles from midtown Manhattan on the New York Central (Amtrak) commuter rail line, whereas Gary is located fifty-five miles from downtown Chicago on the South Shore commuter rail line. However, Stamford had by 1987 twelve Fortune 500 headquarters, mostly refugees from a crowded New York City that located there between 1970 and 1985. These corporate headquarters generated a magnet effect that attracted related white-collar service-oriented jobs so that by 1985 over 55,000 new jobs of this type had replaced over 30,000 lost manufacturing jobs over a twenty-year period.[3] By 1990 Stamford's population had increased to 108,050. Similar scenarios have taken place in Macon, Georgia, ninety miles south of Atlanta; the Ann Arbor/Ypsilanti area of southeast Michigan, thirty miles from Detroit; and San Bernardino/Riverside, California, sixty miles east of Los Angeles.

Gary's Unique Constraints

Why have these cities had at least a modicum of success while Gary has failed miserably? My experiences in Gary during the 1980s indicate that at least six factors not affecting the cities previously mentioned produced unique constraints for Gary. These included, not necessarily in the order of importance, (1) the character of the regional economy, (2) influence of the State of Indiana, (3) the peculiar nature of the local judicial system, (4) the lack of major corporation headquarters, (5) lack of a strong longstanding academic infrastructure, and (6) institutional racism of a higher degree than found elsewhere. While these characteristics were unique to Gary in the 1980s, as more cities become majority black, these six constraints will apply elsewhere. A description of each constraint follows.

The Regional Economy. Gary's export economy as always consisted of steel and closely related industries such as metal fabrication and cement production. U.S. Steel during the 1920s and 1930s had a conscious policy of keeping out a variety of manufacturing operations that would have diversified Gary's economy.[4] Therefore, because of an increased percentage of imported steel, the cumulative effect of high wages, the gradual obsolescence of mill facilities, and the major recession of 1979-1982, the number of jobs in Gary area mills fell from 30,000 in 1974 to fewer than 6,000 by

1987. In the metropolitan region during the same time, steel employment fell from 70,000 to less than 40,000.[5] The steel companies forecast no improvement in this picture for at least the next ten years, despite the fact that more steel is being made here than ever before because of automation and the fact that this region leads the nation in steel production. Unlike the auto industry, which rebounded in 1983-1986 after the recession, such a development never materialized in steel. In addition to reductions in the steel mills, the Budd Company, which was a metal stamping operation with 5,000 jobs, closed in 1982 and has not been replaced with a major employer of similar size.[6] In December 1986, while the national unemployment rate was less than 7 percent, it was 13 percent in the Lake and Porter County job market and estimated conservatively at 20 percent for Gary.[7] This figure of course did not include those who had dropped out of the job market and were no longer seeking work.

Attracting new industry is a real possibility even when one considers the national shift from a manufacturing to a service economy because Gary has excellent highway and rail transportation, waterway access to Lake Michigan, a full service airport, and large, level, vacant plant sites. However, there are several major difficulties with industrial promotion. First of all, Gary is but one of over thirty incorporated municipalities in the region, and, because of the weak economy, most are vying for the same types of industries. This city is not big enough to dominate its region as Detroit, Cleveland, and Milwaukee do. As all of the region's major financial institutions left Gary during the 1970s, the city does not have a strong voice in the private sector fully committed to its welfare.

The *Post-Tribune,* Gary's local newspaper, was not helpful either. Since the late 1960s, there was an ongoing feud between Mayor Hatcher and this paper. Stories about major plant and even small business closings made page one headlines, as did routine crimes. However, in 1983, when the Prudential Insurance Company closed its regional headquarters in suburban Merrillville, idling almost 1,500 white-collar employees, the stories were subdued and focused on how the company was doing all it could to place these workers in other jobs.[8] With negative publicity by Gary's major newspaper, the marketing of Gary becomes very difficult indeed. Even with the election of Thomas Barnes as Gary's mayor in 1987, and his reelection in 1991, it will take years of positive imagery to counter the negative publicity created during the period of 1968-1988.

The Role of State Government.   Historically, state governments all over America have sought to maintain their control over cities, but the effect has been more pronounced in Gary than elsewhere, especially in recent years. First of all, Gary and Lake County are Democratic strongholds in a traditionally Republican-dominated state. While relations improved greatly between Mayor Hatcher and the governor's office between 1985 and 1988 and especially after Barnes's election, Gary has yet to receive full support of the state's economic development arm.

However, it is the state taxation board that caused the most trouble for Gary. Under state law, no Indiana municipality can raise their tax rate without permission of this board. Because of the decline in the steel industry and the refusal of private investors to build almost anything in Gary, assessed valuation has dropped in this city since 1977, while in other Rust Belt cities with black mayors, it has risen considerably or at least remained constant. Since 1980, the Indiana State Taxation Board, while granting increases in other cities, has refused every request by Gary for a tax increase, saying that taxes are "already among the highest in the state."[9] Gary's tax rate, high as it may be, is still lower than that for Detroit, Newark, and Chicago, but all of these cities have been able, at least incrementally, to increase taxes to meet rising expenses coupled with federal budget cuts.

Not only does the tax board routinely deny Gary the right to raise its own tax rate but it has the right to reduce property assessments. U.S. Steel, Gary's largest taxpayer with 40 percent of the city's assessed valuation, appealed to the tax board in 1985 to reduce their assessment by $16 million because of its employment decline, even though the Gary Works made over $60 million in profits in 1984. After months of lobbying, the appeal was granted, and it resulted in a 10 percent revenue shortfall for both the city government and the Gary Public Schools.[10]

The Judicial System.   The local judicial system under the firm control of county and state governments frustrated Gary city officials when they attempted to stem decay and blight. In the period of 1969-1973, the city strengthened its provisions for dealing with building and housing code violations and developed a strong property maintenance ordinance. However, these measures proved to be effective only with holders of small single properties who are often impoverished themselves. Large property holders with financial resources (most of whom were white suburbanites) simply requested a change of venue to an isolated rural county. Once the case was transferred, the owner then usually appealed to the court that he was simply a poor property owner being harassed by the city to make improvements that the tenants would destroy anyway. Between 1976 and 1984, twenty-one cases involving code violations were granted changes of venue; all were lost by the city. The results were a demoralized inspections staff, lax enforcement, and accelerated physical decay.[11]

The Lack of "Native Wealth."   It is known that business firms will make their primary financial, social, civic, and philanthropic commitments in those communities where they are headquartered. However, unlike Chicago, Philadelphia, Los Angeles, and almost all other cities with populations of 100,000 or more and with black mayors, Gary does not have a major Fortune 500 corporation headquarters. The northwestern Indiana mills are headquartered in Chicago, Dallas, Pittsburgh, and Bethlehem, Pennsylvania. In addition, all the local financial and related institutions, including banks, savings and loan associations, real estate firms, and business/financial consultants are headquartered in suburban Merrillville, which is just south of Gary. Though retail shopping nationwide has tended to shift from the central core to the suburbs over the past thirty years, this has not been true for financial and related institutions. Indeed, in nearby South Bend and Ft. Wayne, it is the newly constructed bank towers that dominate the central core.

Indeed, during the 1920s, U.S. Steel made significant civic commitments to Gary. They donated land for the lakefront park, the city hall county complex, and the YMCA and gave direct financial assistance to a variety of programs. In 1934, the Democrats captured city hall for the first time since 1909, and U.S. Steel, which was closely aligned with the Republican party, withdrew their support and has not played an active role in Gary's civic life since.[12]

The Lack of a Strong Academic Infrastructure.   Most midwestern U.S. industrial cities developed strong locally based universities during the period of 1890-1929. These institutions of higher education served as a boost to the cultural and civic life of their regions and tended to mitigate the debilitating impact of institutional racism. Just a few metropolitan areas of this type with populations equal to or smaller than Gary's include Toledo, Ohio (University of Toledo); Akron, Ohio (University of Akron); Youngstown, Ohio (Youngstown State University); and Dayton, Ohio (University of Dayton and Wright State University). All have enrollments of between 20,000 and 25,000, offer strong graduate-level programs, and have significant research capability. One, the University of Akron, offers a Ph.D. in Urban Studies. Table 4 shows that of ten selected Metropolitan Statistical Areas (MSAs) in the East North Central Census Division, Gary ranks ninth in university enrollment.

Northwest Indiana's 600,000 residents are served only by two small branches of large state universities. Indiana University's branch campus in Gary enrolled 5,000 students in 1991, while 7,200 students were served by Purdue University's campus in Hammond. Both branches are relatively new, with Purdue opening in 1958 and Indiana University's in 1960. They offer only undergraduate-level work for the most part, and their connections with local government are weak compared to the universities mentioned earlier. Also, the faculties at both universities are, with few exceptions, not

Table 4. University Enrollment in Ten Cities in the East North Central Region

MSA	1984 Estimated Population	Major Universities with 2,000 or more Students in 1985	University Enrollment in 1986	Comm. College Enrollment in 1986	% of Univ. Students in Population[a]
1. Akron, Oh.	650,100	Univ. of Akron	25,900	26,500	3.9
2. Dayton, Oh.	940,000	Univ. of Dayton, Wright State, Central State	22,500	27,655	2.3
3. Flint, Mich.	445,000	Baker College, Univ. of Michigan at Flint	10,500	11,650	2.3
4. Gary and Hammond, Ind.	629,600	Indiana Univ. Northwest, Purdue Univ. at Calumet	11,800	None	1.8
5. Grand Rapids, Mich.	626,200	Grand Valley State College, Calvin College	12,500	15,600	2.0
6. Lansing, Mich.	416,200	Michigan State Univ.	44,100	26,600	10.6
7. Louisville, Ky./ southern Ind.	968,300	Univ. of Louisville, Indiana Univ. Southeast	24,700	22,500	2.5
8. Saginaw, Mich.	411,900	Saginaw Valley State College	5,400	11,400	1.3
9. Toledo, Oh.	610,800	Univ. of Toledo, Bowling Green State Univ.	39,000	18,400	6.4
10. Youngstown, Oh.	518,100	Youngstown State Univ.	15,000	16,300	2.9

Sources: U.S. Census Population Estimates, 1984; Rand-McNally Commercial Atlas, 1990; Directory of Community Colleges, 1987.

Note: Cities are Metropolitan Statistical Areas in the East North Central Census Division with populations between 400,000 and 1,000,000 in 1984.

[a]Applies only to university students, not those enrolled in community colleges.

interested in urban issues. There are no degree programs in urban studies at either institution, and although IU Northwest has a degree program in Afro-American studies, that program is generally isolated from the mainstream faculty. There are no community colleges in northwest Indiana that compare with statewide systems in Ohio, Michigan, and Illinois. Coupled with the underrepresentation of university students in Gary, the lack of a strong academic presence takes on additional significance.

With an extremely weak academic infrastructure, Gary and northwest Indiana lack another significant resource capable of providing civic leadership, political enlightenment, and forward-looking approaches to the current problems of a troubled economy and racial divisiveness. The prospects for change in this area are extremely dim, as the Republican-controlled state legislature is not anxious to spend meager funds in this Democratic party stronghold.

Institutional Racism. While most U.S. cities have been the scenes of longstanding racial conflict, few if any have seen worse than Gary's. Table 5 shows the gradual increase in Gary's black population from 1910 to 1970 when this city had a black majority for the first time. In 1910, Gary's blacks numbered fewer than 500 out of a total population of over 17,000, with most gainfully employed in the mill, on the railroads, or as private household workers. Yet the *Gary Post-Tribune* ran headlines such as "City to Rid Itself of Worthless Negroes."[13] When blacks arrived in significant numbers during World War I, there was little conflict with white immigrants with whom they lived, dispersed among various blocks in the southside slum district. However, by the early 1920s, a clear pattern of institutional racism had set in. As early as 1908, the school superintendent had transferred almost all black students to a segregated school.[14] In 1926, plans were announced to build an all-black high school, although an existing school of this level was less than one mile away from the proposed site.[15] In 1917, U.S. Steel decided to build housing for blacks only, setting the stage for residential segregation, which was totally complete by 1940 when this group made up 18 percent of the 112,000 residents. Until the 1930s, blacks were not admitted to the two city hospitals, and black physicians were not given staff privileges. There were two golf courses, one with eighteen holes for whites, the other with nine holes for blacks, and blacks were not able to use the Lake Michigan beach until the mid-1960s. These actions by public officials and leading private businesses encouraged working-class whites, most of whom were new arrivals to this country, to adopt strong antiblack attitudes that persist to this day.[16]

While it is difficult to identify racism as such, some actions on the part of leading individuals, private firms, and county/state government are so contrary to the basic laws of economics and public administration that they can only be charged to virulent racial prejudice.

Table 5. Gary's Increasing Black Population, 1910-1990

Year	Total Population	Black Population	% Change in Black Population from Previous Decade	% Blacks in Total Population
1910	16,802	383	n/a	2.3
1920	55,378	5,299	+ 1383.6	9.6
1930	100,426	17,922	+ 238.2	17.9
1940	111,719	20,394	+ 13.8	18.3
1950	133,911	39,123	+ 92.3	29.2
1960	178,320	69,123	+ 76.2	38.8
1970	175,415	92,695	+ 34.1	52.8
1980	151,953	107,644	+ 16.1	70.8
1990	116,646	93,982	− 10.2	80.6

Sources: Statistics derived from selected annual decennial federal censuses.

Note: Gary not mentioned in 1900 Census of places with populations of more than 2,500.

For example, in virtually all American cities with populations over 50,000, retail shopping had drifted to the suburbs, but banks, related financial institutions, and other components of the "office" function remain headquartered downtown. Not so in Gary. When the major hospital planned to leave Gary in the late 1970s for the suburbs, it was scheduled to move into an area where existing full-service hospitals were less than two miles away.

According to the U.S. Census of 1980, 99.5 percent of the region's black population lived in the central ghettos of Gary, Hammond, and East Chicago, and when blacks attempted to move to the suburbs they found hostility, petty vandalism, and even fire bombing from their white neighbors.[17] Even by 1990, the U.S. Census showed that of 116,000 black residents in the metropolitan area, only 3,500 lived outside the ghettos in Gary, Hammond, or East Chicago.

The Gary airport is another case in point. Designated as a reliever for O'Hare International by the Federal Aviation Administration (FAA), it is adjacent to the Indiana Toll Road (the major New York-Chicago route) and is an expressway interchange. It is thirty minutes by expressway and forty-five minutes by commuter rail to Chicago's Loop. It is within a thirty-minute drive for over one million residents of northwest Indiana and the Chicago South suburbs. Noise pollution is no problem, as it lies in an area that is vacant and industrial. In 1977, a plan was approved by the FAA to expend $40 million in federal monies to extend the runways, construct a new terminal building, and make other improvements. By 1985, the terminal building was completed, and several corporations pledged support for scheduled airline service to Indianapolis and Detroit. However, they did not keep their commitments, and air service was discontinued that summer. In the 1986 legislative session, a bill was passed that committed up to

$500,000 to study a location for a possible new airport in rural Newton County, more than two hours from downtown Chicago. All of this was done at a time of fiscal austerity because of the Gramm-Rudman federal deficit reduction bill and its resulting budget cuts.

During the 1980s, most whites in the Gary suburbs did not want to be associated with the central city in any way whatsoever. When the local tourism board decided to promote the region in 1985, it did so with the slogan "Lake's Got It" rather than "Greater Gary" or words to that effect. There is a Lake County, Illinois, located just north of Chicago, so that message must have been confusing to would-be tourists. The newly constructed civic center, in downtown Gary is the only one of its kind in the region, yet by 1990, no major suburban Lake County group had met there. After Mayor Hatcher was elected, the nearby all-white town of East Gary changed its name to Lake Station. The anti-Gary bias was so bad that the Indiana Highway Department refused to put Gary directional signs on the interstate highways until early 1983. In 1982, the Gary National Bank, the region's largest financial institution, changed its name to Gainer Bank. Finally, the *Gary Post-Tribune,* the major daily founded in 1909, removed "Gary" from its masthead in 1976 and is now known simply as the *Post-Tribune.*

The *Gary Post-Tribune* must bear the responsibility for helping to foster a climate of racial divisiveness. It was created in 1921 by a merger of two newspapers—the *Post* founded in 1909 and the *Tribune* founded in 1907—both mouthpieces for the U.S. Steel Corporation in civic affairs. It was run by the Synder brothers, both prominent Republicans, one of whom had served on the Board of Public Works during Gary's early years. During the New Deal, the newspaper bitterly fought the efforts of the Congress of Industrial Organization (CIO) to organize the steel industry. Virulently racist, the newspaper, in addition to printing the headlines cited earlier, described, for example, a black criminal defendant as having an expression of "childlike irresponsibility characteristic of his race."

In the 1970s the *Post-Tribune* was purchased by a national chain, the Gannett Newspapers, but it continues under the same editorial leadership and continues to support U.S. Steel, the suburban Lake County business interests, and the Lake County Democratic party machine. Until the early 1980s, the editorial staff was all white, and the reporters assigned to city hall during the Hatcher administration were hostile to city employees, consultants such as myself, and black people in general.

The *Post-Tribune'*s negativism toward Gary slowly beat down the morale of its citizens, both black and white. When I moved to Gary in 1982, countless Garyites—students, city employees, church members, and others that I met—remarked, "Why would you want to live in Gary? I would live in Chicago or Merrillville if I could." I found Gary to be a place with a massive inferiority complex. The voice of the *Post-Tribune* is pervasive. Gary has no local network television; all major television channels come from Chicago or national cable outlets. Even the major urban contemporary radio stations come from Chicago. Having a virtual monopoly on reported news for Gary and northwest Indiana, the *Post-Tribune* did not live up to its journalistic responsibilities until 1988, when Thomas V. Barnes became mayor.

Some Faults of the Hatcher Administration

Despite these conditions, the Hatcher administration's record was not entirely without blame. In past years, the administration was very anti-business in its rhetoric and actions. Dialogue wasn't established with the business community until the late 1970s, after most firms had moved from Gary to the suburbs. Relationships with state government were very rocky until Hatcher openly extended himself to the Republican-dominated legislature in 1985. By 1988, although these overtures were sincere, it became a case of "too little, too late" even for the new Barnes administration.

The city's personnel system was archaic and riddled with political patronage, a holdover from past decades. Only the police and fire departments were subject to relatively strict civil service regulations, and this was only because of state law. All other personnel appointments were not subject to a merit system of any type. There was no formal system of job classification with titles, qualifications, duties, and responsibilities. There was no formal procedure of recruitment, testing, or selection. Promotion, retention, or layoff was not based on a formal, periodic system of evaluation, even though employee performance reviews were collected and filed.

In the absence of a formal structured merit system such as that which exists in California and in other western cities, appointments were based mainly on "connections" with high-ranking administration officials and supporters. Whereas in most merit systems top department heads are exempt from the protection of civil service, in Gary's city government even a lowly clerk typist or sanitation department laborer owed his job to good standing with elected officials. In addition to the usual set of problems that is inherent in such a system, the Hatcher administration was in office for twenty years without interruption.

The extremely long tenure of the Hatcher administration created an obsolete pattern of organization. The government consisted of four divisions, as shown in figure 2: protective services, community services, physical and economic development, and "city operations." All reported directly to the deputy mayor, who can coordinate day-to-day operations, thereby freeing the mayor to perform his duties without interruption. Actually, the post of public safety director was an anachronism from the

Figure 2. City of Gary Organizational Chart, 1984

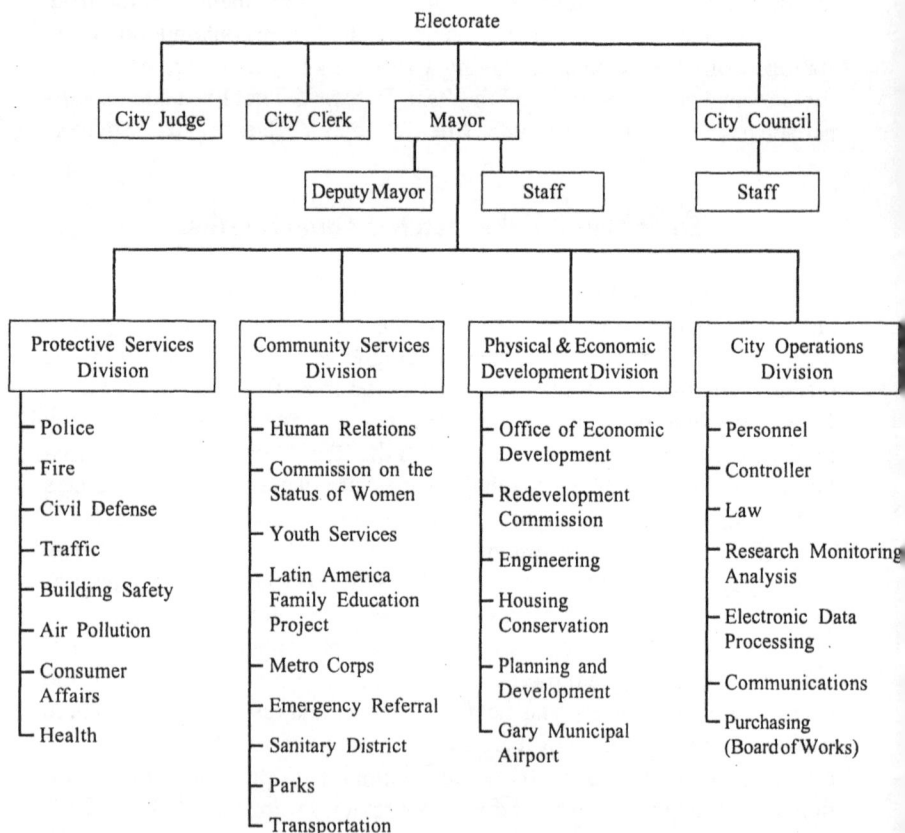

Electorate

City Judge	City Clerk	Mayor		City Council

Deputy Mayor   Staff   Staff

Protective Services Division	Community Services Division	Physical & Economic Development Division	City Operations Division
– Police	– Human Relations	– Office of Economic Development	– Personnel
– Fire	– Commission on the Status of Women	– Redevelopment Commission	– Controller
– Civil Defense	– Youth Services	– Engineering	– Law
– Traffic	– Latin America Family Education Project	– Housing Conservation	– Research Monitoring Analysis
– Building Safety	– Metro Corps	– Planning and Development	– Electronic Data Processing
– Air Pollution	– Emergency Referral	– Gary Municipal Airport	– Communications
– Consumer Affairs	– Sanitary District		– Purchasing (Board of Works)
– Health	– Parks		
	– Transportation		

1960s when Hatcher had to create this position in order to subordinate the police chief, who by state law could not be fired by the mayor.

So by mid-1982, Gary was a study in problems and opportunities. Since the early 1960s, the city had steadily lost population with whites fleeing to the suburbs and black migrants no longer coming to the city in large numbers as the steel industry's employment first leveled off then plummeted in the late 1970s. The city was clearly showing evidences of decay, and, for reasons explained earlier, the regional business community, state and county governments, and suburban civic leaders were not willing to help. But the opportunities were clear. Gary had a prime location, at the center of our nation's highway and railroad system. Chicago, with its recreational, cultural, and business advantages, was just thirty miles away. How Gary was able to reconcile its problems and opportunities during the 1980s will be shown in the following chapters.

4

Getting Started

On June 29, 1982, I received a telephone call from F.C. Richardson, dean
of the Division of Arts and Sciences at Indiana University Northwest. Dr.
Richardson offered me the job of chairman of the Department of Minority
Studies at IUN. It was a small department: only four full-time faculty
members in contrast with the position I held then at the University of South
Florida, where I chaired the seventeen-member Department of Political
Science. But Richardson offered me a full professorship with tenure and
$5,000 more than I was earning at USF. As an associate professor, light
years away from promotion to full professor at USF, this was reason enough
to come to Gary, and the pay increase didn't hurt either. But the main factor
as to whether or not I would accept the job in Gary was that I felt I could
make a difference there, whereas if I stayed in Tampa, I would be just
another professor. For five years I had tried working as a "concerned
citizen" with local government in the Tampa area but to no avail. As a
member of the Hillsborough County Planning Commission, I seemed
always to be on the losing side with the other environmentalists when it
came to decisions made by that body, which was dominated by bankers,
realtors, and developers who wanted growth with no strings attached. As a
member of the Hillsborough Area Regional Transit (HART) board, I tried
repeatedly without success to sell that body on building a light rail transit
line to ease the monumental traffic congestion experienced daily by Tampa
commuters. The majority of that board and the executive director of the
transit agency only understood buses and didn't want to get involved with
any technology, however simple, that they didn't, and wouldn't, understand. And in both cases, I was one of only two blacks on the board, and my
fellow commissioners, all whites, didn't like the idea of taking suggestions
from a black man.

But Gary was different. During my interview I had the opportunity to meet Mayor Hatcher and members of his administrative staff. Unlike their counterparts in Tampa, they welcomed me with open arms, urging me to take the job at Indiana University Northwest and, as Deputy Mayor Jim Holland put it, "help them build this city." So when Dr. Richardson called and made the offer, I said yes almost before he could finish speaking. I was to start work in late August of 1982.

In the weeks before moving, I read everything I could find on Gary. *City of the Century* by James Lane, an IUN history professor, detailed the growth and development of Gary from its beginnings as a new town in 1906 to the early 1920s under Mayor Hatcher. *Black Power Gary Style* by Alvin Poinsett dealt with the rise of Richard Hatcher to power and the phenomenon of black governance: a city with a black mayor *and* a majority black city council. Edward Greer's *Big Steel,* written from a Marxist perspective, detailed not only Gary's history but issues in that city during the 1970s such as housing, police-community relations, and environmental protection. And articles in scholarly journals by IUN professors Raymond Mohl and Ronald Cohen chronicled the history of racism in that city from 1915 when blacks first started to arrive in large numbers through the late 1960s when Hatcher came to power.[1] So in August 1982, when I headed north to Gary, I knew, or thought I knew, quite a bit about our new city.

Arriving in the city, my wife Ethel and I looked in several neighborhoods for a home. There was a very attractive neighborhood just south of the campus and another, about five minutes south of IUN, known as Morningside, a small division laid out in the 1940s, and occupied by U.S. Steel executives until white flight occurred in the early 1970s. However, there were no homes available in either location that met our needs, and we then turned to the Miller neighborhood in northeast Gary.

Miller is located just east of the U.S. Steel plant on Lake Michigan. U.S. Steel, while preempting most of the lakefront for its mill, did leave a two-mile stretch at Gary's eastern end unspoiled. In the 1920s, U.S. Steel donated land just east of the mill to the city of Gary for use as a park. The city created Marquette Park on that site, a 200-acre facility with one mile of lakefront beach. A pavilion and bathhouse was built in the late 1920s, and this park became Gary's showplace. Blacks were banned from the park and beach and did not gain access to either one until the early 1960s. The remainder of Miller was developed between 1920 and the late 1960s as a place of residence for Gary's upper classes. Along almost one mile of Lake Michigan beachfront a variety of homes were built, some for seasonal residents, others for permanent Garyites. All white until 1970, Miller was about half and half at the time of the 1980 U.S. Census. Some whites, mostly ethnic, had fled and were replaced by upwardly mobile black professionals, government workers, and small business owners. However, the majority of whites, largely Jewish, remained. In 1980, Miller's 11,000 residents had the highest socioeconomic profile of all Gary neighborhoods. The homes for the most part were meticulously maintained. Miller was cut off from the rest of Gary by the steel mills and railroad lines, but it possessed its own network of shopping districts, elementary schools, a junior high and senior high school, and it functioned as a self-contained small town all unto itself.

Searching with a local realtor, we found an incredible house. Located on St. Joseph Street, a half-block from the beach, it was designed in art deco by a student of Frank Lloyd Wright and built in 1941. Made of steel and reinforced concrete, it sat on Gary's highest hill on one half acre of land. It had 3,500 square feet of living area on three levels, including four bedrooms, three baths, and a massive living room with a picture window featuring a full view of Lake Michigan and the Chicago skyline. The asking price was $115,000. I negotiated the price down to $90,000, an unbelievable bargain for such a dwelling. Our realtor told us that the house would be worth $150,000 or more if it were located in Ogden Dunes, an all-white village just next to Miller with housing of lesser quality and a shallower beach. Just because it was outside the Gary city limits, its value was greater. I did not care because racism's loss was certainly my gain. I relished my good fortune; a marvelous house, twenty minutes from work, ten minutes from city hall, and an hour's drive to Chicago or—if I wanted to catch the train—a five-minute drive to the South Shore railroad's Miller station, then a fifty-five-minute ride to the "Loop." The schools were Gary's finest with test scores above the national average; the lake Michigan beach, hundreds of feet deep and two miles long, was a priceless asset; and there was even a great restaurant one block away, the Beach Cafe, which served the best lake perch I have ever tasted.

We moved into the house, enrolled our younger daughter Janell in kindergarten at Nobel Elementary School, and settled into our new jobs. I looked forward to becoming involved in the community, and the chance to do so came before I could really settle in. The opportunity was to help elect Katie Hall to the U.S. Congress.

The Election of Katie Hall

In 1976, Adam Benjamin was elected to the U.S. House of Representatives from the first congressional district in Indiana, which includes all of the Gary metropolitan area. He replaced Ray Madden who had held the seat since 1942. In thirty-four years in Congress, Madden had not passed any major legislation and was virtually unknown outside his district. He was, however, a regular in the Lake County Democratic machine whose soldiers got out the vote for him on a regular basis. Serving until his early eighties, Madden rewarded the faithful with small favors as his staff helped constituents in matters such as Social Security eligibility, obtaining visas, and appointments to service academies. Madden was even helpful in greasing the wheels for federal aid to Gary, something Hatcher remembered well when in 1972 a young black Garyite chose to run against Madden in the Democratic party and didn't receive any support whatsoever from Hatcher. Madden won easily with a majority of the black vote going to him.

Unlike Madden, an easygoing, laid-back politician, Adam Benjamin, the son of Lebanese immigrants, was extremely hardworking and driven. As a liberal Democrat, he quickly rose to a position of chairman of the House subcommittee on transportation and public works. He was able to obtain over $100 million for his district in capital improvements in just six years, the most impressive being a $65 million package to revive the old Chicago South Shore and South Bend electric interurban railroad. These funds replaced the entire fleet of aging and obsolete passenger cars that were built in 1925 and had been continuously in use since that time. Other monies from this package included track improvements, a new maintenance facility, and several new stations, including the Gary Transportation Center referred to in Chapter 2. Articulate and well liked, especially by blacks, he won reelection by huge margins in 1978 and 1980. Unopposed in the 1982 Democratic party, he was set to face Thomas Kreiger, who was considered by his Republican party supporters a "throwaway" candidate as Benjamin was thought to be unbeatable.

On Tuesday, September 7, 1982, Adam Benjamin was found dead of a heart attack in his Washington apartment by his aide Peter Visclosky. Benjamin had been in the apartment alone over the Labor Day weekend and had not seen since that previous Friday. On September 10, stunned leaders of the first district Democratic party committee convened to select a successor as provided for by Indiana election law. One stipulation of this law is that all candidates who are currently on the ballot for a general election are ineligible to switch to a slot that suddenly becomes vacant because of resignation, incapacity, or death. Therefore, the pool of available candidates to fill Benjamin's shoes was already limited. Speculation as to Benjamin's successor filled the air almost from the moment that his death was reported. I can still remember having lunch with some faculty colleagues at a restaurant near the campus that was popular with white ethnic steelworkers and overhearing it said that "if Hatcher becomes Benjamin's replacement, at least we'll get him out of Gary." Mayor Hatcher had no aspirations to succeed Benjamin. After all, he was already a national figure, having been, along with Carl Stokes, one of the first two black mayors of a major American city. As a freshman congressman, he would be just one of twenty members of the Congressional Black Caucus with no seniority.

The party committee consisted of Mayor Hatcher, Robert "Hollywood Bob" Pastrick, the flamboyant mayor of East Chicago who was a staunch supporter of the Lake County Democratic party machine, and Mary Cartwright, a Democratic party worker. All members initially agreed that Benjamin's widow should be selected to serve out the two months of his remaining term, provided that she would endorse the committee's selection for the full term beginning January 1983. After hours of deliberation and negotiation, Pastrick nominated himself for the full term, and Hatcher and Cartwright cast their votes for Indiana State Senator Katie Hall, a black woman. Upon the nomination of Hall, Benjamin's widow refused to lend her support, and Mayor Hatcher, who, as committee chair, had the exclusive authority to select a replacement for the partial term, chose Hall over Pastrick's opposition.[2]

Katie Hall, forty-three years old in 1982, was born and raised in the rural Mississippi town of Mound Bayou. In 1960, she received a bachelor's degree in political science and education from Mississippi Vocational College, and she and her husband moved to Gary that same year to begin careers as public school teachers. In 1970, she received a master's degree in education from Indiana University and in 1972 was elected to the state legislature as a member of the House of Representatives. In 1974, she won election as one of two blacks in the Indiana State Senate and was reelected every term without serious opposition.

Hall's opponent Thomas Kreiger, the Republican sacrificial candidate, was fifty-eight years old, a bachelor, and a former public school teacher who quit in disgust because, in his own words, "the kids were a discipline problem and the pay was lousy." He became a computer programmer but at the time of the campaign was out of work.[3] His position on Social Security was to replace the system with private insurance, and he favored the use of robots in the steel industry, which at that time was operating at 60 percent capacity, with 50 percent of the region's work force tied to that industry in a congressional district with an 18 percent unemployment rate. With Democratic registration outnumbering Republican six to one, the election should have been no contest except for two factors—race and, to a lesser degree, sex.

Immediately after Hall's selection by the party committee, disgruntled whites led by Mayor Pastrick filed suit to block the nomination even though the process had been approved by Indiana Secretary of State Edwin Simcox. The Pastrick forces felt that Hall was but a puppet for Mayor Hatcher, whom they hated, and that a vote for her was a vote for him. However, the suit heard in rural Warsaw, fifty miles from Gary, was thrown out by Circuit Court Judge Marvin D. McLaughlin on September 27.[4] On the following day, after reviewing his options, Pastrick announced that he would not file an appeal and instead called for party unity.[5]

Katie Hall's campaign opened on Saturday, September 18, during a dreary rainy afternoon in the vacated Radigan furniture store on Broadway in Gary's all but deserted downtown. It was ironic that the campaign to elect the first black and the first woman to congress in Indiana's history would begin in the store once owned by the Republican who opposed Hatcher in the 1967 general election and, aided by the Lake County Democratic machine and thousands of "Republicans for a day," almost stole that election. I attended this meeting, having met the Halls when I visited Gary for my job interview that June. John Hall, Katie's husband, in addition to his law practice and full-time job as a Gary public school administrator, taught as an adjunct in my department. I was soon impressed with Katie Hall, who possessed a keen understanding of state and local politics not only from a practical point of view but from the perspective of a political scientist as well. I could also sympathize with her as she told about the insults she experienced as a member of the Indiana legislature, including the time white pages, still in their teens, tried to address her as "Katie" while calling the other legislators Mr. and Mrs. or Representative this or that. So as I saw her speak at the initial campaign meeting at Radigan's, I was proud to be involved in a process that could make history. Only twenty to twenty-five people, mostly those who could play significant roles in the campaign, were invited to that meeting. I quickly volunteered to be an adviser on housing and community development, my academic specialty, and during the week ahead would write several position papers on this subject mainly dealing with the impact of the Reagan administration's cuts in subsidized housing and the decimation of U.S. Department of Housing and Urban Development's entire budget.

As soon as Judge McLaughlin handed down his decision, the political "submachine" of Mayor Hatcher began to develop a strategy for Hall's election. This machine had been almost twenty years in the making, starting with a small group of young black professionals in the early 1960s known as Muigwithania, which loosely translated from Swahili, means "to come together and go forward."[6] Unlike mainstream middle-class blacks of that period (or the present time, for that matter) Muigwithania identified strongly with the aspirations of the lower-income, less educated black masses. In Hatcher's 1967 primary election, he had solid support among lower-income blacks but only mild support from middle-class residents, quite a few of whom were aligned with incumbent Mayor A. Martin Katz as tokens.[7] In fact, Hatcher only won 75 percent of the black vote citywide in the 1967 primary election, and analysis shows that in the lower-income Central District, the historically black community, he won by margins of 80 to 95 percent, but in the middle-class black neighborhoods on Gary's West Side, populated by homeowners who moved there in the 1950s and early 1960s replacing whites who fled to the suburbs, his plurality was only slightly higher than 50 percent. Over the years, Hatcher consolidated his support among all blacks, and his candidates defeated blacks and whites alike who were aligned with the white-dominated Lake County Democratic party machine. By 1982, seven of the nine city council members, a majority of the school board, both members of the Indiana State House of Representatives (Assembly), and the state senator from Gary, Katie Hall, were Hatcher supporters.

Still, there were strong forces in the black community opposed to Hatcher. After all, he had been in office over fifteen years and there were by that time several pretenders to his throne, local politicians who had advanced to a point where only ascendency to the mayor's office would satisfy their egos. Gary, by 1982, had not only the lingering problems of physical decay, crime, and neglect on the part of county and state government, problems that had been festering for decades, but new issues to deal with as well. These included inadequate city services such as an aging fleet of police cars, which would frequently break down on the way to reported crimes, and garbage trucks so old that their transmissions would fall out when they hit a bump on the city's pot-holed streets. The major new problem was unemployment as the steel mills, northwest Indiana's only major industry, had cut back from 70,000 workers in 1979 to only 40,000 by 1982. Though Hatcher wasn't responsible for that, his opponents, aided and abetted by the *Post-Tribune,* accused him of driving away potential new industry because of his militant positions on affirmative action, business disinvestment in South Africa, and public sector equity.[8] City Councilman Thomas Crump had all but announced his candidacy for mayor, and in the spring 1983 Democratic primary and later, he would run against Hatcher and lose by only 4,600 votes out of just over 50,000 cast. But sensing a once-in-a-lifetime opportunity to elect a black to Congress, Crump and Dozier Allen, Hatcher's other opponent, agreed to a truce and worked very hard for Hall's election.

Katie Hall's strategy was to ignore Kreiger and to run against President Reagan. Her slogan was clear; elect a Democrat to Congress who will fight for those things dear to a working-class, labor-oriented constituency: (1) contesting the Reagan administration budget cuts in housing, community development, job training, and education programs, (2) expanding unemployment benefits and public assistance aid for impoverished residents, (3) taking a strong stand against unlimited military spending, (4) fighting against high interest rates and economic measures favoring large corporations at the expense of small businessmen and working people, and (5) improving Social Security benefits, including a revamping of the system that at the time was heading toward bankruptcy. Her campaign was designed to make full use of the resources of organized labor with their large mailing lists and cash contributions. Hall intended to reach out strongly to blacks,

Hispanics, women, and suburban liberals, as I projected that she needed at least 90 percent of the black and Hispanic vote and one-third of the white electorate to win, given that blacks only accounted for 30 percent of all registered voters in the district.

With the strategy in place, Hatcher's precinct workers went out to campaign hard for Katie Hall. She was immediately endorsed by a unanimous vote of the Northwest Indiana Association of Labor Leaders after they interviewed Kreiger and her. On October 2, the campaign headquarters were officially opened in the old Radigan furniture store building, and $5,000 was collected on that day alone, in donations ranging from $500 from the leading black churches to one and two dollars from unemployed and elderly persons. The local county Democratic party, the old-line political machine that bitterly fought Hatcher's election in 1967 and had opposed him ever since, began to rally around Hall. They realized that a victory for Kreiger would not only be embarrassing but would also drag down the rest of the ticket and negatively influence several hotly contested races in the suburbs for the state legislature as well as the U.S. Senate race between incumbent Republican Richard Lugar and former Democratic Congressman Floyd Fithian. Although they did not welcome Hall's candidacy with open arms, they were not about to support Kreiger. When the U.S. Department of Labor announced on October 16 that unemployment nationally had risen to double-digit levels for the first time since the Great Depression, the *Post-Tribune,* in a marked departure from its usual anti-black rhetoric, commented on the positive effect of her campaign, stating that "people are now concerned with her stand on the issues, not the color of her skin or sex."[9] A countywide group of white women was formed to introduce Hall to suburban liberals not familiar with her background. By October 18, the Hall campaign had collected a total of $34,000. Of this amount, some $15,000 came from organized labor, a strong ally of the local county Democratic machine, and another $6,000 from the Democratic National Committee. Kreiger was only able to raise $25,000 because the Republican National Committee considered him an embarrassment and did not want to alienate black voters unnecessarily.[10]

The entire campaign was brief; only eight weeks in length from the time of Benjamin's death until election day. Campaign costs were relatively low for both candidates because the Gary area had no local television stations: all television came from Chicago, so advertising was by newspaper, radio, signs, and bumper stickers. Personal appearances were the rule rather than the exception, and Katie Hall excelled in speaking before groups, absolutely crushing Kreiger in the two public debates held in October. The *Post-Tribune* early in the campaign tried to erode Hall's credibility by constantly referring to her record of absenteeism while a state legislator. When Hall responded by pointing out that she was absent on several occasions during the 1982 legislative sessions because her sister was dying of cancer and she had to care for her sister's children as well as her own, the *Post-Tribune* backed off. Kreiger constantly put his foot in his mouth so that by late October, Republicans such as Indiana Senators Richard Lugar and Dan Quayle quietly disavowed him and begged off on even appearing on the same platform. Finally, in an editorial ten days before election, the *Post-Tribune* endorsed Hall with the comment that "if she distances herself from the Hatcher people she could make an excellent member of the House of Representatives." [11]

As the race entered its final week, the winner was still in doubt. Though the Democratic party organization was strong in the old steel mill towns of Gary, Hammond, and East Chicago, its strength was waning in the suburbs where long time Democrats mingled with white-collar Independents and Republicans, who commuted to executive and professional jobs in Chicago. As the election approached, we estimated again after taking some polls that with 70 percent of the electorate being white, Hall would need 98 percent of the black vote and about 40 percent of the white vote, assuming that the turnout rate of registered voters would be the same for both groups. The degree of white backlash was unknown, and Kreiger shamelessly appealed to racist sentiment by indicating over and over that a vote for Hall was a vote for Hatcher.

On the weekend before election day, the Hatcher machine really flexed its muscles. Hundreds of city workers and volunteers went out on Saturday and Sunday with computer printouts containing the names of every registered Democrat in their precinct. [12] The coverage was virtually 100 percent. Their task was simply to find each voter, ask if he intended to vote, admonish him if he dared to say he wasn't planning to do so, and then tell him to "be sure to vote straight Democratic" to avoid any mistakes with the old and cranky voting machines. Indeed, about 10:00 P.M. on Saturday Thomas Brown, my neighbor and precinct captain, rang my doorbell. We had met several times at rallies for Hall and other Democratic candidates, and he said with a wink, "Doc, you are going to vote Tuesday, right? Be sure to vote straight Democrat." I answered him, also with a wink, "Of course."

Election day, Tuesday, November 2, was cold and overcast with a light but steady rain. During the morning and early afternoon, turnout was heavy, peaking around 4:00 P.M. when the mills emptied out workers fresh from the day shift. The polls closed at 7:00 P.M., and the first returns looked good for Katie Hall. By 9:00 P.M., the campaign headquarters on Broadway was filled to capacity with curiosity seekers driving and walking up and down the street, greeting each other in front of the burned-out and vacant buildings of a once vibrant downtown, and remarking that the traffic and activity reminded them of the old days. As the returns came in, the crowd became more and more animated, even boisterous just like football fans at a sports bar watching their favorite NFL team in the Super Bowl. First it was announced that she had won Michigan City by 1,000 votes, and the crowd cheered lustily. Then came the announcement to everyone's surprise that Lake Station, the all-white blue-collar town that changed its name from East Gary after Hatcher's election, had also gone for Hall by a margin of just 58 votes. This was followed by another announcement that Hammond, with a 90 percent white population, had given Hall victory by just 98 votes. What had taken place was that the Lake County Democratic party machine by urging a straight Democrat vote had apparently given Hall victory in spite of their most serious reservations. Then came the words everyone had been waiting to hear. Charlene Crowell, Hatcher's press secretary, proudly announced the result of the Gary turnout: a 45,000 vote plurality for Hall. Pandemonium broke out as Katie Hall's supporters, black and white, young and old, college graduates and high school dropouts alike, cheered and hugged each other, some even broke into tears. No sooner had the cheering died than came a second, more anticlimatic announcement. "At 12:45 A.M. Thomas Kreiger conceded defeat." The crowd cheered once more, then waited for Katie Hall's appearance.

At just past 1:00 A.M. Katie Hall entered the building to thunderous applause. Standing on the platform with her husband and children by her side, she acknowledged the crowd's salute. Mayor Hatcher, also on the platform, was smiling broadly. After all, his hated enemies, members of the Lake County Democratic party machine, caught between a rock and a very hard place, were forced to eat crow and actually work for his candidate. Hall thanked her supporters, then twisted a knife in the Lake County machine's side by personally thanking Mayor Hatcher for his help. Said Hall, "This just goes to show that in America even if you are black and a woman, people will vote for you if you are the best qualified candidate." This was a true understatement. Despite the fact that blacks accounted for only 30 percent of the electorate, Katie Hall won 63.3 percent of the vote in the special election for the unexpired portion of Benjamin's term and 57 percent of the vote for the full term. One hundred fifty thousand votes were cast; about 65 percent of all registered voters turned out, with blacks voting at about the same rate as whites. Hall won 97 percent of the black vote and 51 percent of the white vote.

As we left and went out into the night to drive home on icy roads, all of us felt better. Yes, I thought, this really is America.

Serious Problems Come to the Surface

The winter of 1982-1983 was the mildest in over sixty years. There were only two light snowfalls, and on Christmas Day it was 65 degrees and people were out washing their cars. Most days were marked with bright sunshine and cool, crisp air rather than the cold, dull midwestern weather usual at that time of year.

But conditions in Gary were perhaps more dismal than ever. The euphoria of Katie Hall's victory had worn off, and, in the weeks following the holiday season, Gary professionals, business people, and institutional leaders in hospitals, the university, and social service agencies were beginning to face up to the harsh realities of the times and wondering out loud what the Hatcher administration was prepared to do about the serious problems of unemployment, crime, decline of the physical environment, and, most important, the near collapse of public services.

It was apparent that the only way to combat the loss of jobs in the steel industry was to attract new jobs to northwest Indiana in general and Gary in particular. Gary had numerous plant sites with rail and highway access, all necessary utilities, and a tax structure and workman's compensation package that didn't scare off potential employees. Located in the nation's heartland at the center of its rail and highway network, Gary was perfect in terms of access to raw materials and the distribution of finished goods, which is why it was founded by U.S. Steel in the first place. Even though other cities in the region, such as Hammond, East Chicago, and Michigan City, were competing for new plants along with Gary and the demand for new industry was limited as the United States moved from a manufacturing to a service economy, the attraction of new industrial jobs was still a very real possibility for a number of reasons. First, the steel industry had decided to implode—center their operations in northwest Indiana—so, even though employment in the industry had dropped by 40 percent in the past five years, the mills were not going to close altogether as they did in Chicago and Birmingham. Now, they were actually producing more steel than at any other time and had spent over $100 million on new equipment. Second, although research and development in steel wasn't a viable option (this was going to take place in Pittsburgh where the University of Pittsburgh and Carnegie-Mellon are located), there was a need for the production of specialized steel products, items that couldn't be made overseas. With a skilled work force in place, there was good reason to believe that Gary and northwest Indiana could be the national and even worldwide center for production of these goods. However, it was apparent that unless the problems of crime, physical appearance, and services were solved, new jobs, even those that were "placebound" to the Midwest, would go elsewhere.[13]

In early 1983, crime was the most discussed topic in Gary. The *Post-Tribune* was quick to let everyone who would listen know that in 1982 there were eight-six murders in Gary, giving the city a rate for this crime second in the nation, after Detroit. As anyone who has taken Criminology 101 knows, murder occurs most frequently among people who know each other, family members, lovers, acquaintances. In fact, Gary's Police Chief Virgil Motley repeatedly stated that eighty-one of Gary's eighty-six murders during that year were by people who personally knew their victims. The murder rate was understandable because of the problems of unemployment and poverty, which produced alcoholism, drug addiction, despair, mental disorder, and other behaviors leading to violence. However, the *perception* was that anyone walking Gary's streets would be accosted by an unknown assailant and blown away before he had a chance to surrender his cash and jewelry. The *Post-Tribune* also sensationalized home invasions, robberies, rapes, and possible arsons when they took place in Gary, and, though these occurrences are always frightening, the newspaper *did not* report that the highest rate and incidence of stolen automobiles was at the mammoth Southlake Mall regional shopping center in surburban Merrillville. These articles led the unsuspecting to believe that crime occurred only in Gary. The FBI uniform crime reports for 1982 showed that, in terms of total Part I crimes (murder, robbery, burglary, rape, auto theft, etc.), of 313 central cities in the U.S., Gary's crime rate ranked 151 or about the 50th percentile. Actually, among the cities with the ten worst crime rates (Detroit was first) were four in Florida—Miami, Ft. Lauderdale, Gainesville, and Tampa—but in these cities, gleaming new buildings and warm, subtropical weather hid the ugliness of violence. The perception of crime in Gary magnified its reality and deeply hurt the city's, and region's, chances of landing new jobs.

The problem of the physical environment was not the residential areas. These, for the most part, were clean, well maintained single-family homes built after World War II. Gary's worst slums in the historically black Central District had been torn down by Mayor Hatcher's administration during the period of 1968-1975 and by 1983, although 3,000 units of low-cost slum housing had been demolished, 2,300 units of new subsidized housing had replaced them. The problem was the quality of commercial districts and the entrances to the city. As stated in Chapter 2, business disinvestment in Gary began after World War II and accelerated after Hatcher's 1971 reelection. There had been virtually no new commercial construction in Gary since 1945, with the exception of a few fast food restaurants. Signs had not been replaced since World War II, and building exteriors were poorly maintained. The "coup de grace" was in October 1982 when Gainer Bank, formerly known as Gary National Bank, removed the large attractive electric time-temperature sign from its former headquarters building at the corner of Fifth and Broadway and replaced it with a small, cheap "Gainer·Bank" sign. A Gainer executive was quoted as saying, "We don't consider electric signs like the one we took down appropriate." [14] He forgot to mention that, only a few years before, Gainer built a spanking new headquarters complex in Merrillville, complete with a large, prominent time-temperature sign. The city's entrances were unattractive; small "Welcome to Gary" signs were dwarfed by weeds and views of ugly abandoned buildings awash in a sea of trash and litter. In addition to the decrepit storefronts, some occupied, some vacant, Gary's main streets were lined by tire storage yards, converted warehouses, and weed-infested (and rat-infested) vacant lots. In short, the entrances and main streets made Gary look like a very, very ugly place, certainly much less attractive than it really was.[15]

Perhaps the most serious obstacle to attracting new jobs to Gary was the inadequacy of public services. While the public schools were well financed, well maintained, and scoring higher on standardized tests than the public school system in nearby Chicago, services run by the city—police, streets, sanitation, and parks—were clearly inadequate. Perhaps the major reason for this inadequacy was the heavy cutback in federal funds by the Reagan administration. Although, of course, these cutbacks were national in scope, Gary was more heavily impacted than other cities because (1) through effective lobbying by Hatcher, coupled with the city's needs, Gary had one of the highest per capita aid ratios in the nation, and (2) while other cities were able to offset the federal aid losses with an increased tax base, higher taxes, and the imposition of user fees, Gary did not have that advantage. The poor economy prevented expansion of the tax base, major property owners refused to permit the city to increase taxes (as discussed in the previous chapter), and the administration refused to impose user fees on a population almost 30 percent whom were now below the poverty level.

During the period of 1975-1979 when federal Law Enforcement Assistance Administration (LEAA) money was flowing like water, the city was able to purchase an entire fleet of patrol cars with these funds, but in 1980, the LEAA money was cut off and, by early 1983, these once new and attractive cars were now three to seven years old, and the city had no funds to replace them. Rusted out, dented, and creaking, the old cars could not catch speeding teenagers from the suburbs driving newer high-performance autos. As stated earlier, the cars would often break down on the way to a call. The police force was well trained but terribly underpaid; in 1983, a Gary patrolman with five years experience earned only $16,000 per year compared to $21,000 for his Merrillville counterpart who had a new personally assigned automobile in addition to his salary. This low pay, coupled with the indignity of having to use old, obsolete, and unreliable equipment, drove morale way down. White officers, who comprised almost half of the force, would quit as soon as a suburban opening came available even though some would do so reluctantly because they would miss the challenge of policing in a high density, higher crime-prone city.[16] But more than anything else, it was the daily appearance of Gary's ragged police cars and tired officers that hurt the city's credibility when it came to economic development.

Because of federal aid cutbacks, streets were poorly maintained. Also, the Indiana Highway Department, which should have maintained at least major state-aided streets, chose not to do so in Gary. Every spring, streets would break out in a new rash of potholes and other deformities. As local wags put it, "You didn't need a sign to tell you where Merrillville ended and Gary began. All you had to do was wait until you felt the bumps." Garbage service, which was scheduled for once every week, was sporadic, as trucks broke down from wear and tear. As the city had no money to fix or replace the equipment, some neighborhoods were going weeks without pickups. We all dreaded the arrival of spring when warmer weather would bring rotting garbage and hordes of rats.

In the early weeks of 1983, the city administration was extremely defensive every time these problems were publicly mentioned. They were quick to blame the Reagan administration, state government, white flight, and the *Post-Tribune* but had no concrete proposals for solutions. The 1983 primary election was to be held in May, and the administration didn't want to make promises that sounded weak and hollow or that could not be kept. The public had to know that things were going to get worse before they got better. The Reagan administration had zero-funded the Comprehensive Employment and Training Administration (CETA) for the coming fiscal year, and all knowledgeable observers knew that by summer the city would have to lay off hundreds of employees. Given the administration's inability to deal with these problems head-on, Dr. F.C. Richardson of IUN and John Bettjeman, chief executive officer of Methodist Hospital, quietly organized what was to be called "the study group" to come up with some plans to get Gary back on track.

The Study Group

Both Richardson and Bettjeman had good reasons to find answers for Gary's plight. Richardson had lived in Gary since 1967 in the Morningside section of Glen Park. A dean at IUN and a Hatcher supporter since the 1967 general election campaign, Richardson was worried about the administration's refusal to deal squarely with the city's nagging problems. He had too much invested in Gary, both financially and personally, to walk away without trying every possible option to make things better. Bettjeman was equally committed to Gary for different reasons. Methodist Hospital, Gary's largest, had been forced by the Hatcher administration to enter into a consent decree pledging to spend one dollar to renovate and expand their Gary facilities for every dollar they spent on new facilities in the suburbs. This meant that Methodist Hospital had to commit a total of just over $30 million in capital improvements within Gary, and certainly they wanted to do everything possible to protect their investment.

Richardson and Bettjeman were longtime friends, and Richardson was chairman of the board of Methodist Hospital and, in effect, Bettjeman's boss.

The two decided to form a panel of about twenty citizens, all of whom were professionals in various areas of urbanism. Dr. Richardson asked me to join the group because of my background in urban planning. Others invited included the former Gary city attorney then in private practice, lawyers, accountants, bankers, realtors, educators, newspaper executives, and civic leaders. Depending on the session topic, representatives of city and county government were invited to address the group, but no government employees were asked to join because it was felt that publicly their agenda had to match that of their elected officials, and it would be unfair to them to inquire as to their private opinions on various issues. All meetings were to be private, without any news coverage.

The first meeting was held on February 3, 1983, on a Thursday afternoon at the IUN conference center. Meetings were held every Thursday after that until the end of April. The goal was to prepare a series of recommendations that could be conveyed to Mayor Hatcher and private sector leaders who were made aware of the group's existence and purpose. Though the overall goal was to develop a strategy for landing new jobs and investment in Gary, it was decided early on that before the city could actively go out and openly compete for jobs, the government and the private sector must create the proper climate for investment. As study group member Dr. Randall Morgan, Jr., a local physician, put it, "We must set the table before we can begin the banquet." By the time the group was ready to disband, the following "table setting" recommendations were hammered out:

1. Create a perception of safety.

2. Improve city services, especially in the areas of sanitation, park and recreation, and public works.

3. Work with federal and state government in positive joint ventures involving the Indiana Dunes National Lakeshore, Gleason Park, and the local Medical Center.

4. Get the private sector to invest in Gary's local economy.

5. Have local financial institutions invest in Gary's owner-occupied and rental real estate.

6. Encourage the Chamber of Commerce to promote Gary's advantages to Chicago residents and business.

7. Improve the physical appearance of Gary's business and especially the neighborhood strip commercial districts.

8. Improve entrances to the city especially the major boulevards.

9. Develop a Comprehensive Plan.

10. Develop a strong and viable public-private partnership to implement successfully the first nine recommendations.

Creating a Perception of Safety. The study group felt strongly that before any other initiatives could be instituted, it was urgent that the climate of safety be improved. The first step would be to purchase the necessary patrol cars and related vehicles to enable the police department to do its job. About two hundred cars would be needed at a total cost of just over $4 million. There were two possible means of financing: a lease-purchase agreement that could be paid out in three years when the cars would have to be replaced once again or a bond issue with a ten-year payout. The bond issue would cost the city less money in the short run, but the city government would be placed in the position of having to pay for these vehicles years after they were used up and placed out of service. For that reason, the group recommended the lease-purchase mechanism.

Other suggested means of improving the perception of public safety were to station officers downtown on foot patrol and directing traffic, new uniforms for police officers, and higher pay for officers to cut down the need for second jobs. While all these measures, including the purchase of patrol cars, added up to a considerable amount of money, the group felt that, once presented with a concrete plan of action to mitigate the impact of crime, U.S. Steel would agree to a modest tax rate hike, especially if cost reduction measures, including job cuts and elimination of such frills as leased automobiles for department heads, were also employed by the city.

Improving City Services. The study group realized that second only to the need to improve the image and performance of the police department was the upgrading of basic public services. New garbage trucks, snowplows, and street maintenance equipment were needed. It was recommended that a phased program of equipment replacement take place as some rolling stock was adequate, others marginal, and a few pieces inoperable altogether. As sanitation trucks, snowplows, and street-sweeping and related maintenance equipment have a five- to seven-year useful life, it was recommended that short-term (five-year maximum) bond issues be floated to finance these purchases.

The Gary Fire Department was one of the highest rated in the state in terms of training and efficiency, and, as a result, fire insurance rates in 1982 and 1983 were actually lower in Gary than in the adjacent suburbs. However, some equipment was obsolete, and, of the city's twelve fire stations, five were built between 1912 and 1917 and were virtually disfunctional. The study group recommended that a detailed plan be developed by city staff for eventual replacement of old stations and obsolete equipment.

Thanks to the antipoverty and youth development programs financed by federal monies during the late 1960s and 1970s, the Gary Department of Parks and Recreation had established and maintained a variety of programs for all age groups and acquired and developed several new parks as well.

However, the study group knew that by mid-1983, hundreds of city workers, including many in the various recreation activities, would have to be laid off. Already there were reports from the 1982 recreation season of swimming pools closed for repairs, torn nets on the few tennis courts operated by the department, decrepit conditions at the beach bathhouses, restrooms, and shelters, and lack of equipment to facilitate arts and crafts programs. The study group recommended a full and complete analysis of city recreation needs and facilities with the possibility of closing some of the small neighborhood and mini-parks in residential areas with declining populations and of consolidating/upgrading activities in stable and growing neighborhoods.

Joint Ventures. The study group, after reflection and debate, felt strongly that Gary's administration should reach out to county, state, and federal government in the development of joint use programs, namely (1) the National Park Service and Marquette Park/Beach, (2) the State of Indiana (particularly Indiana University and Gleason Park), and (3) the Veterans Administration and the Gary Medical Center.

In 1966, the Indiana Dunes National Lakeshore was incorporated into the National Park Service. The park grounds, containing rare natural sand dunes and beaches, stretched from just outside the U.S. Steel property in Gary's Miller Neighborhood east to Michigan City. During the 1970s, the National Lakeshore was expanded to take in all of the duneland east of Marquette Park almost to the edge of Gary's downtown. The National Park Service wanted to acquire Marquette Park as part of the Lakeshore properties with the payoff for Gary being facility improvements, the widening and repaving of roads in Miller leading to the park, beach renovation, and improvement of related facilities such as the small boat harbor, Children's Park, concession stands, and restrooms. The city would be spared the expense of improving, patrolling, and maintaining Marquette Park. However, the Hatcher administration had long resisted such an arrangement fearing that once the National Park Service took over, its mostly white police officers would discourage use of Marquette Park and its beaches by black Garyites just as the virtually all-white Gary police force did until the mid-1960s. The study group, though sensitive to the administration's concerns, felt that a carefully written joint use agreement could provide the best of both worlds to Gary, a vastly improved park at no cost to the city but with policy formulation and implementations shared by local and federal governments. As John Bettjeman put it, "50 percent of something is better than 100 percent of nothing." The study group was also keenly aware that unless a joint use agreement was quickly crafted, there would be no money to implement its provisions. The Reagan administration had already cut deeply into domestic programs including those of the National Park Service (Department of the Interior), and more cuts were forecasted for the next fiscal year.

Gleason Park, a 400-acre facility, is located on the Little Calumet River in south central Gary. Named for the first superintendent of U.S. Steel's Gary Works it contains an 18-hole golf course,[17] the city's old high school football stadium, and an expanse of picnic areas, baseball fields, and basketball and tennis complexes. By 1983, the facilities were run down, and the city had no money to make substantial improvements. Indiana University Northwest is located on the park's southeast corner on land donated by the Gary Park Board to the state of Indiana in 1956. The university site included only classroom buildings, administration offices, a student union building, and related parking areas. The study group felt that if the city of Gary could be convinced to let the university build a multipurpose recreation building with joint use by university students (30 percent of whom were black Garyites) and community residents on the site of an old recreation building built by the WPA in 1935, a package could be put together including rehabilitation of the old recreation center and refurbishing the 18-hole golf course and tennis courts, creating a putting course and driving range on the abandoned 9-hole North Gleason course, and roadway, pedestrian, and bicycle path improvements, all to be paid for by state funds. The state would get a new recreation building for IUN, and the city would have a vastly improved park at no cost to its government. It was known that the Hatcher administration would react as coldly to this proposal as the one for the Lakeshore, but the study group felt that it should be put on the table anyway.

Gary's Methodist and St. Mary's hospitals are located downtown within two blocks of each other. In 1978, the Gary Community Mental Health Center was built midway between the two at a cost of $10 million. Physicians' offices had sprung up nearby, and the area was formally declared as the "Gary Medical Center" by the city administration in 1981. With Methodist and St. Mary's undergoing millions of dollars in renovations as part of the consent decree and the mental health center brand new and vibrant, the ideal complement would be a Veterans Administration hospital. The only VA hospital facilities in northern and central Indiana were located in Ft. Wayne and Indianapolis, and the closest VA hospital for northwest Indiana residents was Hines in suburban Chicago, over one hour away. There were many advantages to locating a new VA hospital in the medical center area: it would be adjacent to three existing health care institutions, its location just off the Indiana Toll Road was only forty-five minutes by automobile and fifty minutes by commuter rail from downtown Chicago, making it convenient for consulting physicians from that city, and it was twenty minutes closer to Chicago than other potential sites in suburban Merrillville. Also, development of the hospital could provide over one thousand construction jobs and at least five hundred permanent jobs, many of which could be held by Gary residents. The study group realized that a Gary site for the VA hospital would be a hard sell not only because it was a low priority item on the VA's construction schedule but more so because of Gary's reputation for high crime and poor city services. However, it would be worth the effort, and with Katie Hall in Congress it was reasonable to assume that the Democrat-controlled House of Representatives could boost its priority and endorse its location in Gary.

Private Sector Investment. While increasing the number of jobs in the "export" economy was the study group's long-term goal (and that of the city administration), there was no reason not to encourage investment in the local economy as well. The 1980 U.S. Census showed that, based on per capita income, Gary residents generated total personal earnings of just over $1 billion per year. However, by 1983, virtually all chain supermarkets had deserted the city, along with fast food restaurants, movie theaters, and small businesses. The study group recommended that the Gary Chamber of Commerce prepare a "fact book" and distribute it to major franchise operations.

Local Financial Institutions Investment. Gary had in 1983, a sound, relatively attractive stock of single-family and multi-family residences. However, in 1982, the Gary Human Relations Commission found that Gary-based financial institutions only made 6 percent of their residential real estate loans in Gary. While members of the study group who were connected with financial institutions loudly applauded group initiatives directed at the city administration, such as the improvement of public services, safety, and development of joint ventures, they were remarkably silent on this initiative. A few even urged that it be dropped from the list of recommendations to be delivered to the major private sector elites until public safety and city services were improved, but they were voted down by other members of the study group.

Promoting Gary's Advantages to Chicago Residents and Businesses. This recommendation, unanimously adopted by the study group, would highlight Gary's low-cost housing, the lakefront amenities, the airport, and locational assets to Chicagoans. The Chamber of Commerce, with monies provided by private contributions, would take out Chicago newspaper, radio, and public television advertisements. This would be a long-term campaign (three to five years) and would, if implemented, cost about $100,000 per year, with results, if any, occurring well into the future.

Improving the Physical Appearance of Gary's Businesses. As noted before, Gary's business establishments had established a policy of deferred maintenance going back as far as the immediate post-World War II period. With private funds in the form of loan guarantees by local banks for building refurbishment, complemented by local and state government monies for public right-of-way improvements, the condition of Gary's commercial strips and district nodes would be at least incrementally improved.

Upgrading Entrances to the City. As previously explained, first impressions of Gary are formed when one enters the city from major roadways. These include Interstate 94 (also known as the Borman Expressway), the Indiana Toll Road, Broadway (State Road 53), U.S. 12-20, and Grant Street. All are state aided, and the interstates are federally aided as well. The task would be for the city government, assisted by influential private sector participants and Lake County's entire legislative delegation, to work quietly with state government leaders to improve these roadways with repaving, landscaping, new lighting, and related amenities including, of course, directional signs to Gary posted on all interstate routes.

Developing a Comprehensive Plan. The city's last comprehensive plan was adopted by the city council in 1964. Certainly, there had been considerable changes over the past twenty years not reflected in the 1964 plan, such as the decline of downtown Gary and new growth on the city's western edge. The 1964 plan also did not emphasize development of Gary's airport.

The Public-Private Partnership. The study group's final and most important recommendation was that in order to implement the first nine recommendations, a strong public-private partnership must be forged. Mayor Hatcher and the Gary city administration would have to put aside the bitter memories of the 1967 election and abandonment of the city by the white business community in the early 1970s. On the other hand, the white business and institutional establishment now located in Gary's suburbs, along with the Lake County Democratic machine and the Republican-controlled state government, would have to realize that Gary and its 150,000 residents did exist and that to ignore them not only was morally wrong but worked against their own self-interests as well. The study group proposed a "summit meeting" with Mayor Hatcher and representatives from the suburban governments, state government, and the business community in attendance in order to put aside differences and work for the common good.

The study group's recommendations were finalized on Thursday, April 28, 1983. It was decided to present these recommendations simultaneously to Mayor Hatcher and the presidents of Gainer and Bank One, the president of the Gary Chamber of Commerce, and the superintendent of U.S. Steel's

Gary Works after the May primaries. A few private sector members of the study group quietly remarked that the task just might be easier if Mayor Hatcher lost the primary.

The 1983 Democratic Primary

Immediately after New Year's Day, Thomas Crump, a forty-three-year-old city councilman and Gary native, announced his candidacy for mayor. Crump, the owner of a group of nursing homes and holder of a bachelor's degree in administration, pledged that if he was elected, Gary would be run in a "businesslike manner." He would, unlike Hatcher, work with the private sector and open up lines of communication with suburban and state governments. His plan of attack was to denounce Hatcher as an outsider who had been in office too long, was resistant to change, and was a 1960s black militant out of step with the realities of the 1980s. With no specific platform or concrete proposals for change, his campaign slogan was "Enough is Enough."

At the same time as Crump announced his candidacy, Hatcher announced that he was running for reelection for an unprecedented fifth term. He was quick to remind Gary voters of his accomplishments: forcing the city's largest hospital to remain in town, building almost three thousand units of new subsidized housing, hiring hundreds of blacks in city jobs, virtually eliminating police brutality, and raising the percentage of blacks on the police force from only 5 percent in 1967 to 55 percent sixteen years later. He could point from his city hall office window to the Genesis Convention Center, the Sheraton Hotel, the Genesis Towers Senior Citizens Housing, and the emerging Adam Benjamin Transportation Center as gleaming examples of public sector initiatives by him as contrasted with the decaying, vacant, boarded-up, burned-out relics of the private sector's part of downtown. His campaign pitch was essentially "Elect Tom Crump and you will turn Gary back over to the same people who deserted it years ago."

As the campaign moved along in the mild winter days of January and early February, I became repeatedly irritated at Councilman Crump's attacks on Mayor Hatcher, comparing Gary with Indianapolis and accusing Hatcher of incompetence and cronyism. Indianapolis was a much larger city, the state capital with loads of state government investments, and a regional business center serving not only most of Indiana but large parts of eastern Illinois and western Ohio as well. It was the international headquarters of Fortune 500 corporation Eli Lilly and Company, the giant pharmaceutical conglomerate. Gary had none of these advantages. As for cronyism, the traditional old-line machine with its reward of small favors to residents in exchange for votes was much more redistributive and fair than the reform politics that produced the "new" machine where well-connected bankers, architects, builders, and businessmen make campaign contributions to buy television time for candidates who once elected, would reward their contributors with lucrative contracts while the voters, mesmerized by the television spots get nothing but speeches and higher taxes.[18]

I had agreed to present a paper dealing with black mayors and municipal efficiency at the April 7-9 meeting of the National Council for Black Studies in Berkeley, California. My work focused on fifteen cities in the East-North Central Census Division (Illinois, Indiana, Michigan, Ohio and Wisconsin) with populations of over 100,000. I chose to measure "efficiency" by using the variables of municipal bond rating, per capita tax load, number of municipal employees per 1,000 residents and per capita municipal indebtedness. Using regression analysis, I found that Gary ranked eighth among the fifteen in "efficiency," just behind Indianapolis but ahead of Chicago; Youngstown, Ohio; Detroit; Dayton, Ohio; Rockford and Peoria, Illinois; and Flint, Michigan.[19] After presenting this paper, I immediately sent a copy to Jim Holland, the Gary deputy mayor, and told him to use it as he saw fit because I was concerned about the councilman's attacks on the Hatcher administration's competence without the benefit of data. After this paper was made public, the Crump campaign was at a loss to explain in a quantifiable manner why Gary's government was not up to its task managing the city's affairs.

As the campaign wound down, Crump continued his attacks on Hatcher, but, with no specific proposals for change on his part, their sting became weaker and weaker. Although Crump had a sizable army of volunteers and spent over $50,000, Hatcher still had his patronage army of hundreds of city workers plus volunteers. Also, Hatcher made a temporary alliance with Dozier Allen, his onetime supporter who turned and ran against him for mayor in the 1975 primary election. Allen, the Calumet Township Trustee,[20] was able to use his patronage workers in Hatcher's behalf. Newly elected Congresswoman Katie Hall made appearances for Hatcher and was quick to remind voters that with Mayor Hatcher in office it would be easier for her to work to obtain federal funds for Gary. At a campaign rally on Saturday, April 30, she exclaimed, "We have been building an organization for the past twenty years. In 1967, we elected Richard Hatcher as mayor. Last year you elected me to congress as the first black and first woman in Indiana's history. Look all around you at the convention center, Sheraton Hotel, new housing, all brought to you by this administration and this political organization. We have just begun to bring jobs and progress to Gary. Don't desert us now. Vote for Richard Hatcher on Tuesday."

On election day, Hatcher won, with 27,800 votes compared to 23,200 for Thomas Crump. Hatcher's margin of 54.7 percent was his lowest in four reelection campaigns. Though he won an unprecedented fifth term, like any other politician, his liabilities were beginning to catch up with him. It was to be his last hurrah, but, in May 1983 one would never have guessed that by talking to city administrators and campaign workers.

The Study Group Reports

After the 1983 primary election, the study group agreed that Dr. F.C. Richardson and John Bettjeman would first present the recommendations to Mayor Hatcher; then, if the response was positive, a presentation to private sector leaders would be made. I argued that if private sector endorsement came first, it would be easier to "sell" these recommendations to the mayor, but I was outvoted. The two cochairs met with Mayor Hatcher on June 7, 1983, and reported to the group on June 10 that Mayor Hatcher had been receptive but made no commitments, stating that he would "take them under advisement."

As the weeks turned into months and we heard nothing further from the mayor's office, most of the group members quietly assumed that the Hatcher administration felt that the May primary was a mandate for their policies and that business as usual was the order of the day. By September 1983, the group had disbanded, with members going back to their day-to-day duties. I personally felt that it was unfair and unrealistic for a city administration to do an about-face immediately upon the presentation of a group of recommendations by leaders of only *two* of the many major business, institutional, and governmental elites of northwest Indiana. I felt that, in time, the administration would be supportive of all recommendations and would be supportive earlier if they were endorsed quietly by a broad spectrum of external private sector leadership. Time would prove me right. By the time the Hatcher administration turned over the reins of power to Thomas Barnes on January 1, 1988, they had endorsed and begun implementation on every recommendation. The same could *not* be said for the private sector.

As 1983 drew to a close, the Hatcher administration's overall strength was slowly but surely draining away. In July, almost three hundred city employees (one-fourth of the total work force) were laid off as a result of lost federal funds coupled with lower than anticipated tax revenue because of the recession. The VA hospital was downgraded to a clinic, then relocated to Crown Point, a forty-minute drive from Gary in a Republican congressman's district. The patrol cars simply got older, the sanitation trucks continued to break down, and black middle-class Garyites started to talk about moving to suburban Merrillville even in the face of white hostility. I was disappointed that the Hatcher administration hadn't moved forward to deal with the city's problems and returned to concentrating on my university duties. Then, on November 10, 1983, I received a call from Gail Harris, the city's planning director, asking if I could help prepare Gary's new comprehensive plan.

5

The Comprehensive Plan of 1986

Work on the Gary Comprehensive Plan began in November 1983 and continued until December 1986 when it was finally adopted by the plan commission and city council. Its development and eventual passage represents what can be accomplished in a black governance framework when one does not have to worry about constraints external to that city.

Gail Harris's telephone call caught me by surprise. I had no idea that the city wanted to become involved in comprehensive planning, as none of my previous discussions with her or other city officials had indicated any interest in that area. However, as I did some background research, I found that, unlike what appeared on the surface, this city did have, over the past twenty years, some interest in long-range planning.

As mentioned in Chapter 2, Gary began as a "planned" community, although the major (and perhaps only) goal was a site arrangement to best accommodate the mill, with the first subdivision serving the needs of the managers, professionals, and middle-class business types. The mill blue-collar workers and related service personnel, about 80 percent of the total city work force, wound up being placed outside the "planning" area in newly built slums. By 1917, urbanists familiar with Gary, such as Grahame Rohme Taylor, author of *Satellite Cities*, began calling for comprehensive planning. In 1923, four years after the formation of a planning board, a group of consultants from Chicago prepared a plan calling for parks, boulevards, lakefront drives, and landscaped buffers between the mill and residential areas, but the plans were scuttled by U.S. Steel because they would take land needed for mill expansion.[1] Although the city did adopt a weak zoning ordinance in 1925, designed only to protect the mills, commercial areas, and high-grade residential districts, the planning board ceased to function as an active body. Until after the end of World War II, the only planning-related activity on the part of city staff was reviewing proposed zone changes, lot splits, and subdivision permits, all of which were granted without delay as long as the petitioner was well connected with U.S. Steel, the local politicians, or, preferably, both.

After World War II, the city adopted a zoning ordinance based on a state enabling model. This ordinance was an improvement over the 1925 version as it had fourteen specific districts covering every type of existing land use in Gary, relatively strong enforcement powers, and provisions for zone changes, variances, and conditional use permits. However, there was no comprehensive plan, and the plan commission, which existed mainly to make recommendations for zone changes and public acquisitions, took actions mainly based on politics and what the majority of that body felt was "good planning practice." The city had no professional planners on their payroll, and the zoning section was staffed mainly by clerks with high school educations headed by a "planning engineer" licensed by the state of Indiana as a surveyor whose only exposure to planning was regular attendance at the American Institute of Planners annual meeting.[2]

In 1955, the Cornell University School of Architecture was employed by the Gary Chamber of Commerce to prepare a "1980" plan for downtown. The faculty and graduate students came up with a plan that was bold and spectacular. It featured a loop road around the downtown with a pedestrian mall along Broadway. Also included were new department stores along Broadway, a conference center next to the Hotel Gary, and a "commuter railroad station" located on the exact site now occupied by the Adam Benjamin Transportation Center. Other recommendations by the Cornell University group included a steel museum, an Industrial Loop Road, and a marina. Although this plan received considerable newspaper publicity, it was never adopted by the plan commission or the city of Gary.

By the mid-1950s, Gary's political infrastructure was controlled by the white-ethnic-dominated Lake County Democratic machine. This machine was led by Peter Mandich, who was elected mayor of Gary in 1951 in an upset victory over a Republican incumbent who was controlled by business interests including U.S. Steel. After Mandich's election, a rift developed between Gary's government and the business community. The Gary politicians wanted nothing to do with planning because their modus operandi was the distribution of resources on a political basis whereas the essence of planning is allocation based on rationality as defined by more exact disciplines such as urban design, economics, sociology, and geography. Though the business community was by no means supportive of planning, they were guided by economic reality. In 1955, the suburban, auto-oriented "Village" shopping center opened just outside Gary, and the city's retail trade shrank by 20 percent by 1960 in both the number of jobs and dollar volume of sales. Gary's bankers, merchants, and professionals realized that the city's crumbling infrastructure had to be repaired, new schools and parks built, and new housing constructed, in order to retain the white middle class and shore up property values. Therefore, by the end of the 1950s this body came to realize that some form of planning was needed.

In 1960, the Gary business community formed a blue ribbon group known as the "Committee of 100." It contained not only bankers, lawyers, merchants, and professionals, but representatives from organized labor, the religious community, including the city's Catholic bishop, and four black leaders, which for Gary was a real innovation at that time. The group's mission was to promote the city's welfare by the utilization of all "modern" techniques available. One of these techniques was, of course, comprehensive planning. In its report to Gary's Mayor George Chacharis, a Greek immigrant who became a U.S. Steel engineer before going into politics, there was a provision for planning. The Committee of 100 would provide the salary for a professional planner and a secretary, office space, and supplies for an eighteen-month period. At the end of this time, the planner and his staff would move into city hall and be placed on the city's payroll with full benefits. Chacharis agreed to this arrangement, and the Committee of 100 hired William Staehle as the city's first planning director.

Bill Staehle, held a bachelor's degree in architecture and a master's degree in planning, both from nearby Illinois Institute of Technology (IIT), and had worked as a planner in Chicago and a part-time instructor at IIT. He was well trained, energetic, a visionary, and, for Gary, quite ahead of his time as he believed in equal rights for blacks and equitable service delivery to all residents, regardless of income levels.[3]

Staehle began his duties in July 1961 and, by the time he moved into city hall in January 1963, had assembled a small staff, compiled an extensive data base for planning purposes using primarily the 1960 U.S. Census, revised the zoning ordinance using contemporary standards, and engaged the services of a Chicago-based firm, Tech-Search, to prepare Gary's first comprehensive plan.

This plan, completed in 1964, was a state-of-the-art physical development scheme modeled after the highly successful plan for Philadelphia by Edmund Bacon and Larry Reich in 1961. It featured separate elements for residential, commercial, and industrial use, community facilities, circulation, and urban design. As the consultants were hampered by the fact that Gary was almost 100 percent built up and that U.S. Steel wasn't about to part with its vacant land holdings along Lake Michigan, the plan's recommendations for the private use of land were extremely limited.[4] However, the plan did make bold proposals for new schools and parks linked together, upgraded utility systems, an industrial highway (shades of the 1955 Cornell University proposal), and a parkway along the Little Calumet River reserving the 100-year floodplain for open space. The plan was shortsighted in that it predicted that downtown Gary would remain as the commercial and office hub of northwest Indiana for the rest of the century. It also recommended that the city's airport be turned into a regional park. It said nothing about the problems of segregated housing and de facto segregated schools, although it endorsed wholesale redevelopment that would have dislocated almost 40 percent of Gary's black population. In that respect, the 1964 Gary Comprehensive Plan was not unlike hundreds of others being prepared nationally during the period. Physical planning was the order of the day, having been codified by T.J. Kent,[5] and few professional planners had by that time heeded the call of Mel Webber for taking social responsibility for their decisions.[6]

In January 1968, Staehle resigned as planning director to become head of Gary's Model Cities program. The newly elected mayor Richard Hatcher chose Charles Allen as his replacement. Allen, one of the first blacks in America to receive a degree in planning, had over ten years of experience as a professional planner and was well qualified for the job. Allen became frustrated as, over the next several years, Hatcher repeatedly ignored his recommendations for updating and revising the 1964 plan, favoring short-term, highly visible development projects. Between 1968 and the early 1980s, comprehensive planning took a back seat to development activities. The planning department was placed in a "line" arrangement within the division of physical and economic development (see figure 2). The virus of "projectitus" was so rampant that by 1980, the planning department was actually named the "department of development and planning."

Despite the switch to a development emphasis, the planning department always managed to attract well-qualified professionals. In 1981, Gail Harris was hired away from East Chicago, Indiana, as Gary's planning director. Ms. Harris, a black woman, had a bachelor's degree in architecture from Tuskeegee University and a master's degree in planning from Illinois Institute of Technology. In East Chicago, she served as a one-person planning department for this city of 40,000 people, handling zoning, public acquisitions, and long-range planning. Her chief deputy and head of the advanced planning section was Taghi Arsharmi, an Iranian immigrant who held a master's degree in landscape architecture from Iowa State University. Singh Bakshi, a native of India, was the urban designer with degrees in architecture and planning from the University of Illinois. Carol Ann Seaton, a black Garyite, headed the planning section and held a master's degree in planning from the University of Iowa. The staff's transportation planner was Margaret Merhoff, a white liberal from eastern Tennessee, who held a master's degree in planning from the University of Tennessee, Knoxville. The community development coordinator was Helena Smith, a black Gary native who held a bachelor's degree in Afro-American studies from Indiana University Northwest and a master's degree in public administration from the same institution. By contrast, the highest degrees held by the white planning directors in nearby Hammond and East Chicago at that time, were bachelor's degrees in planning and sociology, respectively. And the white director of the regional planning agency, the Northwestern Indiana Regional Planning Commission, held only a bachelor's degree in civil engineering while heading a well-funded 35-member staff. Over a two-month period between November 1983 and January 1984, I had several meetings with Gail Harris and her staff. I found them all to be bright, energetic, dedicated to Gary, and at least as competent as professional planners in cities where I had previously worked, including Minneapolis, San Bernardino, Los Angeles, Baltimore, New York City, and Washington, D.C. The staff was handicapped by a heavy workload that almost always entailed up to 60-hour workweeks without additional compensation. The equipment was virtually nonexistent; while agencies of similar size had microcomputers and were using software packages such as Lotus 1-2-3, the planning department had only one ancient Wang word processor and an assortment of 1960 vintage drafting machines and Frieden mechanical calculators.

The planning department's work was made more difficult by logistics. The director, community development coordinator, and planning technicians were housed in the basement of city hall. The planning coordinator, transportation planner, and drafting section were located on city hall's third floor in cramped quarters shared with the public works department. The advanced planning section, which consisted of urban designer Taghi Arsharmi, a technician, and a secretary, were housed in a former insurance company building one block down the street from city hall in quarters shared with the city's Division of Social Services. Communications among the three dispersed locations was difficult at best, especially in winter when one had to walk along icy sidewalks to get from one office to another.

The arrangement I worked out with Gail Harris called for writing the city's new comprehensive plan over the next two years and preparing "special studies" as needed by the department and the mayor's office. Harris explained to me that Mayor Hatcher had long realized that the city's 1964 plan was hopelessly outdated but that work on a new document had been held up because the present staff was already spread too thin on development projects. Now, she said, I was in town and could help them with this need. I was offered a nice cozy corner office with windows on both sides in the advanced planning section and access to secretarial services and whatever equipment, however meager, that the section had available. I agreed to compensation at the rate of $20 per hour for fifteen to twenty hours of work per week; this was all the money the city had to give planning consultants, and I looked at the assignment more as community service than

actual professional planning consultation. By January 1984, I was settled in
my office at 475 Broadway and ready to begin the replanning of Gary.

Preparing the Work Program

During the first weeks of January 1984, I had several additional meetings
with Gail Harris, Deputy Mayor James Holland, and Mayor Hatcher
himself. I was deeply impressed with Hatcher: he was brilliant, mentally
tough, and sincere in his dedication to Gary. He said that he had realized for
some years that the 1964 plan should be updated but with the pressure of
day-to-day crises plus the necessary staff cutbacks caused by budget short-
falls following the recessions of 1979-1982 and the reductions in federal aid,
such an effort had not been possible until now. He apologized for not being
able to pay me more what he termed "a person of my ability and track record
should receive." I assured him that I was perfectly satisfied with the
arrangement I had worked out with the planning department because, after
all, mayors in places such as Tampa, Florida, and Pomona, California, had
always welcomed any assistance as community service, but this was the
first time an elected official was offering to pay me for my work.

By the end of January it was clear that the following questions had to be
resolved before work on the plan could begin: (1) What elements should be
included in the comprehensive plan? (2) What should the time frame be for
realizing plan goals and objectives: fifteen years, twenty years, twenty-five
years? (3) How should the plan be structured? (4) How much time should
elapse before beginning work on the plan, preparation of an initial draft,
and final city council approval? (5) And, most important, what type of
citizen participation mechanism should be developed?

After conferring with Gail Harris, Taghi Arsharmi, and Carol Ann
Seaton, I decided that the best approach would be initially to develop a
citizen participation strategy and then work with a citizen/city staff body to
develop first the work programs and then the plan itself.

The city of Gary had developed an excellent mechanism for citizen
participation since Mayor Hatcher was first elected. Gary was an active
player in the War on Poverty and Model Cities programs, the urban renewal
Neighborhood Development Program, and, since 1974, was an entitlement
city for the Community Development Block Grant Program.[7] All these
federal assistance programs required active citizen participation. By the
mid-1970s, cities like Gary with an extensive background in federal aid
programs came to realize that instead of every single program having their
own citizen participation element, this function would be better served
being centralized in the office of the chief executive. The citizen participation office could then *coordinate* this activity for all city-run programs

whether federally, state, or locally funded, thus preventing duplication of effort as well as minimizing conflict. Atlanta and St. Paul led the way in establishing citizen participation offices in the mid 1970s, and in 1978 Mayor Hatcher followed suit by establishing the Mayor's Office of Urban Conservation. By 1983, this office had taken responsibility for organizing citizen participation for all city-sponsored activities. Headed by Patricia Carlisle, an energetic, young black woman with a journalism degree from Marquette University, the Office of Urban Conservation was the obvious place to start with citizen participation.

Pat Carlisle and I quickly agreed that, when it came to developing the Gary Comprehensive Plan, quality of citizen participation was far more important than quantity. We both realized that while hundreds of residents would turn out for hearings regarding the annual allocation of Community Development Block Grant funds, few would be interested in monitoring and inputting a planning process that would have as an end product a document that would point out what might happen in twenty to twenty-five years. Unlike Beverly Hills, Boca Raton, Florida, and Carmel, California, where wealthy residents could indulge themselves in the luxury of dreaming about the future while enveloped by a clean, comfortable and shiny new built environment and surrounded by beautiful scenery in a warm climate, Garyites were worried about *immediate* day-to-day issues such as finding employment, chasing rats and roaches out of their homes, driving through blizzards on worn-out roads, and fighting off burglaries and home invasions all amidst dirty, run-down, and ugly physical surroundings. The consensus of scholars of citizen participation had long been that lower income people were present-oriented and therefore that involving them in planning was a much more difficult effort than working with future-oriented middle- and upper-class client groups.[8]

Given this reality, we decided to develop a broad-based citizen participation committee. The Office of Urban Conservation had previously divided Gary into thirteen residential neighborhoods with populations ranging from 6,400 to 21,400. One leader from each neighborhood would be selected by Urban Conservation. These residents would be joined by representatives from citywide entities including "private" organizations such as U.S. Steel, Gary Chamber of Commerce, Gary/Hobart Water Company, Gainer Bank, Northwest Indiana Public Service Company (NIPSCO, the local electric utility company), Methodist and St. Mary's hospitals, and "public" bodies including the mayor's office, the Division of Physical and Economic Development (which was the planning department's parent body), the planning director herself, the Gary Public School Corporation, and the Gary Parks and Recreation Commission. The group was rounded out by one representative each from the National Association for the Advancement of Colored People (NAACP) and the Gary Urban

League. Totaling twenty-five members, this group met regularly over a two-year period, mostly monthly, sometimes biweekly. Attendance was high; at every meeting fifteen to twenty members showed up, sometimes bringing friends and business partners as well. Members of the body, including the neighborhood representatives, were relatively well educated, very well informed, and had extensive records of public service in Gary, with some dating back twenty to thirty years. Though the neighborhood leaders were not necessary indigenous, they were representative. All had lived in their homes for at least fifteen years and possessed firsthand knowledge of their neighborhoods' problems.

When the citizen planning committee was publicly announced, the mayor's political enemies on the city council attacked, claiming that the neighborhood representatives were "political hacks" and tools of Mayor Hatcher's machine. The mayor, who had reviewed and approved the format designed by Carlisle and me, publicly challenged the dissident council members to name people who could better represent their neighborhoods and prepare a written statement with a rationale for making the substitution. When after a week went by with no names submitted, we chose to ignore these statements by opposition council members and begin our work. In order to make peace, Pat Carlisle sent a letter to each of the nine city council members with an attached schedule of meeting dates inviting them or their designated representatives to attend and work with the planning committee. Over the two years of committee meetings prior to the approval of a draft plan document, not one city council member who was opposed to the mayor showed up or sent a representative to our meetings.

During the month of February, I held weekly meetings with the new committee to develop the work program. Our first task was to decide which elements should be included. Unlike the mandated planning legislation in Florida, the Indiana statutes relating to planning gave us a relatively free hand to choose those elements we felt were important. Because Gary had an extensive network of social service programs already in place, there was no need to develop a full-blown social service element. The school board representative, Peter Troupes, an elementary school principal, was adamant that the plan must stay away from matters dealing with curriculum, testing, and education-based community service programs. Noting that school districts are notorious for protecting their autonomy, I promised not to involve the plan with these issues and in return was able to get Troupes to agree to work with us in developing a plan for school facilities in coordination with plans for parks and recreational activities. Finally, we decided that the plan should contain elements including but not necessarily limited to land use, circulation/transportation, parks open space and conservation, and community facilities. With this last element dealing with the physical and spatial aspects of schools, public safety, hospitals/health care, water and sewage, and human services. Before these plan elements, we would place a "background" chapter, including an extensive treatment on the city's history from its beginnings as a "planned" community to its present status. Also before the plan elements would be a summary of research and analysis findings, including population projections and a statement of economic assumptions upon which this plan was to be based.

As for the timeframe and plan structuring, we concluded that the conventional long-range period of twenty to twenty-five years would not work for us. Gary's problems were too pressing for such a treatment: citizens would *really* not pay any attention to our recommendations if we talked about outcomes too far into the future. Some committee members wanted a ten-year timeframe. In order to resolve this problem and come up with a reasonable framework, I made three proposals. First, I proposed that we take just under two years to prepare this plan, look for approval in late 1985, and then have a fifteen-year implementation period. As the implementation period would end around the beginning of the next century we could call our effort "Gary, Indiana Comprehensive Plan for the Year 2000," a potentially useful public relations move. In addition to the long-range (fifteen-year) comprehensive plan, we would prepare five- to ten-year mid-range development plans for the thirteen residential neighborhoods and the mill properties known as the "Gary Industrial District." Finally, the process would include a one-year immediate action plan that would consist of two parts. The first would be a review of developmental actions taken by the city over the previous twelve months in comparison to plan goals. The second part would be a list of priority capital budget items recommended for any given new fiscal year. These projects would be linked to goals articulated in the mid-range development plans.

This 15-5-1 planning sequence was similar to that improvised in Atlanta and Memphis only a few years before. The advantage was that—unlike most comprehensive plans prepared over the past thirty years in which on one end you had long-range policies with a twenty- to twenty-five-year timeframe and on the other end immediate actions involving zone changes subdivision approvals and public acquisitions, with no connection between the two—this arrangement provided a "Middle Range Bridge" espoused in 1956 by Martin Meyerson.[9] The Middle Range Bridge is almost never followed in practice because the plans at that level involve developmental decisions for specific locations that often are controversial and therefore are avoided by politicians. Mayor Hatcher liked the fifteen-year longer range and five- to ten-year developmental plan framework. Because he represented a "strong mayor" form of government and had a working majority on the city council, he was not afraid of plans with specific development proposals because the package had to be approved by "his" council anyway. What Hatcher did object to was the one-year immediate action plan. He did not see the need for an annual review of development actions and the use of staff time to prepare one. So we agreed to a two-part plan; one being the Year 2000 long-range comprehensive scheme and the second part including development plans for the thirteen residential neighborhoods, the Central Business District, and the Gary Industrial District, which was comprised mainly of U.S. Steel Corporation holdings.

Issues during the Planning Process

In late February, we were ready to initiate the planning preparation process. Our goal was to have a draft plan ready for review and adoption by the plan commission and city council by late 1985, giving us approximately twenty-one months to do the job. We knew that the overriding issues that had to be addressed in the plan were unemployment, decaying infrastructure, deterioration of the low-income housing stock and neighborhood commercial strips, and, most important, an eroding tax base that made it difficult to retain industry and other job-producing economic activities, repair infrastructure, and stabilize public facilities and services, especially schools and parks. We were aware even as early as 1984 that Gary's substantial black middle class would soon begin to leave this city for the suburbs and was willing to trade off white hostility for freedom from crime, drugs, poor schools, and inadequate shopping and recreation. Gary's last "picture show," the Dunes Twin Cinema, had closed in 1983 and now Garyites had to leave town in order to see a movie as well as do major shopping. Even the grocery stores were beginning to close down. In spring 1984, the giant Jewel Supermarket in Gary's black middle-class West Side closed because of repeated thefts and parking lot robberies, leaving some 20,000 residents who lived within a two-mile radius of their store no choice except to go to nearby Hammond or Griffith for day-to-day shopping needs. By early 1984, the first black pioneers moved into North Merrillville just across the Gary line. We forecasted that by 1990, Merrillville would be 10 percent black (the 1990 census found it to be 5.1 percent black). Retaining the black middle class was a "catch 22" dilemma. In order to maintain police protection, fire safety, schools, parks, and streets, one needed the stable homeowning group to remain and pay taxes, but in order to keep this group in Gary, one needed first to provide and maintain these basic services by initially correcting deficiencies and then, once caught up, moving quickly to ensure their maintenance and vitality.

But these were problems that we were aware of and prepared to deal with in the plan. One thing about planning is that, no matter how carefully you strategize, invariably during the process events change and it's "back to the drawing board." That is why the texts on planning always talk about feedback monitoring and evaluation as integral parts of the planning process.[10] During 1984 and 1985 and even later before the plan was finally adopted in late 1986, new issues developed that forced us to shift gears, rethink what we were trying to accomplish, and move in slightly different directions. These issues included (1) the need to produce a separate parks and recreation plan in order to maintain the city's eligibility for federal open space funding, (2) the defeat of Katie Hall in her bid for the Democratic party nomination for congress, (3) the need to fight off the city administration's "projectitus" while we hastened to complete the comprehensive plan, and (4) inadequate funding and resentment on the part of some administration staffers who were jealous over the progress we made in the face of adversity.

The Parks and Recreation Plan. On February 23, 1984, the planning committee approved our work program, and I was all set to begin drafting the comprehensive plan. The next day I received a telephone call from Gail Harris. In a near panic, she informed me that she had just received a letter from the Indiana State Department of Natural Resources, which administers all federal monies for open space. The letter stated that Gary's parks and recreation plan, written and approved in 1978, was now out of date and unless the city prepared and adopted a new one by June 30, 1984, Gary would no longer be eligible for federal open space funding. Harris went on to state that because of the 1983 budget cuts by the city administration, which had reduced the planning department by one third, no one was available to prepare this document. Would I do the parks plan now and start on the comprehensive plan in July?

I really wanted to begin the comprehensive plan, but I could not let Harris down. The professional staff was, by that time, working 60-hour workweeks including some evenings and weekends without additional compensation. Doing the parks and recreation plan was relatively easy because the state guidelines were concise, clear, and extremely helpful. The detailed 1980 census data had been available for about six months, and we could easily put the information into the planning process. The parks and recreation department had excellent, up-to-date information on site sizes, facilities, and equipment, and their pet projects had an excellent change of being funded given the state formula that gave a relatively high priority to factors such as percent below the poverty line. I had also written a parks and recreation plan for the city of San Bernardino, California, about eight years before and was familiar with recreation standards and criteria.

The question was "What could I do with the planning committee until work resumed on the comprehension plan?" I decided to turn a negative into a positive. The planning committee could serve as the citizen participation arm for the parks and recreation plan. Their input and the process itself would serve as an excellent pretest for the comprehensive plan. Lessons learned from the process of developing the parks and recreation plan, especially in terms of citizen feedback, could be directly transferable to the comprehensive plan itself. I called a meeting of our planning committee for Thursday, March 4, 1984. At that meeting I told the group about the need to drop the comprehensive plan and work on parks and recreation and how preparations of that element would help us with the comprehensive plan itself. The group unanimously agreed to serve as the citizen body for the parks and recreation plan. We decided to have another meeting later in March to go over inventory findings, an April meeting to discuss goals and objectives, a meeting in May to discuss preliminary plan proposals, and a June meeting to review and approve the plan itself.

Our inventory study produced some interesting findings. Surprisingly, Gary met the National Recreation and Parks Association standards for overall open space, although the city fell far short of the federal open space requirement of 2.5 acres per 1,000 residents in neighborhood and community parks. Marquette Park, with 255 acres located on the Lake Michigan beach, and Gleason Park, with 450 acres including an 18-hole golf course, boosted the city's overall park lands over the National Recreation and Parks Association threshold. During Mayor Hatcher's sixteen years in office, his administration was successful in obtaining federal funds to develop seven new parks including five new public swimming pools, all in previously deprived, inner-city neighborhoods. These were the positives. The negatives were the failure of almost two dozen mini-parks and the wholesale deterioration of equipment and facilities. The mini-parks, located on isolated vacant lots mainly in the historically black Central and Pulaski neighborhoods but scattered in other residential areas as well, were built as playgrounds for small children (up to ages 5-6) with federal open space monies during the late 1960s and 1970s. By 1984, because of cutbacks in federal aid programs, there were no funds for properly maintaining them. Broken equipment could not be repaired or replaced and, abandoned by the children, junkies and winos became the primary users of the mini-parks. Even in times of relatively adequate funding, the mini-parks were trouble because they were too small to justify the placement of even a single full-time custodian. According to Parks Superintendent Ed Chalko, a Polish-American World War II veteran who received his degree in recreation from Indiana University courtesy of the G.I. Bill, management of the mini-parks was an administrative nightmare.

"I wish they would close them all and move whatever equipment is left to the real parks," fumed Chalko as we discussed this problem. The most significant problem, though, was the gradual deterioration of the park system owing to federal budget cuts coupled with the city's inability to raise taxes because of the intransigence of U.S. Steel, whose properties represented 40 percent of Gary's entire assessed valuation. The park system's problems also stemmed from the inability of the city government to impose user fees on a poor and largely black population already suffering from inflation and high unemployment. The imposition of user fees was primarily responsible for wealthier cities and middle-class suburbs being able to stay afloat in the sea of Reaganesque budget cuts amid an ailing economy. For example, in nearby wealthy and mostly white Flossmoor, Illinois, in 1984, the Homewood-Flossmoor Park District charged $50-60 dollars apiece for about 500 eight- to twelve-year-old boys to play little league baseball for a single season. The money was used not for uniforms (that were provided by local businesses) but for park maintenance. There was no way that type of charge could be assessed to Gary youngsters.

By field-checking Gary's major parks, we found swings, most with broken seats; broken playground equipment such as carousels and see-saws; fieldhouses with leaky roofs, peeling paint, and inoperable toilets; and baseball fields littered with weeds and broken glass. In the summer of 1983, of eleven public swimming pools, only two were kept open during the entire July 1 through Labor Day season, with three being closed altogether. When pumps broke down and filters clogged, they went for weeks without repair; sometimes they were not repaired at all.

Our plan called for long- and short-term recommendations. Our major long-term policies were to push for the development of regional recreation areas in the 4,300-acre Little Calumet River floodplain and the 250-acre Grand Calumet River basin (assuming that the Grand Calumet, which runs along and through the south end of the U.S. Steel Corporation's mill property, could ever be cleaned up) and to enhance the expansion of the Indiana Dunes National lakefront in Miller. Other long-term recommendations included preserving Gary's remaining open land, almost all of which is environmentally sensitive, for conservation as opposed to development of any kind, including landfills, and proposing only two new parks, both in areas that actually grew in population between 1970 and 1980. Our short-term recommendations included phasing out all of the mini-parks—abandoning them entirely in some cases or turning them over to community organizations if any were prepared to take over their maintenance and operation—and repairing facilities and equipment in existing neighborhood and community parks. Mayor Hatcher was not pleased with our proposal to eliminate the mini-parks because they were products of his administration and were located mostly in neighborhoods that invariably gave him strong support in elections. But when we explained the problems and difficulties with the mini-parks to him and the councilmen in whose wards they were located, he decided not to challenge our recommendations publicly. He was concerned that if the City of Gary didn't present a united front in support of the parks and recreation plan it would be rejected by the State Department of

Natural Resources, resulting in the loss of federal funds. On Thursday, June 7, the planning committee approved the Gary Parks and Recreation Plan of 1984, and on the following Wednesday this document was formally adopted by the city's Parks and Recreation Commission. We sent it down to Indianapolis for review by the Department of Natural Resources immediately after this approval. On August 5, we received formal notification by the state that our plan met their guidelines and was approved unconditionally and that Gary was eligible for open space monies through 1989. Even before we completed the parks and recreation plan, work had begun on drafting a proposal to the State Department of Natural Resources for funding with open space monies. We had to choose between two alternatives: improvements to Grant Park, a community-level recreation area located in the historically black Central neighborhood, or improvements to Marquette Park on the Lake Michigan beach.

Mayor Hatcher supported the Grant Park location; since 1967, its neighborhood had consistently been his greatest source of election support whereas Miller, located adjacent to Marquette Park, had always given a majority of votes to his opposition. We favored Marquette Park because it was a citywide (actually regional) facility and had a better chance for funding as we could pick up additional points on the state's rating scale because of the weight given to "water-related" activities. When we explained to Mayor Hatcher that Marquette Park had a better chance for funding because it was on the water and that more of his supporters were now living in Miller than in the past, he agreed to our preferred project. Our plans called for repairing the beach concession stands and restrooms, building new picnic shelters, and restoring a footbridge over one of the park's lagoons. The U.S. Naval Reserve had a nearby facility that housed a Seabee battalion, and we were able to get a written agreement with them to provide technical expertise and labor for rebuilding the footbridge as part of one of their training exercises. With this inkind assistance, we knew that our project stood an excellent chance for funding.

Our funding package was for $200,000, not a large sum by any means but, given the scarcity of resources, any new monies were welcomed. Our document had to be in to the Department of Natural Resources offices by 5:00 P.M., August 31, 1984. Our proposal was ready for typing by mid-August, and we felt we could make the deadline without any problems. But on Monday, August 20, things started to unravel. I found that the secretary who was supposed to type our final draft had left unexpectedly for vacation and would not be back until after Labor Day. After a frantic but successful search for a replacement clerical person, the old word processor broke down and the entire report had to be hand-typed. The weekend came and went with the report still not finished. On Tuesday, August 28, the word processor was patched up, and the clerical people began retyping the proposal on it. Even by Wednesday evening, we felt no sense of urgency because as long as the report was proofed, corrected, and sealed by Thursday at 5:00 P.M., good old Federal Express could pick it up and it would be in the state office by 10:30 A.M. on Friday, August 31, the deadline.

However, by 5:00 P.M., Thursday, the report wasn't ready. The word processor still had some problems. Lines were skipped, some pages were missing altogether, and the old photocopier ate some of the original maps. So we stayed all night putting all the pieces together. By Friday morning, the report was finally completed. We then took it out to Merrillville for photocopying (there was no full-service photocopying business in Gary). By 2:00 P.M., we finally had a complete project package, checked, sealed, and ready to go to Indianapolis. The question was how to get there before the office closed at 5:00 P.M. Fortunately, three planning staffers climbed into the departmental car, a 1978 Ford Pinto Wagon with 140,000 miles on it, and made the 160-mile trip to Indianapolis in record time. The package was stamped "received 4:57 P.M." by the clerk at the State Department of Natural Resources, and we were home free.

Our grant application was approved in full. Today the picnic shelter is up in Marquette Park, and other improvements have been made as well. In August 1990, I visited Marquette Park and saw the shelter crowded with picnickers on that warm summer day. I had to smile a bit when I remembered what it took to get it built.

Katie Hall's Defeat.   After going to congress in November 1982, Katie Hall quickly developed an exemplary record. She was selected chairperson of both the census and population subcommittee and the civil service and post office committee in which she coauthored and led the successful fight for passage in the House of a bill to commemorate Dr. Martin Luther King, Jr.'s birthday as a national holiday for federal employees in November 1983.[11] She received a 100 percent positive rating from the AFL-CIO political education committee for her strong pro-labor stand and a 95 percent rating from the NAACP. Although she was not able to get the Veterans Administration facility in her district, it was not her fault, as site locations for VA hospitals and clinics are chosen by federal bureaucrats who report to officials appointed by the president. Republicans controlled the federal bureaucracy, and Democrats were unable either to get a two-thirds majority in both houses to override a presidential veto or to "trade" with Republicans for supporting a facility in Gary. It was no wonder that the VA clinic found itself in Crown Point, thirty miles south of Gary and in the district of Republican Congressman "Bud" Hillis.

Early in 1984, two prominent whites from south Lake County announced themselves as Democratic primary candidates for Katie Hall's

House seat. One, Jack Crawford, was a young attorney with a Kennedy-style mystique. As Lake County prosecutor, Crawford was a law-and-order advocate who managed to have all of the right answers for organized labor, civil rights groups, and the well-organized anti-abortion Roman Catholic Church. The other, Peter Visclosky was a thirtyish attorney, soft-spoken, and single. Visclosky was the son of former Gary Mayor John Visclosky who served briefly from 1962 through 1963 when Gary Mayor George Chacharis was sent to prison on racketeering charges.[12] Peter Visclosky finished college and law school while residing in Merrillville, and in 1980 became an aide to Congressman Adam Benjamin. It was Peter Visclosky who, to his horror, found Benjamin dead of a heart attack in his apartment on September 7, 1982.

Going into the primary campaign, Crawford had the most money, eventually collecting over $200,000 mostly from small contributors and religious organizations. Visclosky raised only $60,000, also mainly by small contributors. Hall raised $70,000, although, unlike the other two, her funds came mostly from labor and other special interest PACs. Crawford aimed his campaign directly at Hall, whereas Visclosky emphasized his relationship with Adam Benjamin. Hall campaigned on her record, citing passage of the King holiday bill and the national publicity surrounding it. Neither Crawford nor Visclosky mentioned the race issue, although both campaigned heavily in white neighborhoods and paid little attention to blacks in Gary and Hispanics in East Chicago.

Unlike the furor that marked the 1982 general election, Hall's 1984 campaign was quiet and laid-back. Her appearances were limited and almost nonexistent in white communities. Although she received strong endorsements from U.S. House Speaker "Tip" O'Neill and Mayor Harold Washington of Chicago and constant support from Mayor Hatcher, her campaign clearly lacked the enthusiasm of 1982. The Reverend Jesse Jackson made only one appearance in Gary for her before some 3,500 cheering fans in a hall that held 8,000 people. The campaign organization made several crucial errors, the most significant being the scheduling of a major fund-raising dinner on the same night as the anniversary celebration of the *Gary INFO*, the city's largest black-owned newspaper. Crawford and Visclosky ran much better organized campaigns. Crawford relied heavily on newspaper and radio advertising, and Visclosky personally visited 3,300 homes. Still, Hall needed only a plurality, as there is no second primary in Indiana elections. With blacks comprising 30 percent of the total registered voters in the district, her incumbency and the Hatcher submachine available for precinct work, she was the clear favorite going into the election.

The election was held on May 8, 1984, a sunny spring Tuesday. To many people's surprise, Visclosky won, tallying 44,712 votes to Hall's 42,345. Crawford trailed with 40,755. Hall received only 3,500 votes outside the central cities of Gary, Hammond, and East Chicago. In her concession speech, she charged racism as being responsible for her defeat saying, "In northwest Indiana, if you are black and a female there are people who won't accept you no matter what you have accomplished."

Shouting racism is like crying "wolf." If you state it too often without solid evidence, no one will notice when racism really is the case. Analysis of the primary election results tell another story. Hall lost because of complacency among her campaign workers who did not turn out the Gary vote. The campaign staff felt that the two strong white candidates in the race would split the white vote just as in the case of Hatcher's 1967 primary campaign and of Harold Washington's Chicago effort in 1983. They were 2,400 votes wrong. In 1982, there were 76,692 registered voters in Gary, 39,946 votes for Katie Hall, and a turnout of 60 percent. In spring 1984, registration in Gary rose to 86,544, an increase of 10,000 potential voters. All six Gary city council districts experienced an increase in registration mainly because Jesse Jackson was running for president. However, in the 1984 primary, Congresswoman Hall received only 32,446 votes in Gary, 7,500 fewer than in 1982, with only a 50 percent turnout. Not only did she lose votes in every council district, but, in the four predominantly black ones, she lost a total of 4,800 votes from the 1982 count. If Congresswoman Hall had retained the same number of votes in the four predominately black districts that she had in 1982, she would have won the election.

Katie Hall's defeat in the 1984 Democratic primary was a tremendous blow to Garyites. It was the first major loss for the Hatcher submachine since 1967. It was entirely unexpected because, in recent years, over 90 percent of incumbent congressmen had been reelected to office every two years if they choose to run. It was a major setback for the comprehensive plan. With Hall reelected, she would have quickly attained the stature of Adam Benjamin and would have been able to make the "deals" necessary to bring big-ticket capital improvements to Gary, thus helping with plan implementation. Just before the election, Congresswoman Hall stated that one of her priorities for 1985 fiscal year was funding to rebuild the Gary airport as a regional center for the U.S. Postal Service overnight mail operation. She was also quietly working with representatives of the U.S. Department of the Interior to expand the National Lakeshore, including a marina for Gary. All of these hopes were dashed with Hall's defeat, and we had to scale back our draft plan recommendations and our dreams as well.

Fighting the Virus of Projectitus.   With declining economics, out-migration of the middle class, and a deteriorating physical plant, black mayors of central cities, especially those located in the Rust Belt, must resort to highly visible developmental projects to enhance their images. At the same time, emphasis on development projects leaves little or no time for comprehensive planning. June Manning Thomas's and Wilbur Rich's portrayals of Detroit Mayor Coleman Young serve to illustrate that point.[13] In Gary, during the period of 1980-1983, Mayor Hatcher's pet development projects included the Genesis Convention Center, the Hotel Gary, and the Sheraton Hotel, described in Chapter 2 of this book. During 1984 and 1985, when I was actively working on the comprehensive plan, the Adam Benjamin Transportation Center and the parks administration building were large projects commanding the attention of the mayor and the city planning staff as well.

When I signed on to prepare the comprehensive plan, the arrangement with the City Planning Office was that I would have at my disposal technicians from the advanced planning section, one to prepare graphics, the second to do basic fieldwork. Also, Margaret Merhoff, the city's transportation planner, was to prepare the transportation element. By September 1984, the parks and recreation plan and the Marquette Park Improvement Package had been completed, and I was ready to begin work once more on the comprehensive plan. At that time, Merhoff was serving as the general manager in charge of construction for the Adam Benjamin Transportation Center, working at least fifty hours per week on that effort. She had no time to write a plan element. Also, both technicians were occupied by another pet project of the mayor's office, the designation of a portion of the city as an enterprise zone. So I quickly found myself in the position of having to write the entire plan with the help of only a single secretary. As I was trained in architecture at Illinois Tech, designing and preparing graphics was no problem except that it would be time-consuming, thus extending our self-imposed deadline for drafting the plan. Knowing where the mayor's priorities lay, I simply decided to do whatever it took to prepare the plan, extending the date for submission of a draft to our planning committee to February 1986, with submission to the plan commission and city council in September of that year. Gail Harris had no problem with that change and extended my consulting contract through December 1986 with more money for my fees and a limited budget for supplies.

Dealing with Internal Jealousy. Although Mayor Hatcher, Deputy Mayor James Holland, and Robert Farag, director of the city's Division of Physical and Economic Development, approved of my new contract, knowing they would get a comprehensive plan by a member of the American Institute of Certified Planners (AICP) for less than one-fourth of what it would cost if prepared by a full-service planning consulting firm, some staffers in the Division of Physical and Economic Development resented the new arrangement. I would be receiving more in consulting fees for part-time work than some full-time technicians and junior-level planners were earning for working, in some instances, fifty-hour weeks. Quickly, rumors began to spread around city hall that the planning department had hired another consultant that would soon leave them with a worthless package, if indeed anything at all, and just pick up the checks. This had happened many times in the planning department and other city agencies during the 1970s when federal money was running like water, and, if these rumors persisted, they could hurt my relationship with the planning staff. Some members of the planning staff were all too quick to buy into this argument for nefarious reasons. For years, especially from 1975 to 1981 when funding was plentiful, they had argued that preparation of a comprehensive plan was impossible. Now, with extremely limited funding, one was about to be prepared without them, and they were jealous. Even though I had written the parks and recreation plan, which had been approved by the state and submitted what would eventually become a successfully funded program for improvements to Marquette Park, these products would soon become outdated just like last month's hit recording or last year's fashions. I knew I needed another credible product on the table well before the 1986 comprehensive plan submission deadline.

I then contacted some of my planning colleagues across the country whom I knew had similar problems at one time or another. After talking to a few, I hit on what turned out to be a successful idea. I would first prepare a set of goals, objectives, and policies for each element of the comprehensive plan: land use, including residential, commercial, and industrial; transportation/circulation; economic development; utilities; housing; community facilities (recreation, education, sanitation, health, and human services); conservation; and public safety (police, fire/rescue). Then, once that package was approved by our planning committee, I would prepare the draft mid-range plans for the thirteen residential neighborhoods. In the plan, every neighborhood would have sections on history and general background, a census profile comparing its characteristics with those citywide and the Gary-Hammond-East Chicago Standard Metropolitan Statistical Area (SMSA), a list of assets followed by a list of problems, and then treatment strategies. The treatment strategies included (1) *prevention*— compliance with codes, minor infrastructure upgrading, and spot clearance, (2) *rehabilitation*—concentration of housing rehabilitation monies, infill with new construction, and infrastructure improvements such as street repaving, new sidewalks, street lighting, and water, sewer and drainage improvements, (3) *reconstruction*—total clearance limited to only three small areas of the city, none being larger than five city blocks, and (4) *Gateway*—improvement and beautification of expressways and arterial streets leading in and out of the city.

After these mid-range plans were complete in draft form we would place them in a book titled *Development Strategies for Gary's Neighborhood*. Stamped "draft" at every opportunity, this document would serve as an interim report until the full comprehensive plan was completed. Then I would go back to the development strategies document and rewrite the mid-range plans as per the comprehensive plan. The strategies document could be ready by mid-1985, as we had a complete set of background data, and the plan itself would be ready exactly one year later.

In October 1984, Gail Harris resigned and returned to her hometown of Philadelphia, accepting a position with Mayor Wilson Goode's staff. The new planning director was Arlene Colvin, the assistant city attorney who specialized in zoning, building, and housing cases. A graduate of Indiana University College of Law and a practicing attorney before joining the city government, Colvin was brilliant, thorough, warm, outgoing, and sensitive to the human condition, as she was a black woman who grew up in Gary's public housing projects, attending college on an academic scholarship. While Colvin had taken only an introductory course in planning during law school, her work on zoning matters plus her quick inquisitive mind gave her an insight on the profession possessed by few planners, even those who are AICP recognized.[14] Colvin asked some keen and pertinent questions about my revised planning program: What was in the present background data base? Were the strategies tied to specific program recommendations with funding sources identified? I made revisions based on Colvin's comments, and we both presented our proposal to Mayor Hatcher. He loved the idea of a development strategies document because it would give him a tangible product useful for potential project funding. We stressed that the strategies document wasn't the plan but just an interim measure. He understood, stating that just in case the plan never was completed, at least the city would have a product that could be helpful in setting development priorities.

With background information fully available, I prepared a set of plan goals, objectives, and policies. This set was reviewed and discussed at length by the planning committee before being adopted with minor revisions in March 1985. By July 1985, the strategies document was drafted and approved by the planning committee. The document was sent directly to Mayor Hatcher's office, and we waited for weeks without an answer. Then on August 29, 1985, Colvin and I were summoned to Mayor Hatcher's office for a meeting. We both wondered immediately, "What did we do wrong? Is the mayor unhappy with our work?"

We went to his office, were ushered in, and found him beaming, a copy of the strategies report on his desk. He told us both that it was an excellent piece of work, thorough, complete, and usable. He scheduled a news conference for the following day, and Colvin and I presented the report to the press. Mayor Hatcher said "for some time, the press, especially the *Post-Tribune* has accused this administration of throwing together projects without any relationship to an overall planning strategy. That has been false because in recent years, the Genesis Convention Center, Hotel Gary,

Sheraton, and Transportation Center were all projects that evolved from the 'Negotiated Investment Strategy' monitored and approved by the U.S. Department of Housing and Urban Development. If you take the time to read this 200-page report entitled *Development Strategies for Gary's Neighborhoods*, you will find that we have prepared a set of five- to ten-year mid-range plans that will guide us in setting development priorities over the years." The press reports were generally favorable. The *Post-Tribune* highlighted one of our observations: "Gary's commercial establishments are generally in shoddy condition. Most merchants for a variety of reasons have not seen fit to make improvements. The result creates a very negative impression for both city residents and visitors alike."[15]

The citizen reaction was most positive. The planning department and mayor's office received dozens of letters and telephone calls praising announcement of the report. One elderly lady wrote, "It's bout time someone tries to make these store owners fix up their places. They need better goods too." Over the next few months several embarrassed merchants did fix up their shops' facades. Impressed by our background studies that showed Gary's residents with a total disposable income of one billion dollars per year, several fast food franchises started telephoning the Mayor's Office of Economic Development requesting more information on Gary. And once the development strategies were announced by the mayor, there were no more rumblings of discontent from my former detractors in city hall, at least not out loud.

Finished Product

With the development strategies document completed and approved by the planning committee and the mayor's office, we were able to finish the comprehensive plan without further delay. A full draft plan was prepared by October 1985. Workshops with our planning committee were held in October and November almost weekly with spirited discussion over the contents. For example, Pete Troupes, the school board representative, vehemently disagreed with including a map and related text showing those schools the board was considering for closure within the next five years. The mayor's office objected to our population forecasts showing Gary declining from 151,953 in 1980 to 138,000 in 1990. I agreed to drop the map Pete Troupes objected to in return for a chart showing enrollment/capacity ratios and enrollment changes since 1970, so that interested readers could at least get some idea as to which schools *might* be closed. Only two schools out of thirty-five were involved, and the district's enrollment was still strong at 30,000 students, virtually unchanged from that in 1980. My response to the mayor's office was that we utilized for population projections a modified cohort survival methodology similar to that employed by the Northwestern Indiana Regional Planning Commission (NIRPC), which did all the area-wide forecasts. We used slightly lower out-migration rates than did NIRPC, as their 1990 estimate was 125,000. The 1990 census showed Gary's population at only 116,646, so we were way off.

The planning committee's Miller representation was extremely upset with our recommendation to endorse the National Park Service proposal for a roadway through their property in Gary to West Beach. West Beach is the most popular destination for National Lakeshore visitors, especially in summer. Located just outside the Gary city limits, West Beach attracts over ten thousand visitors from northwest Indiana and the Chicago South suburbs every summer weekend day, creating massive traffic congestion on the sole access road to the beach, which is only two lanes wide. The National Park Service wanted to place a three-lane parkway directly from Interstate 94 to the beach. It would use mostly an abandoned railroad right-of-way in their property and would bridge U.S. 20, U.S. 12, and two active railroad right-of-ways. We objected to bridging U.S. 20, as the road would pass directly over two shopping centers we were trying to revitalize. Our alternative called for an at-grade intersection at U.S. 20, enabling the travelers to stop at either shopping center for "goodies" before heading to the beach and to stop for gasoline on the way back. We also proposed an intersection with a connector street in Miller, which would have enabled these residents to use the National Park Service road throughout the year as a direct connection to the interstate system, cutting the travel time to Chicago by at least ten minutes. As we felt strongly that neighborhoods like Miller could be promoted as a relatively inexpensive place of residence for Chicagoans tired of the dirt, noise, poor schools, and crime of that city, this connection was extremely important to us. As part of our alternative, we also set forth a condition that the National Park Service spend money to repave Miller streets and improve Marquette Park in exchange for our support for their access road. The Miller representative wanted no road at all. A staunch environmentalist, he preferred that the abandoned right-of-way return to its natural state. He was not concerned with the present congestion or with the advantage of having badly needed improvements in his neighborhood paid for by the National Park Service with no obligation to Gary taxpayers. However, he could not get a single supporting vote from other committee members.

On December 16, 1985, the Comprehensive Planning Committee unanimously recommended approval of this document.[16] Our final plan was in two parts: a fifteen-year (Year 2000) long-range plan and a five- to ten-year mid-range plan for neighborhood development based on the strategies document revised to fit with the long-range plan.

The long-range plan consisted of population forecasts, economic as-

Figure 3. Gary Planning Districts, 1980

Lake Michigan

Gary Industrial District

Miller

Brunswick

Ambridge-
Mann   Downtown   Downtown
         West   East
                  (Emerson)

West side
                              Aetna
         Tolleston
                  Central

                      Pulaski

Black Oak

Glen   Glen
Park   Park
West   East

Neighborhoods	1980 population
1. Aetna	7,045
2. Ambridge-Mann	8,577
3. Black Oak	9,999
4. Brunswick	7,203
5. Central	21,423
6. Downtown East (Emerson)	7,165
7 Downtown West	10,027
8. Glen Park East	18,153
9. Glen Park West	14,246
10. Miller	12,400
11. Pulaski	9,223
12. Tolleston	9,805
13. Gary Industrial District	319
Total Population	151,953

Source: 1980 U.S. Census.

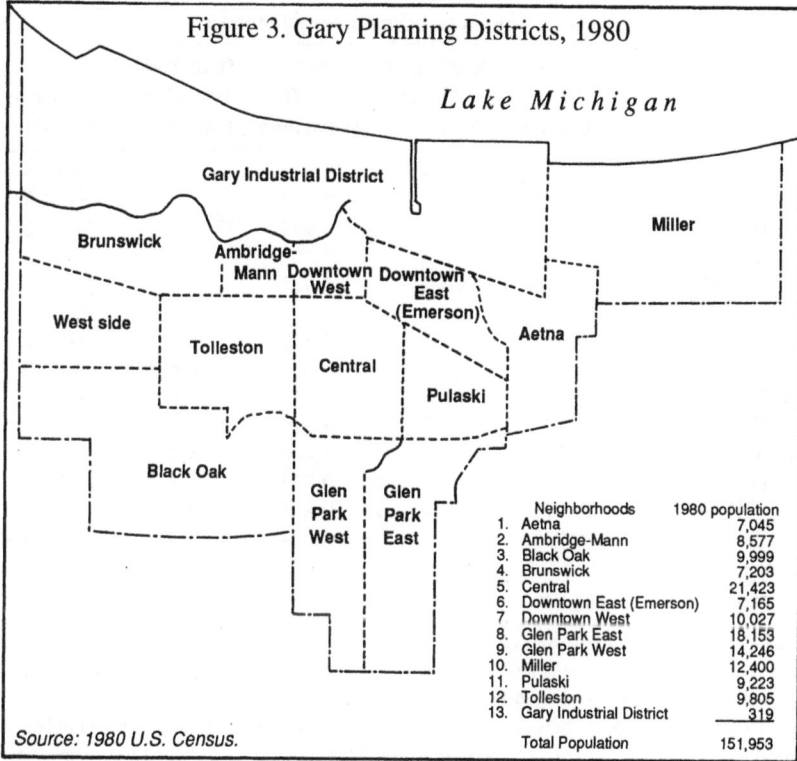

sumptions and elements for land use, transportation and circulation, and community facilities, which included physical plan recommendations for water, sewer, police, fire protection, libraries, and multi-purpose social service centers. It concluded with a detailed section on implementation. The mid-range neighborhood plans section began with an overall rationale followed by a list of observations and descriptions of our four treatment strategies—prevention, rehabilitation, reconstruction, and Gateway. Following these were the neighborhood plans along with a detailed list of projects that must be undertaken between 1985 and 1995 in order to meet plan objectives. We figured the cost of these 75 projects at $234,465,000 in 1985 dollars. The breakdown included $123,800,000 for housing rehabilitation at $20,000 per unit for 6,190 units, $3,215,000 for economic development, $30,000,000 for water and sewer improvements, $15,725,000 for local and collector street repair, $2,200,000 to replace four fire stations, and $25,575,000 for park and recreation improvements including a marina on Lake Michigan.

Details of the plan are really not that important. Figure 3 shows the thirteen residential neighborhoods and their 1980 populations. Tables 6 shows the population change between 1970 and 1980 of Gary's thirteen

Table 6. Gary's Residential Neighborhoods

Neighborhood	1970 Population	% of Total 1970 Gary Population	1980 Population	% of Total 1980 Gary Population	% Change 1970-80
1. Aetna	8,272	4.3	7,045	4.6	−14.8
2. Ambridge-Mann	8,920	4.7	8,577	5.6	− 3.8
3. Black Oak[a]	12,983	6.9	9,999	6.6	−23.0
4. Brunswick	8,144	4.3	7,203	4.7	−11.6
5. Central	37,804	20.0	21,423	14.1	−43.3
6. Downtown East (Emerson)	9,458	5.0	7,165	4.7	−24.2
7. Downtown West	15,391	8.1	10,027	6.6	−35.0
8. Glen Park East	18,179	9.6	18,153	11.9	− 0.1
9. Glen Park West	14,492	7.7	14,246	9.4	− 1.7
10. Miller	11,694	6.2	12,400	8.2	+ 6.0
11. Pulaski	11,825	6.3	9,223	6.1	−22.0
12. Tolleston	25,875	13.7	19,805	13.1	−23.4
13. West Side	5,920	3.1	6,368	4.2	+ 7.6
Total Population	188,957		151,634		−19.8

Source: Gary, Indiana, Department of Planning.

Note: Preliminary figures for the 1990 U.S. Census show Gary's population at only 116,646, a 23.2 percent decrease from that in 1980.

[a]In this table the total population for Gary in 1970 includes the Black Oak area, annexed in 1977. About 300 residents resided in Gary's Industrial District in 1970 and 299 in 1980 according to the U.S. Census.

neighborhoods. Only two neighborhoods, Miller and West Side, showed a population increase between 1970 and 1980. Our socioeconomic composite analysis showed Miller, Glen Park, West Tolleston, Ambridge-Mann, and Brunswick to be strong and the old Midtown areas of Central, Pulaski, and Downtown East and West to be weak. The same pattern held true for housing. The executive summary, along with a map showing the thirteen neighborhood units and their 1980 population, is in the book's appendix. However, the economic assumptions upon which this plan's goals, objectives, policies, and programs are based do deserve some attention. These assumptions and their rationales included the following.

1. Employment in the steel industry will at best, remain at present levels. The major industry of northwest Indiana was, is, and will be at least until the year 2000, steel production. In the early 1970s, U.S. Steel's Gary Works and allied mills employed over 30,000 workers. By 1985, that figure had dropped to 8,000, and by 1990, only 6,000 workers remained at that mill. For all of the steel mills in northwest Indiana, employment dropped from 70,000 in 1979 to 40,000 in 1985 and 36,000 in 1990. At the same time, because of automation and related new technology, actual steel production is at an all-time high. The only way 1985 employment levels could be maintained or increased would be for northwest Indiana and Gary to find a special niche in the worldwide steel market, namely to excel in specialized steel products that cannot be made elsewhere in the nation or overseas.

2. *There is a good possibility of attracting additional small shop diversified manufacturing to Gary.* Despite the national shift from an industrial to a service economy, we felt that with perfect location, excellent transportation facilities (including intersecting interstate highways, navigable waterways, and an airport capable of handling all types at commercial aircraft except widebody jets), and a large supply of vacant land suitable for industry, complete with all necessary utilities, Gary could not only attract diversified manufacturing but serve as a major truck transportation center. The land-use plan designated areas adjacent to I-80-90 and I-94 for truck-related facilities such as parking areas, service shops, repair facilities, restaurants, and motels. That Gary was designated as a federal "enterprise zone" with benefits for job production activities helped, along with the fact that taxes and workman's compensation rates are much lower in Indiana than in Illinois or Michigan. Implicit in this assumption is that Gary must have good schools (testing at least around the 50th percentile nationally), well-developed parks, police protection, and fire safety systems in order to attract and maintain a stable work force and management component.

3. *The Gary Regional Airport is a major element in any strategy geared to attract diversified light industry and services.* Gary's airport is located thirty minutes from downtown Chicago, actually closer in terms of time than O'Hare. The runways can accommodate even small and medium-sized jet airliners such as 707s, 727s, and 737s. Also, even as early as 1985, we observed that O'Hare was becoming overcrowded, with airline companies forced to divert flights to Midway Airport and even Milwaukee. Midway was not a suitable alternative because it is surrounded by residential land use and cannot be expanded. Milwaukee is ninety minutes from Chicago. In 1978, the Hatcher administration prepared an expansion plan for the airport, including a passenger terminal, new access roads, and an industrial park. The comprehensive plan endorsed this proposal and extended its recommendations because of the increased need for an additional full-service facility for the Chicago area. Development of the Gary airport would stimulate the economy not only in terms of motels, restaurants, and related facilities to serve passengers but also in the generation of aviation-related economic activities such as air express carriers. After the comprehensive plan was developed, the planning department prepared a detailed design scheme for an expanded Gary airport. The dynamics of the Gary airport development will be discussed in Chapter 7.

4. *Gary's population will decline between 1985 and 1990 but will begin*

to rise incrementally in the early 1990s as plan recommendations are implemented. We felt that even if Gary didn't grow from our 1990 projected population of 138,000, this number wouldn't decrease drastically by the year 2000. Some 140,000 residents still required goods and services, and these "import" functions should be exercised in Gary rather than residents being forced to do shopping for groceries and other basic needs in Hammond, Merrillville, Hobart, or Griffith, suburbs adjacent to this city. According to the 1984 U.S. Census estimates of per capita income, Gary residents earned just over $1 billion annually. This translated into significant purchasing power. The land-use plan identified sites for new or rehabilitated neighborhood and community shopping centers.[17] We strongly recommended that downtown Gary intensify commercial uses on Broadway between Fifth and Seventh avenues, attract a major tenant such as Wal-Mart, and serve the 35,000 residents who lived within a two-mile radius of the CBD.

5. *Given the stagnant economy in northwest Indiana, Gary residents should be encouraged to train for available positions in the service and technology sectors in the greater Chicago area.* We realized that no matter how successful our efforts were in stabilizing employment in the steel industry, attracting other diversified manufacturing jobs to the factories adjacent to the old mills, or expanding the airport to include new industrial parks, there would still be a need for considerable numbers of Gary residents to commute to work outside of northwest Indiana. So we hit upon the rather novel idea of conceding defeat on the economic development battle and retreating to the position of Gary as a partial bedroom community in an attempt to win the economic war. We knew that we did not have a ghost of a chance of landing any of the new Japanese automobile plants that eventually wound up in rural Illinois, Michigan, Tennessee, and Kentucky. On the other hand, new job opportunities in the service-technology sector were being created in Chicago's "Loop" area, along the Tri-State Expressway, and other locations in that city's south, west, and northwest suburbs, all within a one-hour drive of Gary. At the same time, Gary residents would be encouraged to remain in the city in its relatively low-cost, sound housing stock. In order to make this assumption work, private developers would have to be willing to provide market, state-of-the-art single-family, townhouse, and apartment complexes to retain upwardly mobile Garyites who commuted to Chicago. Also, the Gary Public Schools, Indiana Vocational-Technical College (a two-year career-oriented state-supported school), and Indiana University Northwest would have to gear themselves to prepare Garyites for the new service-technology economy.

6. *Gary should encourage upwardly mobile workers from Chicago, particularly those who work in the "Loop," the south suburbs, and the Tri-State Tollway area to settle in Gary.* Our fairly extensive historical analysis

showed that as early as the 1920s there was a strong "Come to Gary" movement on the part of business leaders promoting Gary as a place of suburban residence for Chicago workers.[18] During the 1950s, black and white developers built housing on Gary's West Side for middle-income black Chicagoans denied single-family, detached housing in that city and its suburbs because of racial discrimination. These developments, known as the Tarrytowns, are only a forty-minute drive from the largest black community in Chicago, the South Side. We felt that in addition to the previous recommendation geared to returning Gary's upwardly mobile population, we could attract Chicago blacks to Gary because of better schools, lower levels of gang violence, and most important, low-cost attractive housing, half the cost of comparable shelter in Chicago or its suburbs. We also felt that middle-income blacks and whites could be attracted to the Lake Michigan beach area of Miller for the same reasons. The key ingredient was that in order to make this scenario come true Gary would have to provide good schools, parks, and other public services. The Gary Chamber of Commerce would have to "sell" the city's attributes by advertising in Chicago newspapers and magazines and on radio and television stations.

7. *Federal and state aid will continue to decrease until at least 1988, but after that it can be expected to rise to at least mid-1970s levels in constant dollars.* We felt that reliance on federal assistance even in the future was not the way to go. Improvement of Gary's airport, new housing construction in the middle-income Miller, Miller Beach, Glen Park, and West Side areas, and the influx of new industry to the abandoned plants near U.S. Steel's Gary Works could take place simply by "market" factors and public-private cooperation. Whatever federal and/or state funds would become available could be used for low- and moderate-income housing and infrastructure improvements. We did not anticipate the election of George Bush, the savings and loan fiasco, or Operation Desert Storm when this plan was written.

The plan's history and implementation sections deserve at least a passing note. Our history section was eleven pages long, whereas usually this subject is treated in a comprehensive plan in one or two pages. We felt that it was important for Gary citizens to know that the city was poorly planned from the very beginning. The mill took up virtually the entire lakefront with the town designed in a unimaginative rectilinear gridiron and placed below the mill. We felt that Garyites must know that the city's decline began not with the election of Richard Gordon Hatcher in 1967 as the *Post-Tribune* would have one believe but as early as the mid-1950s when the region's business elites decided to emphasize suburban development and neglected renewal of the central city. We felt that it was important for all Garyites, even those whites who fled the city in the 1970s, to know that the business/institutional elite composed of the bankers, realtors, U.S. Steel management, and professional class, largely Anglo-Saxon and Protestant, despised the white Catholics and Orthodox ethnics (Poles, Slovaks, Hungarians, Greeks, and Serbians). These elites ran from the ethnics in the 1950s when they took over Gary's government just as the ethnics ran from Gary when blacks took over the reins at city hall, and we felt that the ethnics living in the Gary suburbs of Merrillville, Hobart, Crown Point, and Valparaiso ought to know that.[19]

Our implementation section stressed that the comprehensive plan as adopted would have to be consulted and reviewed with respect to zone changes, variance, subdivision and plot plan applications. Also, the capital improvement program preparation, Community Development, Block Grant allocation, and related federal and state funded improvement programs would have to be in concert with the comprehensive plan. We also stressed the importance of intergovernmental coordination and the development of good working relationships with our neighbors, not only the central cities of East Chicago and Hammond but also the suburbs of Merrillville, Griffith, and Hobart.

Our neighborhood mid-range plans were straightforward, practical, and focused simply on what was possible over a ten-year implementation period, given the scarcity of resources. In Aetna, we recommended that a large section be designated for targeted housing rehabilitation. This neighborhood had been virtually all white until the late 1970s. Then, blacks moved into single family housing built in the early 1950s to minimal construction standards. Most needed repair when racial change began to occur, and, with the 1979-1983 recession and mass layoffs in the steel industry, many new black homeowners could not afford the monthly payments, to say nothing about ongoing maintenance. By 1985, almost every block in this community had at least two or three vacant boarded-up homes repossessed by FHA and VA. Most of the remaining units were in various stages of disrepair. However, the city administration had always viewed Aetna as a stable area not in need of assistance and, more important, "enemy" territory, as Hatcher's opponents had carried Aetna in every mayoral primary election since 1967. Our recommendation was designed to alert the administration to the fact that Aetna needed help and that recent residents, unlike the previous ones, were inclined to vote for Hatcher if they felt that help was coming and against him if the administration turned a deaf ear to their pleas.

Ambridge-Mann was a middle-class white neighborhood, heavily Jewish, until the early 1970s when racial change occurred. The new residents were middle-income blacks who purchased high-quality housing at bargain basement prices. By the mid-1980s, this neighborhood was beginning to show signs of wear. Some blocks had vacant, boarded-up homes; others had vacant, weed-infested lots. We recommended a "prevention" strategy with strict building code and zoning enforcement and a program to expedite the sale and reoccupancy of the vacant homes, all of which were FHA, VA, or "Fannie Mae" (Federal National Mortgage Association) repossessions.

Black Oak, in the city's southwest section, was the only predominately white neighborhood in Gary. Occupied mainly by lower-income residents living in mobile home parks and modest single-family homes, this neighborhood, built in the 100-year floodplain of the Little Calumet River, had a serious problem with storm drainage. We recommended that Black Oak receive top priority for federal funds for storm sewers and repair of major streets. We also recommended as an interim measure that present culverts and drains be routinely cleared of debris in order to reduce flooding at least incrementally.

Brunswick was another neighborhood occupied by white ethnics until the 1971-1975 exodus. The new black families that moved in were mainly lower-middle-income mill and factory workers. By 1985, most residential blocks were still being meticulously maintained, but the merchants on Fifth Avenue, which bisects the neighborhood, had allowed their shops to become run down. We recommended elimination of the strip commercial uses, and especially the unfenced junkyards, with remaining businesses clustered at key intersections. The plan also recommended the construction of new low-cost housing on vacant lots, preservation and upgrading of the neighborhood's schools and parks, and housing rehabilitation in three small locations. To facilitate expansion of the Gary airport, we recommended clearance of a small dilapidated section of single-family homes sandwiched between the Indiana Toll Road and U.S. Steel's Gary Works, as they were in the airport's flight pattern.

The Central neighborhood, or Midtown, is Gary's historically black community. Before 1950, virtually all of Gary's 40,000 blacks were squeezed within its borders, mostly in run-down dilapidated housing. By the 1960s, this neighborhood began to empty out as residents found new homes in areas vacated by fleeing whites. The 1970 population was 37,804, and, by 1980, the population had dropped to 21,423, still 99 percent black. Central still had a considerable amount of substandard housing, but almost 2,000 units of subsidized units had been built in the Midtown urban renewal area by 1985, and there were some sections with attractive single-family housing, well maintained by their occupants. We recommended "prevention" treatment for the well-maintained areas such as Means Manor, "Gateway" treatment for the decaying Broadway commercial strip, and adaptive reuse for the vacant Froebel High School. A final recommendation was the purchase and restoration of the first home of Gary's most famous citizen, pop megastar Michael Jackson.

Downtown West and Emerson made up the original first subdivision laid out by the U.S. Steel Corporation in their original plan for Gary. This area was originally the place of residence for Gary's upper classes at the western end and craftsmen, foremen, and other skilled workers at the eastern extreme. Virtually all white until the mid 1970s, both neighborhoods experienced considerable deterioration by 1985. We recommended preservation of the remaining sound blocks in Emerson, a combination of rehabilitation and reconstruction for the remainder of the area, "Gateway" treatment for Fifth Avenue, and the creation of a "Medical Center of Gary" by unifying Methodist and St. Mary's hospitals with the newly built Gary Community Mental Health facility, as all three institutions were only four blocks apart. Structures between the three could be renovated for use as physicians' offices, board and care facilities, or medical laboratories.

Glen Park East and West lie in the southernmost portion of Gary, separated from the remainder of that city by the Little Calumet River floodplain and Gleason Park. All white until 1970, by 1980 the population was about 45 percent black, 45 percent white, and 10 percent Hispanic. Its major asset was a strong housing stock, mostly consisting of solid brick and wood frame single-family homes built between 1920 and the early 1960s and available in 1985 at prices ranging from $25,000 to the low $40,000s. Other assets were the Indiana University Northwest campus and Gleason Park. Our recommendations centered on preserving the housing stock and upgrading schools and parks, particularly Gleason Park and Golf Course. For the latter, we urged implementation of the University Park concept that Bill Staehle, Gary's first planning director and then an administrator at the IUN campus, and I developed. This program essentially consisted of improvements to Gleason Park financed by the state of Indiana and joint use by IUN students and community residents.

Miller was viewed by us as the crown jewel in the set of neighborhood plans. Originally a place of residence for the white middle and upper-middle class, this neighborhood was by 1980 52 percent black, 44 percent white, and 4 percent Hispanic. The new black residents were largely middle-class professionals. Housing quality was the best in the city, and the majority of the housing stock had been built after 1960. The major asset was Marquette Park and the two miles of wide beachfront on Lake Michigan running the entire length of this neighborhood's northern edge. We recommended preservation of the housing stock including strategies to lure Chicago "yuppies" and "buppies"[20] to the inexpensive beachfront community with its electric commuter rail stop, a fifty-five-minute ride to downtown Chicago. Other recommendations included reconstruction of all at-grade railroad crossings, expansions of the National Lakeshore, and the development of a marina along the U.S. Steel Corporation breakwater at the western end of the public beach.

Pulaski is an inner-city neighborhood settled by white ethnics between

1920 and 1950. By the mid-1950s, racial change occurred, and the whites were replaced by blacks who, like the former residents, were upwardly mobile mill and factory worker families who kept the modest well-constructed homes neat and clean. We recommended "prevention" treatment for this small neighborhood of 9,200 residents with strict code enforcement and expedition of the process to sell and reoccupy the small number of vacant and boarded-up homes that were beginning to erode neighborhood quality.

Tolleston is the neighborhood bordering the historically black Central or Midtown district to the west. All white until the early 1960s, Tolleston is best known as the place where astronaut and former Eastern Air Lines President Frank Borman was born and raised. By 1985, Tolleston's eastern end closest to the Central district was occupied mainly by lower-middle-income blacks; the western end containing newer single-family homes built during the 1950s and early 1960s were occupied by middle-income blacks and a few remaining whites. While prevention treatment was recommended for most of Tolleston, the eastern end was designated for rehabilitation. A special targeted rehabilitation program was recommended for the Tarry-towns-Oak Knoll area of Tolleston. Tarrytowns was a series of subdivisions consisting of small single-family homes built for upwardly mobile Chicago blacks during the late 1950s and early 1960s. Oak Knoll was a 400-unit subsidized housing development built in the early 1970s as a section 236 project. Both had seriously deteriorated by 1985, but we felt that a concerted rehabilitation effort would restore these developments to standard housing condition.

West Side, located on Gary's fringe, developed after 1960 in a pattern similar to many unplanned suburbs. Originally slated for industrial development by Gary's 1964 Comprehensive Plan, the area was invaded by speculators who built isolated housing tracts, some of which were located next to the city's landfill. The late 1960s and 1970s saw new subsidized housing, mostly section 235 and 236 developments. By 1985, some tracts were in excellent condition with well-maintained homes and apartment complexes. Others were in various levels of decline. We recommended a combination of prevention and rehabilitation treatment depending on sub-area condition. We also recommended phasing out the city's landfill and constructing a waste-to-energy facility in the Gary Industrial District, north of the Indiana Toll Road.[21]

With the exception of the waste-to-energy facility and the proposed marina, actually to be developed as a part of a planned unit concept with motels and condominiums, we made no other proposals for the U.S. Steel property known as the "Gary Industrial District." U.S. Steel officials were protective of their property even though less than 50 percent of the site was used. They were extremely secretive on their plans for the vacant parcels.

We felt that U.S. Steel was simply being antagonistic to the administration because Hatcher attempted to get them to pay their fare share of taxes and stop polluting Gary's air. But after talking to Bill Staehle, I found that U.S. Steel had shunned him too when he was overseeing preparations of the 1964 Comprehensive Plan.

In summary, the Gary Comprehensive Plan was a straightforward, no-frills, realistic proposal for the city's future. The long-range plan sought to attract new industry to Gary. Another source of jobs and economic development was expansion of the city's airport, a strong recommendation made in the plan. But the plan's major orientation was redirecting Gary from thinking of itself as a central city of the same order as Detroit, Pittsburgh, or Cleveland to the realization that its best hopes rested upon becoming a bedroom community for Chicago. This was a real possibility because Gary was only one hour away from this metropolis, with some neighborhoods on the western end being only forty to forty-five minutes removed. The city's housing stock was strong and, by Chicago standards, cheap. The Lake Michigan beach was a valuable, overlooked asset. To make the bedroom community concept work, Gary had to find ways to upgrade its infrastructure, schools, parks, and overall city services. The plan's recommendations were remarkably similar to ideas presented to the city administration in 1983 by Dr. F.C. Richardson's study group, but now these recommendations were backed by detailed data and observations. Mayor Hatcher warmly embraced the proposed plan when it was presented to him in draft form in late 1985. He would have also embraced the study group's recommendations, had they given him adequate time to reflect and respond.

The Plan Adoption Process

Once the comprehensive plan was accepted by the Citizens' Planning Committee, we were free to turn our attention to having this document adopted by the Gary Plan Commission and the city council. The plan commission presented no problem at all. An advisory body whose members are nominated by the mayor and confirmed by the city council, this group must, under Indiana law, adopt a plan for it to have any legal status whatsoever. As Hatcher had been mayor since 1967, he had the opportunity over time to appoint every one of the plan commission members. As these members knew that Mayor Hatcher approved of the plan, they were inclined to approve of it also. We knew that some members would ask questions and request specific information, and we were ready to answer these questions and supply necessary data. Still, we did not expect any serious problems from this group.

The city council was altogether different. A nine-member body, this council has six members elected from specific districts in which they must reside, and three members elected at large comprised the remainder of this body. Three council members could be considered staunch allies of the mayor. These included First District Councilman Gardest Gillespie who represented the Aetna, Miller, and Emerson neighborhoods, Gerald Hayes of the Second District who represented the Downtown West, Ambridge-Mann, and Brunswick neighborhoods, and Dharathula Millender, council-woman-at-large. There were two relatively neutral councilmen, Zeke Comer of the Third District, which contained the middle-income Tolleston and West Side neighborhoods along with Black Oak, and Cleo Wesson, who represented the historically black Fifth District. The mayor had four opponents on the council. Dr. Vernon G. Smith of the historically black Central or Midtown district, Sixth District Councilman Rick Bartolomeo, an Italian-American who represented Glen Park, and Councilmen-at-large Clemmons Allen, Jr., and Roy N. Pratt. All members of the city council except Bartolomeo were African-Americans.

The six neutral and opposed councilmen presented our biggest potential problem. None of these councilmen had attended any planning committee meetings even though they, or their designated representatives, had been openly invited. The strategy Pat Carlisle, Arlene Colvin, and I decided on was that I would hold a series of private meetings with the council members informally on a one-to-one basis before going to public hearings. I would meet first with the pro-Hatcher council members, all of whom had attended several planning committee meetings and were aware of the process. Then I would meet with the neutrals and finally with the four anti-Hatcher council members. We felt that several questions and comments posed by the pro-Hatcher and neutral factions would be raised by the anti-Hatcher group as well. By being able first to formulate answers to these questions made by council members friendly to the mayor, and to us, we could be at least be better prepared to deal with the same questions or similar ones posed by potential antagonists. The procedure that we decided on was to mail each council member an executive summary and, if they so requested, a copy of the complete plan. Then, within a few days of the mailout, Pat Carlisle's Office of Urban Conservation would call to set up an appointment for the councilperson to meet with me.

The mailings were prepared and sent to each council member in February 1986. Telephone calls were made to the council members in late February and March. Many council members were pleasantly surprised to receive the materials and follow-up telephone calls, with more than one stating that this was the first time that the city administration had given them information and then a request for private meetings well before the matter was brought to them in public. Not a single member of the city council refused to meet with me concerning a discussion of the comprehensive plan. Encouraged by this response, we set our meetings with individual council members between April and June 1986. For each presentation, I gathered five 30-by-40-inch illustration boards upon which colored maps were mounted and a slide projector with a special built-in screen fabricated by one of the employees in the public works repair shop, a 30-year veteran of U.S. Steel's Gary Works Sheet and Tube Division who had been forced into early retirement at the age of 56 during the 1979-1982 recession.

My initial presentation was to First District Councilman Gardest Gillespie. First elected in 1983, Gillespie was an energetic public school teacher in his thirties employed by the Gary School Corporation. An avid Hatcher supporter, Gillespie had attended several of the planning committee meetings, especially when Miller area issues were on the agenda. He was not thrilled about our decision to endorse the National Lakeshore's Parkway to transport visitors from suburban Lake County and Chicago to the West Beach through Gary, agreeing only if the National Park Service would provide an interchange in Miller for local residents, repave streets in that neighborhood, and pay for beach improvements in Marquette Park. Councilman Gillespie was definitely present-oriented. He objected to our mid-range plan proposal for the South Shore commuter rail station to be moved about one-half block to the west of the present location where additional parking could be provided. He stated to me that he had just completed discussion with the South Shore Railroad management, and they assured him that renovations to the existing stations would be made that summer, and he didn't want to go on record as supporting a proposal that could jeopardize the renovation project. I assured Councilman Gillespie that I was aware of the renovation project and that in my discussions with the South Shore's director of planning and development we agreed that *eventually* the station should be moved but that, for the time being, the existing station had to be renovated. With that hurdle cleared, Councilman Gillespie endorsed the plan, agreeing to vote for its approval when it would be submitted to the council that coming fall.

My next meeting was with Councilwoman-at-large Dharathula "Dollie" Millender. Millender, a retired Gary public school teacher, had been an avid backer of the comprehensive plan since the process began in late 1983. She had attended almost all the planning committee meetings, and her expertise on education matters and overall knowledge of Gary's past were extremely valuable not only to myself and the planning department staff but more so to other members of the committee. A history teacher, Millender had written a book on the history of Gary's black community[22] and contributed greatly to the history section in the comprehensive plan. Millender needed no presentation. We had a pleasant two-hour informal conversation, discussing the plan's overall goals. She felt that we should emphasize attempting to bring new high-technology steel-related jobs to

Gary and deemphasize relegating the city to the role of a bedroom community. A Gary resident since 1962, Millender had come to the city when it was at its economic height, when it stood right along with Toledo, Akron, and Youngstown and very close to Detroit, Cleveland, and Pittsburgh as a major U.S. industrial center. Councilwoman Millender understood that our nation was in a transition from an industrial to a service/information-based economy and that the larger cities just mentioned had Fortune 500 companies headquartered in them *and* strong academic infrastructures, both of which are needed to bring high-technology industrial-based jobs to a metropolitan area, and that Gary lacked both. However, apparently Millender did not really want to believe this dim reality. We agreed to disagree on this point, and, as she was quite pleased with all other aspects of the plan, she agreed to support it when it came before the city council.

The next appointment was with Gerald Hayes of the Second District. A Hatcherite since the mid-1960s, Hayes sometimes disagreed with the mayor but felt overall that he was doing a good job, given the recession, federal aid cutbacks, and opposition from state, county, and suburban governments. Hayes represented the Downtown West, Ambridge-Mann, and Brunswick neighborhoods and was most concerned about maintaining and preserving the housing stock, especially in the latter two. He had attended those plan committee meetings that focused on neighborhoods within his district. Those meetings, like the ones in all other neighborhoods, were held in three parts, the first to review funding, the second to decide on goals and objectives, and the final to review and approve plan proposals. Having attended these meetings, Hayes was quite familiar with our findings and recommendations and approved of them. Councilman Hayes, to my mild surprise, wanted to talk about overall plan goals and objectives. He, like Councilwoman Millender, favored emphasizing attracting new jobs to Gary. I pointed out to Councilman Hayes that certainly that was one of our major objectives but that we must keep our options open. After further discussion, Councilman Hayes seemed satisfied with my explanation and promised to vote for the plan.

With the first three presentations completed, we knew that the easy part was over. We learned that city council members and the public in general would question our economic development strategy of less reliance on attracting new jobs and more on becoming a bedroom suburb of Chicago. So we prepared new charts showing distances and times from Gary to Chicago's downtown, the South Suburbs of that city, and the newly developing service activities along the Tri-State Expressway, all of which were directly linked to Gary by interstate highway and in the case of Chicago's downtown or "Loop" by electric commuter rail as well. We produced charts showing the vast difference between Gary and the Chicago area in prices of comparable homes and apartments. We noted that test scores for all Gary public school students were slightly higher than for all Chicago public school children and much higher than for schools in Chicago's mostly black south and west sides. With this new presentation material we felt better prepared for the remaining meetings.

My next appointment was with Councilman Zeke Comer of the Third District. This district covered the middle-income Tolleston and West Side neighborhoods and the mostly white Black Oak district. Comer had been a longtime Hatcher supporter but had in recent years moved toward a position of neutrality. I was expecting a tough sell, but Comer greeted me warmly as I walked into his office. He stated that while he was unable to attend any of the planning committee meetings he was aware of the group's work and was pleased with the recommendations made for neighborhoods in his district. A thirty-year employee at Inland Steel in nearby East Chicago, Councilman Comer prided himself on being the first black electrician admitted to journeyman status with the local branch of the International Brotherhood of Electrical Workers (IBEW). He strongly agreed with our economic development strategy and felt that Gary's days as a steelmaking center were just about over. Feeling that U.S. Steel and other area companies would close their mills altogether within a few years, Councilman Comer confided that he would soon retire. He felt that our land-use plan wasn't bold enough. "Why didn't you just take all the mill property and make a nice big park right on the lake? Then call the Walt Disney people and get them to build a Disneyworld North on the land. This will solve all of our job problems." I told Councilman Comer that was not a bad idea at all but I was afraid U.S. Steel would not go for it. "They don't even like the idea of parting with a few acres on the east end of their land for a marina complex." We both had a good laugh on that one, and Councilman Comer agreed to support the plan.

My next meeting was with Cleo Wesson, councilman of the Fifth District and "dean" of the city council, having served continuously since 1954. Wesson's district included the lower- to lower-middle-income areas of Midtown, Pulaski, and part of Central. Wesson's concerns were mainly over how to preserve the housing stock in Pulaski and eliminate the remaining pockets of slum housing in Central. He wished that we had put more emphasis on completing the Midtown urban renewal project, a program that had begun in the early 1970s and by 1985 had replaced 4,000 dilapidated slum units with 2,000 units of new low- to moderate-income dwellings. When I responded by saying that we could no longer depend on federal funding as we had done in the past and that it was better in the long run to emphasize preserving the existing stock, he agreed in principle and decided to support the plan.

With the Hatcher supporters and neutrals accounted for, it was time for the hard part. Clemmons Allen, Roy Pratt, and Dr. Vernon Smith were former supporters of Mayor Hatcher, but all three had become disillusioned with him as the city declined and he remained in office without any new agendas to stem blight. Rick Bartolomeo was the long holdover from the old white ethnic machine that ran Gary from 1951 until Hatcher's election in 1967. Opposed to the mayor from the start, Bartolomeo was planning to move to Crown Point, some twenty miles south of Gary. He would not be a factor in the plan adoption process, but Councilmen Allen, Pratt, and Smith certainly would, and I had to be on my toes to deal with them.

On Wednesday, August 20, 1986, I had my meeting with Councilman-at-large Clemmons Allen, Jr. Allen, a twenty-year sargeant with the Gary Police Department was known as a tough guy.

I was expecting a cold, formal meeting and was surprised by Councilman Allen's warm greeting. He was pleased that I had taken time to send the plan summary to him well ahead of time and then arrange for a private meeting. Said Allen, "Doc, you have made history. This is the first time at least since I have been on the council that anyone from administration did things your way. Their usual practice is to hand us something the day before the council meeting and then talk about us *bad* in public if we have questions." He requested a full explanation of the plan and, after I went through everything with him, seemed impressed. He liked the proposed marina location and decentralized police stations in the Miller, Brunswick, and Glen Park neighborhoods. He was especially pleased with our plan for a public safety and service center located on Broadway just south of downtown and including a new police headquarters, fire headquarters, the county welfare department headquarters, a major multi-purpose service center, a county courts building, and office buildings to accommodate attorneys, bail bondsmen, and social workers. Allen then endorsed the plan, promising his full support when it came to the city council for a vote.

Councilman Roy Pratt, who, like Allen, was elected at large, was warm and friendly. A public school teacher and a summer recreation leader with the Gary Park and Recreation Department, Pratt approved of eliminating the mini-parks and putting money into the renovation of existing neighborhood and community parks. He especially liked the idea of our proposed waste-to-energy facility in the U.S. Steel industrial area. He felt that a not-for-profit corporation locally based in Gary could build the facility. I agreed and told him that was an implementation matter and that once the plan was adopted we would be preparing special system plans for the airport, public safety service center, fire stations, and the waste-to-energy facility. He then promised full support for the plan.

At the close of our meeting, Councilman Allen came by to discuss another matter with Pratt. I got ready to leave, but both insisted that I stay. Allen stated to Pratt, "Doc is all right, isn't he? He respects councilmen." Pratt looked at Allen and said, "You know, this is something anyone can use. When we get a new mayor we can use these recommendations to do some real good in Gary. It can be our plan too."

Rick Bartolemeo called and said that we didn't have to meet. He had read the 13-page single-spaced executive summary and thought it was a fine piece of work, one that he would certainly vote for. This left only Dr. Vernon Smith. Born in the Fourth District, which he represented, Smith grew up in the Central or Midtown neighborhood when it was the only place for black Garyites to live. Valedictorian of his Froebel High School class, Smith went on to earn bachelor's, master's, and doctorate degrees in education at Indiana University. A 15-year veteran of the Gary Public School System, Dr. Smith started out as a teacher and became an elementary school principal in just ten years. He was principal of Nobel Elementary School in the Miller neighborhood, where he developed a strong reputation for leadership, fairness, and promotion of academic excellence in this, one of the few remaining racially mixed schools in Gary. He had just been transferred to a principalship at Williams Elementary School in the Pulaski-Midtown neighborhood. Rumor was that school superintendent Dr. Ernest Jones, an ally of Mayor Hatcher, transferred him to keep the politically ambitious Dr. Smith from developing another power base in the high voter turnout Miller area in addition to his traditional base in Midtown. Regardless, Dr. Smith was a force to be reckoned with. The fact that he was an outspoken opponent of the mayor and a possible candidate for that position in the upcoming 1987 primary meant that he intended to do no favors for the present administration, especially helping to pass *their* comprehensive plan without a good reason to do so.

On Tuesday, September 9, 1986, Dr. Smith and I met in his office at Williams School. I noticed that Dr. Smith had a complete 350-page copy of the plan with at least a dozen yellow self-stick notes protruding, and I knew I was in for a long afternoon. First, Dr. Smith questioned my population projections. How did you get them? he asked. What methodology was utilized? I replied that the cohort-survival method had been used, the same methodology employed by the Northwestern Indiana Regional Planning Commission, except my out-migration rates were lower than theirs. Smith seemed pleased with my answer, noting that one of his doctoral degree specialties was educational statistics, and we discussed the use of SPSS and Lotus 1-2-3 in terms of their application to social science research. He felt that we had erred in not preparing at least a sketch Central Business District Plan that would tie together the CBD with the public safety and service complex, the Midtown Renewal Area, and our proposed 35-acre theme park. He felt that our recommendation for neighborhood park improvements in Midtown were vague when compared to those made for facilities in Miller, Glen Park, and other middle-income neighborhoods. He pointed out numerous typographical errors and statistical inconsistencies. Actually Dr. Smith's nitpicking was a big help. Only Jackie Gissendamer, the secretary who typed the plan, and I had proofed it; no one else on the planning staff had the time. Now we were getting a proofreading job free of charge.

I thanked Dr. Smith for his comments and his assistance. He requested that I make his suggested changes and send a copy to him for review. I agreed to do so, and the changes were made and sent out to him at Williams School. On September 24, I received a telephone call from Dr. Smith. He had indeed received the revised plan. It was now acceptable to him and he would vote for it. The entire city council was now accounted for.

The Gary Plan Commission could not be taken for granted. Like the city council, the plan commission members had been invited to all of the planning committee meetings. Some members, such as Jerome Fifer, the city engineer, Douglas Grimes, the city attorney, and Bob McGaffney, a U.S. Steel supervisor and park board member, had attended regularly and understood the plan. Others, such as Maurice Preston, the commission president, Frank Neal, the vice president, and Eric Washington, a young ambitious realtor, had not attended these meetings. So during September and October, I offered a series of workshops for the entire plan commission. As the plan commission's work was almost 100 percent devoted to implementation matters, zone changes, lot splits, plot plan approvals, and public acquisition, most of their questions were about the implementation element. They agreed with my recommendation for concurrency and that once the plan was adopted, zoning should be changed to reflect the plan provisions. They also liked the concept of drafting the capital improvement program according to mid-range development plan priorities. On November 18, 1986, the plan commission unanimously adopted the Gary, Indiana Comprehensive Plan, Year 2000.

We were now set to go before the city council. Mayor Hatcher decided to hold public hearings in all six city council districts during late November and early December. The hearings were well advertised and publicized on local radio. Still, attendance at the six hearings ranged from a high of just under fifty people in Miller to a low of one dozen in Ambridge-Mann. No one had any real opposition, and resident's questions were similar to those expressed by the city council. I witnessed the same level of attendance and overall public interest in 1977 when the Tampa-Hillsborough County Horizon 2000 Comprehensive Plan was proceeding toward passage and again in 1991 when the Gainesville, Florida Comprehensive Plan process was under way (which to me was surprising for a college town and home of the University of Florida). People, regardless of race or class, tend to be somewhat apathetic about something as esoteric as a comprehensive plan but will come out in droves against a LULU or NIMBY such as a sanitary landfill or prison. In that regard, Gary was little different from any of the thirty or so cities I have worked in as a staff planner or consultant.

In addition to the public hearings, during that time I made a series of presentations to the city-wide community organizations, including the Chamber of Commerce, the NAACP, the Gary Urban League, and the Civitan Club. Most meetings went smoothly, but at one presentation before the Frontier's International one of the club members, a local businessman who had made too many trips to the cash bar, got up and made a rambling speech about government interference in people's lives, stating that planning was communistic and that everyone should be able to do his own thing. "You can't tell people they can't park their 18-wheelers in front of their house. That's the only way they can watch it. Dammit, Catlin, don't you know about crime in this town?" When I pointed out that the comprehensive plan called for a truck-oriented district along U.S. 20, which would include secured parking for large trucks, he replied, "I didn't know you guys had thought that through," sat down, shut up, and dozed off, as I completed the question/answer session with some of the more sober members of the audience. This was not unusual, as an urban planner for almost twenty-five years, I knew there would always be evenings like that.

Our final hearing with the city council was set for Tuesday, December 16, 1986. I called Patricia Carlisle of Urban Conservation and asked her to make certain that at least our citizen representatives on the planning committee came out and were prepared to speak on the need for plan adoption. I said, "Pat, we've been waiting three years for this moment. It's our Super Bowl, and we can't lose." She agreed and virtually the entire planning committee came out to the city council meeting held at the Genesis Convention Center. About two hundred people were in the audience. I made the initial presentation for the plan itself. Arlene Colvin spoke about her department's commitment to long-range planning, and Pat Carlisle talked briefly about the citizen participation process. Then it was time for audience participation. Eleven people, including four citizens representing the planning committee, got up and spoke in favor of the plan. Only one person, John Laue, a Miller resident and environmentalist who opposed our endorsement of the National Park Service's access road to West Beach, spoke against the plan. Laue actually apologized for having to speak in opposition, stating that he strongly supported the rest of our plan.

Before the city council actually voted, several members—Gardest Gillespie, Dollie Millender, Clemmons Allen, and Dr. Vernon Smith—got up and made brief speeches in support of the plan. They all commended me, Arlene Colvin, Pat Carlisle, and the planning department staff for coming up with such a high-quality product on a shoestring budget. Then the vote was taken. Nine were in favor of adoption, none opposed, no abstentions. The Gary, Indiana Comprehensive Plan, Year 2000 was now officially adopted as per Indiana law by a unanimous vote of the city council. It was the mayor's plan, but his enemies on the council didn't care. As Clemmons Allen and Roy Pratt had said a few months before, "This is something anyone can use."

Some Reflections on the Gary Comprehensive Plan

Urban scholars such as Banfield and later Murray[23] have postulated that low-income people and members of minority groups are "present-oriented," not particularly concerned about future occurrences, leaving us to reason by inference that people of these types are not receptive to long-range comprehensive planning. Recent scholarly works by Thomas, Rich, Meir, and Jones[24] tell us that black mayors, at least those in Detroit, Chicago, and Atlanta, tend not to look in favor of planning because it can and does get in the way of development projects. The experience in Gary indicates otherwise. A process fully supported by Mayor Richard Gordon Hatcher was launched in 1983 and almost exactly three years later culminated in the unanimous adoption of the city's first comprehensive plan since 1964. Certainly there were problems. The process took one year longer than initially anticipated because of the lack of available city staff to assist in plan preparation. I and others helping with plan preparation had to tiptoe around petty jealousies of administration staffers who had been saying all along that preparing a comprehensive plan was too costly and time-consuming only to find that one *could* be prepared on time, with limited staff assistance and at one-fourth the cost of similar efforts elsewhere.

The elements basically included only land use, circulation, and community facilities, which fortunately covered a wide variety of urban systems. Still, an education element should have been part of the plan, but, because of the universal resistance and independence of the school board, it was not possible just as was the case in the much more expensive Tampa-Hillsborough County Horizon 2000 Comprehensive Plan[25] and many, many others across the nation. It would have been nice to have the plan printed on glossy pages with color illustrations and maps like the classic 1969 Plan for New York City, but because of budget constraints, we were limited to black and white graphics prepared with a typewriter, correction fluid, and photocopier. The desktop publishing systems so common by 1990 were not readily available in 1985, and, even if they had been, the city of Gary could not have afforded one.

The success in having the comprehensive plan prepared and adopted is owing to several factors. First of all, it was a common-sense document. We knew that any goal date further away than fifteen years would be deemed unrealistic by citizens and elected officials alike. Our goals were modest, realistic, but at the same time thought-provoking and crafted to meet the need demanded by new times. It would have made little sense to assume that U.S. Steel would close the mill and propose an urban designer's dream of a planned unit development on the lakefront in its place. Such a proposal would certainly have attracted a lot of attention, even nationwide and internationally, but it would have been bitterly opposed by U.S. Steel even if they *did* plan to close the mill. U.S. Steel would have shot us down and forced us to back off just as they forced Mayor Hatcher to retreat when he proposed in the early 1970s that the corporation pay its fair share of taxes and clean up their pollution.[26] On the other hand, our proposals to deemphasize running after scarce economic development ratables while falling back on the city's strengths (cheap affordable housing, excellent transportation linkage to Chicago jobs in terms of time and distance, adequate schools and parks, and a relatively pleasant suburban, single-family, detached housing environment) was a major and important innovation. The use of a long-range plan and a mid-range neighborhood-based development program in the same package helped too. This combination produced the type of continuum desperately needed for planning to work. Instead of offering up only lofty goals, objectives, and policies, we were able to link them to tangible programs that citizens, elected officials, and business leaders could grasp and understand. Our citizens' participation model certainly wasn't broad-based and deep, but it was representative. All members of the planning committee, whether citizen representatives, public agency staffers, or private sector representatives, understood their various constituencies and articulated positions in their favor. With a process stretching over a three-year period, there was a give and take that evolved naturally and finally resulted in a consensus that in turn led to unanimous adoption by all parties involved.

The most important reason for the process's relative success, however, is that preparation and adoption of the comprehensive plan was a matter internal to the city of Gary. The Indiana statutes regarding planning are informal. A plan is not required by law as is the case for Florida and several other states. However, if a unit of local government *chooses* to prepare a plan, the statutes suggest certain elements but do not require them. Adoption of a plan by the government's legislative body is required if it is to have any official standing, which in turn is important in maintaining eligibility for various state and federal grant programs. Gary was free to embark upon what turned out to be a successful process without interference from state government, the county, or the surrounding suburbs. As we will see later in the Gary airport case, interference and private agenda-setting on the part of Lake County, suburban governments, private suburban interests, the *Post-Tribune*, and even the state of Indiana, all worked to scuttle a golden opportunity for economic development benefiting the entire northwest Indiana region. These same negative forces had no opportunity to mess up the Gary Comprehensive Plan process.

The only real test of a comprehensive plan's validity is the test of time. By 1990, some of the plan's objectives were beginning to be met. Chicagoans started to discover Gary's high-quality, low-cost housing stock. Local realtor Gene Ayres has built several townhouses near Lake Michigan in Miller Beach, selling them for from $130,000 to $150,000 to eager

Chicagoans and upwardly mobile Garyites who have decided to stay home even if their jobs are in the Chicago area. Marina Village, a 1,400-unit rental complex two blocks from the Lake Michigan beach was originally constructed in 1962 for a white middle-class clientele. With white flight in the 1970s, the complex owners opted for the Section 8 subsidized rental program to fill vacant units, and, by 1985, Marina Village had become almost all black and Hispanic with all tenants receiving Section 8 subsidies. The development had deteriorated physically, crime had risen, and the commercial establishments in and around the complex had closed because of poor sales because of the fear of crime. In 1989, a Chicago-based development firm purchased the entire complex, moved the tenants to other Section 8 properties in Gary, and is planning to renovate the development for a middle-income "yuppie" and "buppie" group. The new occupants will be Chicagoans and Garyites who will be drawn to Marina Village by the nearby beach and the free shuttle bus service to the South Shore railroad's Miller station two minutes away. While the purists might lament over the removal of poor people from the beach, this action meets our plan objective of improving Gary's economy. Property values will be raised, tax collections increased, and the city's image greatly improved. After all, the city of Gary must pay its bills and provide services, whether the mayor and majority population is black, white, or polka dot. Atlanta, Detroit, and Newark have learned this lesson. Gary is learning it too.

6

Metrolake—Racism or Good Government?

Beginning in the early 1950s, cities across the United States became more and more black and/or Hispanic because of increasing nonwhite in-migration and housing discrimination. Whites, sensing that soon they would become a minority in these cities, did not sit idly by and simply allow black governance to take place without a struggle. Several tactics were employed to maintain white domination, some subtle, others direct and heavy-handed. The subtle techniques included annexation, promotion of moderate black mayoral candidates who were actually surrogate whites, and metropolitan consolidation. The mean, dirty, and visceral tactics in-cluded violence, political intimidation, and the rigging of elections.

Sophisticated cities led by well-educated elites and maintaining at least one Fortune 500 corporation headquarters used, for the most part, the subtle means. For example, in 1951, Tampa, Florida, annexed a large suburban area containing 110,000 residents, 98 percent of whom were white, to a city of 130,000. This annexation had the effect of reducing the black population from 36 percent to 20 percent.[1] Coupled with an "at-large" system of city council elections set up in 1946 to keep a growing Latino population from obtaining political power, this annexation and a corresponding drop in the black population percentage created a situation that prevented the election of even a single black to the Tampa City Council until 1984 when the "at-large" system was replaced by one in which four of the seven council members were elected by district. In 1969, Richmond, Virginia's white leaders engineered an annexation of an adja-cent area containing 47,000 inhabitants, of which 45,700 were white. The annexation, upheld by the U.S. Supreme Court in *Richmond v. U.S.* in 1971, decreased the city's black percentage from 51 percent to 43 percent. The "Burger Court" majority found there was no discriminatory *purpose* in the annexation, but Justice William V. Brennan vigorously dissented, stating, "Richmond's focus in the negotiation was upon the number of new white voters it could obtain by annexation; it expressed no interest in economic or geographical considerations such as tax revenues, vacant land, utilities, or schools."[2]

Other annexations during the period of 1950 through 1985 that had the effect of reducing the population percentage of racial minorities took place in cities such as San Antonio, Houston, and Dallas, Texas; Charlotte, North Carolina; Birmingham and Montgomery, Alabama; and Phoenix and Tucson, Arizona. However, by the late 1970s, annexation became more and more difficult because unincorporated area suburbanites feared higher taxes and involvement in "urban" problems such as crime, traffic congestion, and inadequate schools. Also, there was growing state control over the annexation process in order to prevent urban fragmentation and the creation of unincorporated county "urban islands" such as East Los Angeles, West Hollywood, and Willowbrook in southern California.[3]

As opportunities for annexation waned, many cities found that metropolitan consolidation, in addition to avoiding duplication of services, had a side effect of reducing the black population percentage. Although, between 1950 and 1975, no fewer than forty city-county consolidations in Standard Metropolitan Statistical Areas were defeated in voter referendums, three did succeed. These included Nashville-Davidson County, Tennessee, in 1962; Jacksonville-Duval County, Florida, in 1967; and Indianapolis-Marion County (Unigov), Indiana, in 1975. In all three cases, the black population percentage decreased considerably after consolidation. In Nashville, it dropped from 38 to just under 20 percent; in Jacksonville, from 41 to 23 percent; and in Indianapolis, from 35 to 18 percent. The consolidations in Nashville and Jacksonville took place as a result of voter referendum. The Indianapolis consolidation was particularly nefarious; it was enacted by an act of the Indiana legislature, a procedure unprecedented in any state in this century. No local vote was involved, and reorganization went into full effect the year following legislature approval.[4]

However, Gary's less sophisticated and relatively less educated white elites, instead of undertaking subtle actions to head off black governmental control, waited until Hatcher's 1967 Democratic primary win and then took steps to regain power. These included attempts to rig the 1967 general mayoral election, followed by an attempt at deannexation of the all-white Glen Park section of Gary, and then promotion of a surrogate black candidate to overturn Hatcher. When all three plots failed, the next move was the successful incorporation of Merrillville as the site of an alternative power base. When even this failed to achieve desired results, an attempt at metropolitan consolidation known as "Metrolake" took place.

White Attempts to Regain Political Control

In 1960, one did not have to be a genius to see that, with Gary's rapidly growing black population, it would be simply a matter of time before the black minority would become a majority and seize political control. In 1940, blacks comprised only 18.3 percent of the population, a figure that rose to 29.3 percent in 1950 and 39 percent in 1960. By the mid-1960s, the estimate was 50/50 black/white. However, during the early 1960s, Gary's city government, controlled by white ethnics, did not feel that blacks posed a threat to their power. In late 1982, I interviewed former Gary Mayor George Chacharis and was told, "We never considered annexation or consolidation with Lake County when I was mayor. We knew that blacks were about 40 percent of the population in the early '60s, but they were about 30 percent of the registered voters. We thought that if we kept giving them things, a position here and there . . . they would be content. We were going to run Dr. Williams for mayor in 1971. We didn't count on Hatcher becoming mayor."[5]

As shown earlier in Chapter 2, after Hatcher won the Democratic party primary in May 1967, he held discussions with John J. Krupa, Lake County Democratic party chairman. When he refused Krupa's politically intimidating demand to name the city controller, chief of police, and their key officials in exchange for the party's support in the general election, Krupa and other white ethnic Democratic party leaders threw their support to the Republican party candidate Joseph Radigan. Not content simply to support Radigan, Krupa and his followers took to purging black voters from the election rolls and adding nonexistent white voters in their place, a scheme exposed by Marian Tokarski, a white election board worker.[6] Hatcher then filed suit in Federal District Court, charging willful negligence in voting procedures and illegal disqualifications of black voters. Named as defendants were John Krupa, Walter C. Zurbriggen, Jerome J. Reppa, Robert H. Rooda, Anthony Dobis, Jr., Louis G. Karras, Marian Evanseck, Helen Ann Reypa, Bessie Manowski, Elease P. Wilson, Edward Robinson, Erma McBride, Rudy Bartolomei, Meaky Metcaff, Frank Perry, Andrew Atlanis, Marguerite Graves, Ortomease G. Gardeau, Isaac Davis, Steven Mojanovich, Mary A. Dzacky, Martha Pruitt, John Bokaik, Joseph S. Bejgrowiiz, and Dorothy Wakowski. The three-judge federal court panel ruled in favor of Hatcher and issued a preliminary injunction against actions by the defendants that would impair the holding of a fair election.[7]

Despite the Lake County Democratic party's continued intimidation, including breaking voting machines in black precincts, and attempts by white Gary police officers to keep blacks from voting, Hatcher won, with 40,000 votes to 38,000 for Radigan.

Stung by Radigan's defeat, the disgruntled white leadership's next move was a proposed deannexation of all-white Glen Park, Gary's south-ernmost community, which is separated from the rest of the city by the Little Calumet River and floodplain. Attempted in 1968 and led by Gary City Councilman Eugene Kirkland and State Senator Bernard Konrady, the "game plan" was not only to break away from Gary but to combine Glen Park's 30,000 residents with up to 50,000 other white inhabitants in southern unincorporated Lake County to form a new city. Indiana law made such a deannexation next to impossible, and Glen Park lacked a tax base sufficient to cover even minimal service costs. Mayor Hatcher even joked about cutting off Glen Park's water and placing toll gates on major streets connecting Gary with Glen Park, charging whites to enter the city on their way to work in the lakefront steel mills.[8]

With deannexation of Glen Park no longer an option, the next move was to attempt to unseat Hatcher in the 1971 Democratic party primary by use of a moderate black who would serve as a surrogate white. Conve-niently for this group, Dr. Alexander Williams, a prominent black physi-cian, chose to run for mayor against Hatcher. Williams, a light-skinned man with wavy hair, represented Gary's black middle-class elite. This group, composed of physicians, attorneys, public school teachers, and administrators, controlled black social and civic life in Gary through their fraternities, sororities, churches (Catholic and Episcopalian), and clubs. Well connected to the Lake County Democratic party machine, which rewarded them with small favors such as minor positions in city and county government, this group was pushed aside when Hatcher won first the Democratic party primary for mayor and then the general election. Many supported Martin Katz in the 1967 primary election. There was considerable resentment among members of this group (the majority of whom were light-skinned) when Hatcher, a dark-skinned "outsider" from a low-income working-class family in Michigan City, became mayor and thereby Gary's most important black citizen. Understanding this class conflict based on skin color, education, and church affiliation, the white elite felt that, with a coalition of middle-class blacks and most of the whites, they could defeat Hatcher. Williams had been elected Lake County coroner with machine support and was viewed by the white elite as a racial moderate and a reasonable alternative to Hatcher and his militant, pro-black, civil rights agenda.

Actually, Dr. Williams was just about as militant and pro-black as Hatcher. He had fought for desegregation of Methodist and St. Mary's hospitals. He had also fought for integration of Gary's parks and beaches and was an outspoken opponent of segregated housing. His differences with Hatcher were mainly over tactics. In his self-published book *Which Way Gary?* Williams attacked Hatcher for failing to deal with the city's rising crime rate. He attacked Hatcher's tearing down over 4,000 units of housing in Midtown with less than 300 units of new housing built, wasting of federal antipoverty and Model Cities funds, coddling black teenage gang members, and, most important, failing to work with the white business community to resolve Gary's problems. Williams was endorsed by the *Gary Post-Tribune* and a wide variety of white business, social, civic, and religious leaders. He ran with the full support and backing of the Lake County Democratic machine. However, Dr. Williams lost to Mayor Hatcher, winning only 37.5 percent of all votes cast. Hatcher won over 60 percent of the total vote and 90 percent of the black vote. Dr. Williams won 85 percent of the white vote. However, though just over 60 percent of black registered voters turned out for the election, only 32 percent of white voters showed up at the polls. Hatcher went on to defeat a white Republican in the general election by over 50,000 votes. With Hatcher reelected by a landslide, the next move was the incorporation of Merrillville. As late as 1970, this community was little more than a crossroads at Broadway two miles south of the Gary city line with fewer than 15,000 residents. Though Indiana had a buffer zone law preventing new incorporations from taking place less than five miles from previously established cities, Gary's white suburban Lake County legislative delegation, led by State Representative Chester A. Dobis, introduced local bills providing a waiver from this requirement as early as the 1969 session. The Indiana legislature authorized an exemption in 1971, and Merrillville was incorporated as a town adjacent to Gary that same year. At the time of incorporation, the town's population was only 22,000. By 1980, it had increased to 27,677, with only 32 black residents. To put this population increase in perspective, the population for all of Lake County dropped from 545,000 in 1970 to just 522,965 in 1980, a 4 percent *decrease*. After Merrillville's incorporation, not only did thousands of white Garyites move there but Gary's entire business community did likewise. Sears, Roebuck and Company, J.C. Penney, Montgomery Ward, and Goldblatt's department stores all closed their downtown Gary establishments along with over 100 other businesses, all white-owned, between 1971 and 1979. By the late 1970s, most had reappeared in the Merrillville area. Southlake Mall opened in 1978 with Sears, J.C. Penney, newly arrived Carson Pirie Scott, and Ayers as major department store tenants. Montgomery Ward found itself in another new mall just down the street from Southlake on U.S.-30. The two malls had a total of over one million square feet of gross leasable area, five department stores, and two multiscreened cinemas. Other establishments along U.S.-30 included the Holiday Inn complex with a 600-room hotel, an ampitheatre seating 3,500, a "Holidome" and convention facilities. Others included a "Toys-R-Us," headquarters for Gary's two banks, Gary National Bank and Bank One, and several small shops and restaurants. Just south of U.S.-30 on Broadway, Methodist Hospital opened a new full-service facility with 150 beds in 1973. They threatened to close the Gary facility and turn it into a nursing home, but Mayor Hatcher filed suit against them in 1972 and a consent decree was handed down in 1974, forcing Methodist to spend one dollar to remodel the Gary facility for every dollar spent on construction of the new facility in Merrillville. St. Mary's Hospital opened a new 110-bed hospital in Hobart in 1976, but, painfully aware of Gary's successful consent decree against Methodist, they voluntarily agreed to spend an amount of construction money to remodel their Gary facility equal to that for new facilities in Hobart.

Gary's former white elite, now entrenched in Merrillville and suburban Lake County, felt that, with the successful move to incorporate Merrillville and abandon downtown Gary, the old city would eventually collapse under its own weight. With an eroding tax base devoid of commercial ratables, decaying infrastructure, rising crime rate, and a slowly deteriorating physical environment, disgruntled voters would blame Hatcher for the city's plight and remove him from office in favor of a moderate supported by whites who would then promote their agenda for the city they had abandoned. However, much brighter and more resourceful than his enemies, Hatcher outflanked the old white elite once more. The Negotiated Investment Strategy of 1978 described in Chapter 2 gave rise to the refurbished Hotel Gary (renamed the Genesis Towers), the Genesis Convention Center, and the refurbished Holiday Inn, now known as the Sheraton Hotel. These gleaming new and remodeled structures were a distinct contrast to the drab storefronts of commercial establishments abandoned but still owned by whites south of Fifth Avenue. White elites had one more shot at removing Hatcher when Thomas Crump announced his candidacy for mayor in January 1983. Crump, a local black businessman and Gary native, was envisioned as a moderate, and he campaigned as one who would "work with the business community." Endorsed by the *Post-Tribune* and the mainly white Gary Chamber of Commerce, Crump still lost to Hatcher in the May 1983 Democratic party primary. Hatcher won with 27,835 votes, or 54.7 percent, to Crump's 23,150 votes, or 45.3 percent of the total. Although this was Hatcher's lowest voter percentage since 1967, he still won, and whites along with a growing number of blacks had to wait at least four more years for a new and at that time still unknown knight in shining armor to appear and take Gary back from Hatcher and his black militant followers.

The Indiana Legislative Council

In 1984, Indiana State Representative Chester A. Dobis of Merrillville and Jerome J. Reppa of Munster, a south Lake County suburb, assumed a leadership role in the Indiana Legislative Council. That body consists of sixteen legislators, eight from the house, and eight from the senate. Included are the house and senate speakers, president pro tem, majority and miniority leaders, and whips. The Indiana Legislative Council functions as an executive committee of the legislature. Dobis headed the council's committee on government affairs. On July 18, 1984, Dobis announced that the legislative council would undertake a study to find means of improving local government in northwest Indiana by making it more efficient and effective.[9] Measures that could be used to achieve this werc intergovernmental cooperation and coordination, elimination of duplicated services, and the use of regional agencies where appropriate. When questioned by the media as to whether or not consolidation would be considered, Dobis and Reppa replied, "It might be." The legislative council intended to petition the legislature for an enabling act that would provide funds for a study on how best to improve local government in the region. They requested $200,000 to be spent for this purpose during the 1985-1986 fiscal year. Plans called for their support to be made public before July 1, 1986.

Mayor Hatcher in his weekly press conference blasted the proposed study as nothing more than a front for consolidation. He warned the audience about Unigov, the Indianapolis-Marion County consolidation, stating, "When black people went to sleep in Indianapolis, they were 35 percent of the population and when they woke up they found Unigov in bed with them, and they were less than 20 percent of the population." He attacked Dobis and Reppa as people who were not friends of Gary. "They ran away from this city, but now they want it back." Hatcher's remarks were dismissed by *Post-Tribune* columnist Gary Galloway as "the usual racial stuff we've come to expect from Gary's mayor."[10]

It must be pointed out that Jerome J. Reppa was the same person named as a defendant by Mayor Hatcher in his federal court suit in the 1967 general election. Reppa was one of twenty-five Gary and Lake County residents accused of attempting to steal the election from Hatcher by removing eligible black Gary voters from the rolls and adding in their place nonexistent whites. As stated earlier in this chapter, the three-judge federal panel ruled in Hatcher's favor and issued a preliminary injunction against Reppa and the other defendants barring them from taking any and all actions that would impair the holding of a fair election.[11] Another defendant in that case was Anthony Dobis, Jr., the uncle of Chester A. Dobis. Chester A. Dobis himself pushed for the incorporation of Merrillville in 1971, although this action violated Gary's buffer zone as provided for by Indiana law. At Dobis's request, the legislature waived this provision so that the incorporation of Merrillville could take place. Both Reppa and Dobis had been Gary residents who moved to the suburbs after Hatcher's election as mayor. Given the connection of this proposed "study" to the documented actions of both men, Mayor Hatcher had good reason to believe that Chester Dobis and Jerome Reppa might be using the perfectly legitimate concern over good government as a tool to eliminate Gary as a political entity in northwest Indiana.

In 1985, the Indiana legislature passed an enabling act funding the Indiana Legislative Council to conduct a study of local government in Lake County. The study was given to the Indiana State University Center for Governmental Services. There was no competitive bidding, and no request for proposals were prepared and circulated outside the state of Indiana. The study's mandate was an open one: analyze the existing situation of Lake County's local governmental units, cities, towns, villages, townships, special districts, and the county government itself. Then, make a series of recommendations that will improve efficiency and effectiveness. School districts were not to be included in the study. Though the role of state and even federal government would be examined in the context of local government, no recommendations concerning changes in their operations would be made.

One might wonder, in the first place, why the study would be assigned to Indiana State, a university better known for Larry Bird and its basketball team than as a leading institution in the field of governmental affairs. Issues such as regional government and consolidation are politically explosive. Indiana State, being a public institution, is funded by the Indiana legislature, and the study's client group was the legislature's own executive committee, the Indiana Legislative council with the operating committee headed by Dobis and Reppa, two prominent state legislators. Given this dynamic, there would always be the possibility of the Center for Governmental Services giving these legislators what they wanted, which in this case could all too easily be an anti-Gary, anti-Mayor Hatcher package. In order to maximize integrity, the study should have been given to an out-of-state university to make certain that no conflict of interest could occur.[12]

There were several well-qualified university research institutes outside Indiana quite capable of taking on such an assignment. The top three public affairs programs in the nation are the John F. Kennedy School of Government at Harvard University, the Lyndon Baines Johnson School of Public Affairs at the University of Texas, and the Maxwell School at Syracuse University. Any one of the three would have been an excellent choice for a study that no one, including Mayor Hatcher, could claim was politically biased. The same could be said for similar centers at the University of Georgia, University of Southern California, Washington University in St. Louis, and the University of Kentucky. Even if, for some good reason, only an in-state university could be the recipient of public funds, why wasn't Indiana University or Purdue University selected? They are Indiana's two leading public universities, and both have Ph.D. programs in political science and government. Indiana State University has no Ph.D. program in government or political science and therefore lacked the critical mass of scholars and doctoral-level students needed to undertake serious research. Most important, Indiana University's School of Public and Environmental Affairs is the nation's fourth leading institution in public affairs in terms of scholarly productivity.

Despite the possible conflict of interests, Indiana State was chosen. The lead researcher would be William Harader, director of the Center for Government Services and a highly respected political scientist. Their work began in June 1985, and, by August 1986, polished drafts were circulated to the Indiana Legislative Council.

The Lake County Government Study

Through the efforts of Gary's legislative delegation, State Senator Carolyn Mosby, and State Representatives Charlie Brown, Earline Rogers, and Earl Harris,[13] Mayor Hatcher's office had been quietly kept informed about the study's progress. Through some personal contacts at Indiana State, I was able to get various drafts of the report only days after they were prepared and photocopied. I was able to get a final draft only a few days before it was formally presented to the media.

The report, which was over 300 pages in length and titled "Lake County Government Study," opened with a brief background of the evolution of its mission, telling the reader what he probably already knew: Gary, and Lake County, was losing residents and had an eroding tax base and a weak economy. A summary of attitude surveys of Lake County residents taken by the researchers was included. Then some broad goals and objectives were presented, followed by a list of seventy-six recommendations with a rational and detailed explanation for each. The recommendations were organized under five headings: (I) Adequacy of Services, (II) Present and Future Fiscal Capability, (III) Government Structure, (IV) Efficiency of Local Units of Government, and (V) Metrogov.

Sixteen of the seventy-six recommendations specifically dealt with replacing existing Gary agencies, which were "one of a kind" functions in Lake County, with regional agencies and with metropolitan consolidation itself. Specifically, the major regionalization recommendations were:

1. Indiana and Illinois should create a transportation authority patterned after the New York Port Authority to regulate major airports, private transportation operations, and terminal facilities.

2. Combine all sewer systems, sanitary districts, and conservancy districts in the cities of Gary, Hobart, East Chicago, Hammond, Griffith, Whiting, Munster, and Highland into a "Metro" district.

3. Combine library systems in East Chicago, Gary, and Hammond into a "Metro" system.

4. Create a Lake County Economic Development Commission to replace local ones in Gary, Hammond, East Chicago, and South Lake County.

5. Have one planning and zoning board for all of Lake County.

6. Adopt a planning, programming, budgeting system for all of Lake County with computerization of all records.

7. Abolish the township trustees and transfer their responsibilities to county government.

The consolidation proposal was to combine North, Calumet, and Hobart townships into one government known as "Metrogov." This single government would have an elected mayor. The mayor would head an "executive board" consisting of the mayors of the five constituent cities (or boroughs) of Gary, Hammond, East Chicago-Whiting, Hobart, and Griffith-Highland-Munster (see figure 4), and an elected controller. There would also be a thirty-five-member legislative council with seven members each from all five constituent cities.

Mayor Hatcher asked me to look at the Lake County Government Study for some initial observations. I quickly noticed two things. First, the study only included Lake County, though the metropolitan area as recognized by the U.S. Census Bureau included Lake and Porter counties. Porter County (just east of Lake County) was mostly rural until the early 1960s when Bethlehem Steel built new mills on Lake Michigan, quickly followed by new suburban single-family housing tracts. Porter County grew from 87,000 residents in 1970 to 120,000 in 1980, a 32 percent increase. Most of this increase came from former Lake County and especially Gary residents looking for "move-up" suburban-oriented housing. The two counties were intertwined geographically, socially, and economically since 1960, and both must be considered parts of one urbanized area. Second, Metrogov left out Merrillville and the other rapidly growing Lake County suburbs in the U.S. Route 30 corridor including Dyer, Schereville, St. John, and Crown Point. This area was the growth district for Lake County; residences, commercial centers such as the Merrillville shopping mall, hotel-office complexes described earlier, hospitals, and related institutions had been built there in the 1970s and early 1980s. Assessed value was well over $300 million in this area neglected by Metrogov's planners, and, with only 100,000 residents to serve, it would be a valuable addition to any city, new or old.[14] Why was the shiny, new, and lucrative U.S. Route 30 corridor not recommended as part of Metrogov? I did observe that Metrogov's 400,000-plus residents would consist of a population that by 1980 U.S. Census figures would be only 30.8 percent black and 10.2 percent Hispanic. Gary's 1980 population was 71 percent black and 7 percent Hispanic. Blacks counted for 30 percent and Hispanics 35 percent of East Chicago's population. Political advantages then available for blacks in Gary and blacks and

Figure 4. The Metrolake Proposal, 1986

As it appeared in the September 25, 1986 edition of the *Post Tribune*

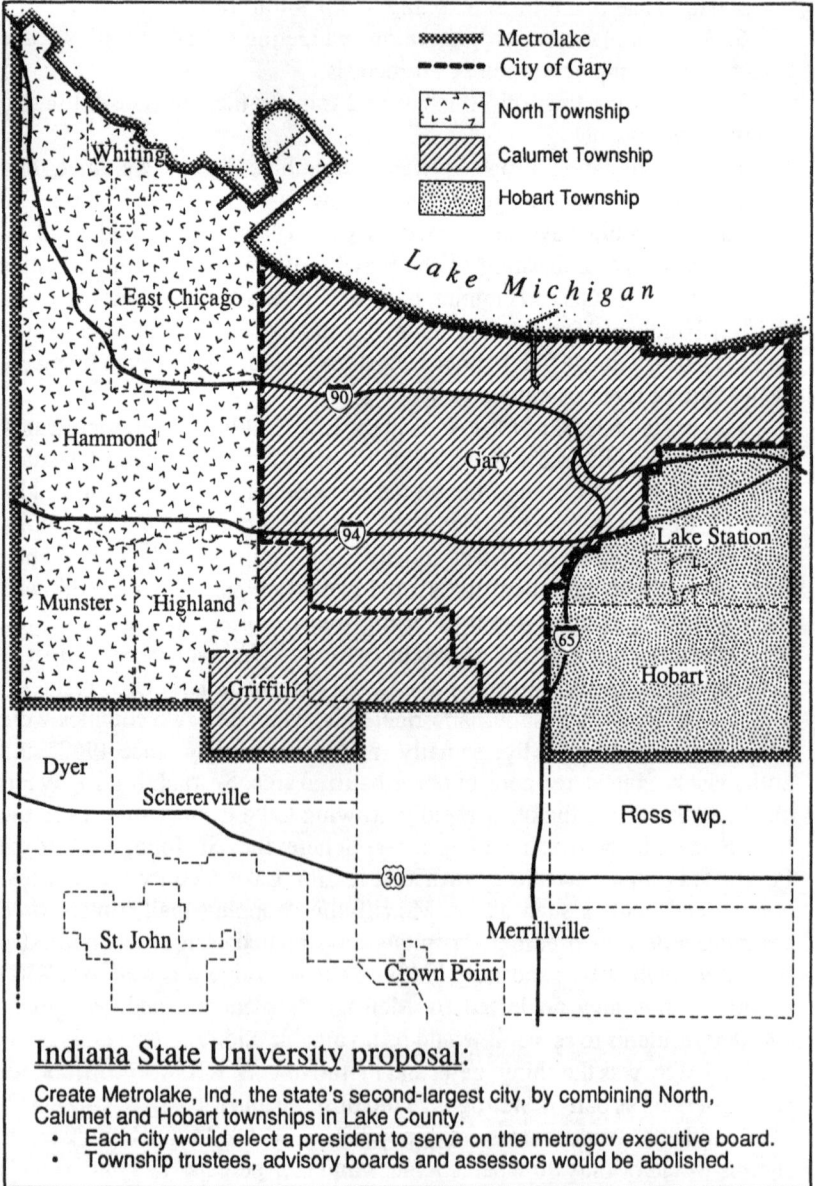

Indiana State University proposal:

Create Metrolake, Ind., the state's second-largest city, by combining North,
Calumet and Hobart townships in Lake County.
- Each city would elect a president to serve on the metrogov executive board.
- Township trustees, advisory boards and assessors would be abolished.

(After Mike Kent / *Post - Tribune* graphic)

Hispanics in East Chicago would be wiped out under Metrogov. Also, the executive board would give Gary only one seat, or 14 percent of the representation, whereas Gary would consist of 40 percent of Metrogov's population.

I told Mayor Hatcher that at first glance Metrogov and the entire study was puzzling. On one hand, more than half of the recommendations seemed to have real merit. On the other hand, some, including the Metrogov proposal, seemed off the wall. With the entire northwest Indiana metropolitan area not covered by Metrogov, especially the U.S. Route 30 corridor, this was a different type of consolidation from all others considered nationally between 1950 and 1985. All it did was neatly eliminate black and Hispanic political power. I recommended that we wait for the study's official presentation, observe initial reaction to it from the region's political, business, institutional, and civic leadership, study all seventy-six recommendations carefully, and then take control. He agreed, and we waited for the study's official presentation to take place.

Metrolake Is Announced

On September 24, 1986, the Indiana Legislative Council formally introduced the Lake County Governmental Study to the press. An article appeared the very next day on page one of the *Post-Tribune* with the headline "Metrolake Would Join Ten Cities." Written by Bob Ashley, the article began with the statement that the consolidated government proposed by the study would be "the second largest city in Indiana, the thirty-third largest city in the nation, bigger than Miami, Florida, Cincinnati, Ohio, and Minneapolis, Minnesota." "Welcome to Metrolake, Indiana," the article went on to state. Although some of the other seventy-two recommendations of the study *not* about consolidation were mentioned in passing, the focus was clearly on Metrogov, now renamed Metrolake by the *Post-Tribune*.

The *Post-Tribune* was quick to report initial reaction by northwest Indiana leaders to the study. State Representative Chester A. Dobis, one of two legislators who initiated the study, said, "Some of the things sound like they are workable." He also said that he had not yet been provided with a copy of the recommendations, a dubious statement, as members of Mayor Hatcher's staff and I had been receiving copies of drafts on a regular basis, and we were not even in the study's information "loop." Representative Jerome J. Reppa said, "There are lots of controversial issues that are worthy of debate. I would like to live long enough to see some of these changes." Dr. William Harader, the study's author, defended the proposed consolidation, saying that "merging the three townships into a single city would lower the risk of financial collapse in the event one of the area's steel mills closes."[15] Harader, for some reason, forgot to say that inclusion of the U.S. Route 30 corridor townships of St. John, Center (Crown Point), and Ross (Merrillville) would lower the risk of financial collapse even more.

In another article published in the *Post-Tribune* that same day, reporter Rich James commented on the northwest Indiana mayor's reaction to Metrolake. Richard G. Hatcher was quoted as saying, "All of this is about racism. The city of Gary has major assets that the rest of the area wants: the lakefront and the airport. I see this as a very real threat to the very existence of Gary as a city. After all these years they have sent people against me and haven't been able to defeat me. So this is the ultimate solution. Just wipe out the city, create a much larger city, and kill any black influence." The *Post-Tribune*, in their usual biased coverage, conveniently left out Hatcher's remarks that, of the seventy-six proposals, some seemed to be very good and that he might be able to support several after further study. Other elected officials were not enthusiastic about Metrolake either. Stanley Jones, the town board president of Munster, a predominately white upper-middle-class community included in the proposed consolidation, stated, "The only thing it does is dilute the impact of the vote of the individual citizen." Not realizing that Mayor Hatcher of Gary was strongly against the consolidation, Jones went on to state, "I do not see the purpose of it other than Gary and East Chicago seeing their tax bases eroding. They see development elsewhere and want to get a piece of it." The mayor of all-white Whiting, Joseph B. Grenchik, said on behalf of his 5,000 citizens, "Our people are happy with their service. We've got enough problems without handing things over to someone in some ivory tower who would never come around here." Thurman Ferree, the town board president of Highland (another white suburb proposed for inclusion), stated, "I think you would lose representative government. It doesn't get better because it's bigger. All communities have a specific flavor and reasons why people live there. Services in the Ridge communities (Highland and Munster) are good." East Chicago City Clerk George W. Cvitkovich said in regards to the proposed thirty-five-member Metrolake city council, "There's too much jealousy here. People are too protective of their own positions. The bottom line is where are they saving any money?"

East Chicago's flamboyant Mayor Robert A. "Hollywood Bob" Pastrick gave measured approval to the idea of consolidation. Stated Pastrick, "I've been an advocate for some time that there should be some form of regional government. I don't know what its composition should be, and it will take more study and meeting of the minds, but there is far too much duplication of services. There has been regional cooperation on building marinas in northwest Indiana, but, in other ways, the cities compete. We're competing in economic development, but we're moving the same jobs from community to community and not bringing any in."

Thomas M. McDermott, mayor of Hammond, felt that Metrolake was a good idea but that the consolidation should have included all of Lake County. He was quoted as saying, "I think in the long range the people would find their services would improve, and then taxes would go lower, and it would give us a lot more strength when talking to people in Indianapolis. I think it's exciting from the standpoint of the size it would give us, the tax base it would give us, and from the standpoint of going after museums and sports franchises." McDermott added that people in Highland and Munster might object, as many of them moved from Hammond and East Chicago for what they felt were better schools, better equipped parks and recreation areas, and newer housing with more spacious yards.

The reaction from black community leaders other than Mayor Hatcher was muted. Calumet Township Trustee Dozier T. Allen was a Hatcher supporter who later turned against him and ran for mayor in the 1975 primary only to lose in a crushing defeat. Under Metrolake, his office would be abolished. However, in a statesmanlike manner, he was quoted as saying that he could see strengths and weaknesses in the Metrolake plan. Allen said, according to this newspaper article, he would want the structure modified to have the Metrolake mayor appointed on a rotating basis from the five "city" presidents elected to the proposed Metro Executive Board. "I don't like the odds of an election at large. That would insure some ethnic groups would never have a mayor," stated Allen. State Senator Carolyn B. Mosby said, "I am not in favor of political consolidation. It gets people excited and protective. The people who left Gary do not want to be lumped with Gary. The people who left Hammond don't want to be lumped with Hammond. They left for a reason."

The interesting thing about Rich James's article was that he took pains to quote Dozier Allen, Carolyn Mosby, Thomas McDermott, Robert Pastrick, and others completely, giving their pros and cons concerning Metrolake. However, the only quote from Hatcher dealt with negatives, namely the notion that Metrolake was a racist plot to eliminate black political power in Gary. No mention of Hatcher's willingness to consider some of the study recommendation was made, even though this acknowledgement was part of the official press release and Rich James attended Mayor Hatcher's press conference on September 24, 1986, when he made his statements concerning Metrolake. Once again, the *Post-Tribune*, which had opposed Hatcher from the time he announced his candidacy for mayor of Gary in 1967, stooped to biased coverage.[16]

The *Post-Tribune* continued to highlight Metrolake. On September 26, 1986, the very next day after the announcements by Bob Ashley and Rich James, an article by Joseph Conn began with the headline "Metrolake Ideas to be Pushed." The article quoted Chester A. Dobis and Jerome J. Reppa, the Indiana state representatives who sponsored legislation for the Lake

County Government Study, as stating they would press for the implementation of "some" recommendations in the coming legislative session. They
were careful not to mention which recommendations might be pushed
because apparently they were waiting for public opinion in northwest
Indiana to register before committing themselves.

Mike Angil of the *Hammond Times,* in an article written on September
26 and headlined "Gary Mayor opposed to Metrolake," took a view more
balanced than the one presented by the *Post-Tribune.* Angil pointed out that
Chester A. Dobis was an employee of Gainer Bank, an institution that had
long opposed the Hatcher administration, and that Dobis was the one who
pushed for Merrillville's incorporation, thereby violating Gary's buffer
zone as provided for by Indiana law. Angil also mentioned Hatcher's
comment that some of the study recommendations seemed well intended
and that he might support them after further review.

On Sunday, September 28, 1986, the *Post-Tribune* ran an editorial
headlined:

SOMETHING NEW IS NEEDED

Maybe a new idea is exactly what this area needs. A sweeping, stunning idea—something to startle leaders and citizens into thinking. The metrogov proposal that came out
of a state study of Lake County government is just that. That doesn't mean there isn't
room for discussion and improvements before implementing any suggested changes.
But there should be serious consideration of the idea, not just knee-jerk reactions.

Anything that might breathe life into this area is worthy of careful thought.
Anything that holds promise for improving economic efficiency of government and
providing better services is worthy of careful thought. Anything that would aid in
making taxes fairer and give the people solid service for their money is worthy of careful
thought. Careful thought with an open mind.

Forming a super-city out of what is now Gary, Hammond, East Chicago, Whiting,
Lake Station, Hobart, Griffith, Highland, Munster, and New Chicago carries great
potential, as presented in the study.

It is not a racist idea, as predictably charged by Gary Mayor Richard Hatcher.
Rather it is racism that keeps it from being accepted as a valid solution to reviving a
dying area. Hatcher and many Gary residents see it as an attempt to dilute black
influence, to eliminate a predominately black political unit. Residents in the suburban
towns see it as an attempt to force them to share life and power with blacks and other
minorities. The challenge of the metrogov idea is to bring people together as people, not
as blacks, whites, Latinos, rich, poor, laborers, yuppies, bigwigs. It will be the inability
to do this that will keep Metrolake from coming into being anytime soon, if ever—that
and the selfish political fiefdoms that split and control various corners of Lake County.
Both attitudes belong in the history books.

The fear of the loss of identity by cities and towns is a legitimate concern. It's
difficult to break with the past, no matter how bright the future might look. But the loss
of identity could well be less than expected, particularly any place where a strong sense
of community already exists. People living in the cities involved already think of
themselves as living in Miller, Glen Park, Brunswick, the Harbor, Hessville, even the
smaller towns have their residential divisions.

Even if there were a Metrolake as proposed there would be five "constituent cities" within the super-city, similar to New York City's boroughs (Brooklyn and Manhattan sure haven't lost their identities). People would still probably think of themselves first as living in Miller, then Gary, then Metrolake, then Lake County, then Indiana. The farther away someone is from home, the bigger the home territory. When in Florida, one is from Indiana. When in Indianapolis, Lake County. When in Lake County, Gary. When in Gary, Miller.

The thing that should determine whether to go with a metrogov system, though, is whether it would help the people. Would it, as the study indicates, lower the tax burden of residents, provide better services, produce an area conducive to strong economic activity? This is what responsible leaders should be considering first and foremost.

Residents, who for years have seemed resigned to corrupt and inefficient government, can lead the way by demanding that their leaders provide something new. Metrolake could mean more for your money and a better standard of living for all. Irrational prejudices should not be allowed to ruin that chance.

The editorial cavalierly ignored northwest Indiana's sorry history of racism that gave rise to the *need* for black political power by dismissing Mayor Hatcher's concerns as "predictable." The editorial also dismissed the legitimate concerns of the white suburbs of Highland and Munster for their self-determination by suggesting they didn't want to share power with blacks. It did not address the issue of the affluent tax-rich U.S. Route 30 townships in south Lake County being left out of the proposed consolidation. It also did not take into account that Mayor Hatcher and Mayor Pastrick of East Chicago saw some of the study recommendations as positive and certainly deserving of further study. The editorial, through slick rhetoric appealing to basic human values of sharing and togetherness, made it appear to the casual reader that those opposed to the Metrolake consolidation were opposed to all seventy-six study recommendations as well. Nothing could have been further from the truth.

On Monday, September 29, I met with Mayor Hatcher in his office. We discussed, at length, the events of the past few days concerning Metrolake and came to these conclusions: (1) McDermott and, to a lesser extent, Pastrick favored the proposed consolidation because they, especially McDermott, felt capable of being elected mayor of Metrolake; (2) Dozier Allen was behaving as a "statesman" because by doing so he would curry favor with white business and institutional leaders for his possible race for mayor the next spring (he could be magnanimous about having his position as township trustee abolished because it wouldn't happen anyway, given the power of the statewide network of Township trustees; (3) Carolyn Mosby's statement was well meaning and accurate; (4) the *Post-Tribune*, by view of the distortion and biased reporting of Hatcher's remarks on the study and their editorial, was acting as a cheerleader for the white elite of northwest Indiana; and (5) the major objective of northwest Indiana's white leadership was not the proposed consolidation, which was simply a smoke screen to divert public attention to something that might never happen;

instead, the objective was to seize control of Gary's airport, library system, sanitary district, and public bus system and the new Adam Benjamin Transportation Center out of which they operated by supply, taking these systems away from Gary and placing them under "regional" control.

I agreed to review the Lake County Government Study, including its recommendations, in detail. We agreed to meet on October 6 and finalize a draft statement concerning the study in time for the mayor's weekly news conference on Wednesday, October 8.

Analysis of the Lake County Government Study

During the week of September 29-October 3, I reviewed the Lake County Government Study. I noticed that while there was considerable notation and review of the literature with respect to taxation budget and finance, organization and management, and personnel administration, there was no mention of the literature about consolidation, either that of entire governmental units or metropolitan systems (transportation, libraries sewage, etc.) in the form of special districts. This was extremely unfortunate coming from an academic institution such as Indiana State University. Given the obvious volatility of a consolidation recommendation, one would think that even a pragmatic academic would have loaded up on literature that supported such a position.

Perhaps the reason Harader did not include as part of his literature review material on consolidation was because, at best, the literature has mixed opinions concerning the wisdom of such an action. From Tuesday, September 30, through that weekend, I devoted practically all my waking hours to a review of the literature regarding metropolitan consolidation, special districts, and governmental cooperation. Concerning consolidation, I found that Brommage wrote in 1969 that problems with consolidation included (1) frequent remoteness from the public, (2) slow progress because of constituent city resistance, and (3) problems in determining criteria to be employed in formulating the new governing body.[17] Bollens and Schmandt in 1982 questioned whether consolidation really presented savings. Instead, they emphasized intergovernmental cooperation as an alternative.[18]

As far back as the early 1960s, Indiana University scholars Ostrum, Tiebout, and Warren noted that individual governments within metropolitan areas tend to develop basic frameworks for cooperation. They note, "Contrary to the frequent assertion about lack of metropolitan framework for dealing with metropolitan problems, most metropolitan areas have a very rich and intricate framework for negotiating, adjuncticating and deciding questions that affect their diverse public interests."[19] Although that type of metropolitan framework had not been put into place in northwest

Indiana because of an individualistic political culture, lack of an academic intrastructure, lack of native wealth, and racial/ethnic divisiveness, Harader if he had followed the literature, could have made an argument for coperation rather than intensifying local divisions by calling for consolidation.

The reactions of the town board presidents of Highland and Munster and the mayor of Whiting could have been predicted had Harader taken time to review the literature on voter behavior. For instance, in 1964, the U.S. Advisory Commission on Intergovernmental Relations stated that "consolidation may lessen the voter's influence on his total government by making his vote relatively less important."[20]

If Harader had taken time to review thoroughly the literature on race relations in northwest Indiana, he might have been more sensitive to the impact of a proposed consolidation on Gary's black citizens and East Chicago's Latino citizens. My review showed that James Lane[21] presented in 1979 a detailed account on racial divisiveness in Gary with a careful review of the 1967 mayoral race, as did Nelson and Meranto (1978), Poinsett (1971), and Greer (1979).[22] Raymond Mohl and Neil Betten, in 1974, showed how Gary's black population moved from a relatively integrated setting to complete segregation and intolerance as a result of public policy.[23] In 1986, Mohl and Betten went further by showing how public policy decisions that resulted in racial segregation and discrimination for blacks encouraged whites to develop, adopt, and maintain prejudicial attitudes toward this group.[24] Greer, in 1979, detailed the history of racial and economic discrimination against blacks and Mexican-Americans by white elites in order to set up and maintain a dual labor market.[25] Jeanne Fox, in 1974, writing about the impact of consolidation on racial minorities, concluded that given experiences with Jacksonville, Florida, and Durham, North Carolina, regionalism dilutes minority political power, adds another layer of bureaucracy, and does not address problems such as housing, employment, tax equalization and zoning.[26]

Some advocates of regional government, including Harader, felt that, despite the obvious loss of political power, blacks gain because of an improved economic environment. But do they? Table 7 shows that after five years of Unigov in Indianapolis, blacks there scored lower in seven of ten U.S. Census indicators than did their counterparts in Gary. In 1970, Indianapolis blacks were below those in Gary in, again, seven of the same ten indicators. In 1980, for example, the median household income for blacks in Indianapolis was $12,827 compared to $16,920 in Gary. In 1970, before Unigov, the corresponding figures were $6,116 in Indianapolis and $7,532 in Gary. Table 8 shows that in the U.S. Census Bureau's 1982 Survey of Minority Owned Businesses—Black, Gary's black-owned businesses did slightly better than those in Indianapolis. Despite the declining

Table 7. Quality of Life Factors for the Black Populations of
Gary and Indianapolis

	1970		1980	
Indicator	Gary	Indianapolis	Gary	Indianapolis
Socioeconomic:				
Median income[1]	$7,532	$6,116	$16,920	$12,827
% Female-headed households	12.0	20.0	38.0	37.6
% High school graduates	39.0	37.1	61.0	52.6
% Below poverty level	18.8	18.0	21.4	20.0
% Professional and managerial jobholders	11.7	10.5	15.1	12.8
Housing:				
Median value of housing[2]	$14,500	$11,400	$25,800	$23,300
% Homeowners	52.0	49.0	61.4	48.2
% With at least one automobile	68.1	64.6	77.0	76.8
% of all units with air conditioning	17.0	18.0	50.0	50.0
% of all units with central heat	80.0	80.0	86.4	83.7

Source: U.S. Census, 1970 and 1980.

[1] In 1970, this indicator was expressed as "Median Income Families and Unrelated Individuals"; in 1980, it was expressed as "Median Household Income."

[2] Applies to owner-occupied housing only.

steel economy in Gary compared with the robust boomtown economy in Indianapolis, blacks did better in Gary because of, among other things, strong affirmative action programs on the part of city government.[27] As one of my students remarked in class while we were studying Metrolake, "What good is it to see a large high-rise building going up when all you can do is watch the construction through a knothole?"

Harader's study was completely insensitive to minorities. Blacks made up almost 75 percent of the city's work force in 1985, including 55 percent of police officers. In East Chicago, Mexican-Americans make up almost 34 percent of all city workers. In a consolidation that results in white political control, given the racial animosity of the past, what was to prevent wholesale discharge and or downgrading of minority governmental employees? Harader's study made no mention of affirmative action or even nondiscrimination; these phrases never appeared in any of the 300-plus pages.

The literature was not too kind to special districts formed on a regional basis. In 1962, the U.S. Advisory Commission on Intergovernmental Relations, in criticizing the Port Authority of New York, stated, "Typically, the limited purpose special district is remote from the voters because of its composition, method of governing body selection and method of financing. The need for covering their costs tends to be a preoccupation

Table 8. Comparison of Black-Owned Businesses in Gary and
Indianapolis in 1982

Indicator	Gary	Indianapolis
Black population (in SMSA)	125,000	157,000
Sales per firm	$51,484	$36,978
Per capita sales (SMSA)	$106.04	$77.79
Percentage of all sales (SMSA)	.8	.4
Total gross sales	$67,445,000	$92,928,000

Source: U.S. Census Bureau Survey of Minority Owned Business Enterprises, 1982.

Note: Despite Indianapolis's robust economy under UNIGOV, it appears that blacks may not have
been sharing equally in this abundance. Strong affirmative action programs in black-
governed Gary allowed minority business there to thrive despite the relatively poor economy
of northwest Indiana.

with the results that they may neglected other related services and resist
efforts that may not be self-supporting (e.g. the New York City subway
systems and the toll roads—bridges)."[28]

In 1963, the U.S. Advisory Commission on Intergovernmental Relations said that, based on their analysis over a twenty-year period, special
districts are resorted to primarily because existing units of government are
either unwilling or unable to provide services.[29] In the case of Gary, this
city already had the region's only large scale airport capable of handling
commercial aircraft. The Gary Sanitary District, in continuous operation
since 1911, is the largest and most comprehensive in northwest Indiana. The
Gary Library System was the largest in the region, closely followed in size
by Lake County's. The Gary Public Transportation Corporation, chartered
in 1949 with the takeover of the city's private streetcar lines, carried ten
times the combined ridership of those in Hammond and East Chicago. It
might have been a better idea for Gary to absorb these smaller services
rather than to form a new special district. Though special districts might be
useful to provide *new* services that at a given time are not available
anywhere in a metropolitan area, they should not be used to replace
otherwise sound existing systems, according to the U.S. Advisory Commission's report.

Another reason for creating a special district is that the services provided by an existing unit of government may not be adequate. For example,
in 1980, the South Shore railroad had only two thousand daily riders.
Saddled with ancient passenger cars, old decrepit stations, and unstable
track beds, the railroad petitioned the Indiana Public Utilities Commission
for abandonment of passenger service. Their trains were late, often broke
down, and, most important, the company wanted to get out of the passenger
service business. Congressman Adam Benjamin took the lead in forming
the Northwest Indiana Commuter Transit District (NICTD). This new

agency, headed by one representative from the state of Indiana and one each from Lake, Porter, Laporte, and St. Joseph counties, took over the passenger service and obtained $64.5 million for new cars, stations, and track improvements. The new cars were put into service in 1983, the new stations were built in Gary and Chesterton in 1985, and, by 1986, ridership had doubled to 4,000 daily.[30]

However, this was not the case for the services offered by the city of Gary proposed for consolidation. The Gary airport, designated by the Federal Aviation Administration as a reliever for O'Hare, is the only one in the region with runways and facilities capable of handling commercial jet carriers and had never been cited for a Federal Aviation Administration violation. Since 1978, it had undergone an ambitious expansion and development program, featuring a new passenger terminal building opened in 1984 with three counters, three baggage ramps, and two rental car booths. The Gary Public Transportation Corporation had a fleet of sixty-two new buses purchased in 1982 and 1983 and one of the lowest accident rates nationwide for an urban public bus system nationally, and it had qualified, in 1985, for a federal grant to build new storage facilities. It operated out of the downtown Gary Adam Benjamin Transportation Center, a spanking new, $10 million facility that served as an interstate bus terminal and the major Gary station for the South Shore Commuter Railroad. The Gary Sanitation District had an environmental record no better or worse than other districts of its type in the region. Its consideration by Harader for combination with the smaller districts in East Chicago and Hammond made no sense, as the Gary Sanitation District treated Merrillville wastes and run-offs, and, of course, Merrillville was left out of the sanitary district consolidation as well as the total governmental consolidation of Metrolake. The Gary Public Library System—debt-free, with a main library, five branches and, in 1985, the largest circulation in the northwest Indiana region—had an excellent collection of African-American literature. Not only was consolidation inappropriate for the Gary Library, as they were doing fine just as they were, but the Lake County Governmental Study made no provision for the enhancement of this collection under consolidation. I doubted if Harader and his associates at the Indiana State University Center for Governmental Services were even aware of the collection's existence.

The Lake County Government Study made numerous references to Unigov, the Indianapolis consolidation of 1975. However, the literature on Unigov is cautious about applying that model to other metropolitan areas. James Owen and York Wilburn's classic work on Unigov, *Governing Metropolitan Indianapolis*, published in 1985 just before the Lake County Government Study began, is critical of Unigov. Though they were generally supportive of Unigov, the authors noted a number of concerns about it.

Table 9. Per Capita Property Tax of Indiana City and County Governments in Cities over 50,000 Population (Fiscal Years Ending December 31, 1982 and December 31, 1983)

		Per Capita Property Tax					
		1982			1983		
City	County	City	County	Total	City	County	Total
South Bend	St. Joseph	$162	$57	$219	$182	$61	$243
Hammond	Lake	129	85	214	165	87	252
Muncie	Delaware	139	60	199	159	66	225
Anderson	Madison	144	46	190	154	52	206
Gary	**Lake**	**137**	**85**	**222**	**151**	**87**	**238**
Fort Wayne	Allen	125	56	181	149	57	206
Terre Haute	Vigo	146	67	213	142	86	228
Evansville	Vanderburgh	120	62	182	134	76	210
Bloomington	Monroe	92	n.d.	n.d.	102	40	142
Indianapolis	Marion	n.d.	n.d.	219	n.d.	n.d.	239
Ave. U.S. City	Ave. U.S. County	149	96	245	153	105	258

Sources: Government Finances, GF 83 No. 4, GF 84 No. 4, GF 83 No. 8, and GF 84 No. 8, Bureau of Census, U.S. Department of Commerce. "Any inter-city comparison based upon these figures should be made with caution, recognizing the variations that exist among urban areas in the relative role played by the municipal corporation . . . . Data . . . related only to municipal corporations and their dependent agencies, and do not include amounts for other local governments overlaying city areas. . . . Variations in the assignment of governmental responsiblity for public assistance, health, hospitals, and public housing, and other functions to a lesser degree, also have an important effect upon reported amounts of county expenditure, revenue, and debt."

n.d. = no data available

Prepared by Gary Department of Redevelopment, September 1986.

1. *The Indianapolis Library retained its quasi-independent status* (as compared to the proposed consolidation proposed by Harader for Metrolake).

2. *Taxpayers were paying higher levels because of increased school taxes not covered by Unigov, and, actually, Indianapolis has one of the highest per capita tax loads among Indiana cities with populations over 100,000* (see table 9). This point was extremely important because one of the possible advantages of Metrolake, as noted by Mayor McDermott of Hammond and the *Post-Tribune,* was the lowering of taxes in the long run.

3. *A very large portion of Unigov's operating expenditures is funded by federal grants, and Indianapolis will need new monies if and when revenue sharing ceases.*

4. *Indianapolis's booming economy caused, among other things, higher assessed values, and this would have occurred with or without Unigov.* As we all know now, revenue sharing was phased out in

1987-1990, and Indianapolis, just like all other cities across the nation, had to raise local taxes to help meet expenditures. Economic growth is owing to strong leadership, not necessarily Unigov, and Mayors Richard Lugar and William Hudnut being Republicans certainly helped.

5. *Unigov's enactment without voter referendum was unique in consolidation experience. Another legislative mandate might fail.* The authors noted that the consolidation of Las Vegas and Clark County enacted by the state legislature was overturned two years later by the Nevada Supreme Court.

6. *Successes during the last fifteen years are not so clearly the product of unified government that they justify the marketing of Unigov as a model for widespread adoption elsewhere.*[31]

Had Harader and his associates chosen to read Owen and Wilburn's analysis of Unigov and other relevant literature, they would perhaps as academics been unwilling to propose consolidation and regional government. One would hate to think they *did* review the literature on consolidation and then chose to ignore it because of a predetermined agenda. Again, it is important to note that the study, which took an entire year to prepare, contained no references to Owen and Wilburn's work or the other literature on consolidation and regionalism that I was able to find and review in a matter of days.

I found in my review that the literature was much more sympathetic to cooperative approaches. For example, Werner Z. Hirsch in 1971 wrote *Los Angeles: Viability and Prospects for Metropolitan Leadership*[32] and advocated a program whereby facilities in place continue to be managed by those cities in which they are located and new services could be operated by either the central city, an urban county, or a regional agency. If Hirsch's model were to be followed, Gary would retain its airport, bus system, library system, and sanitary district. New services such as marinas and light rail transit lines serving the entire northwest Indiana region could then be operated by regional agencies or special districts. As in the case of consolidation and regional government, Harader did not cite any of the literature on governmental cooperation as an alternative to consolidation or regionalism.[33]

Based on my literature review, I wrote a long memorandum to Mayor Hatcher urging him to oppose the Metrolake consolidation and the folding of Gary's airport, bus company, sanitary district, and library system into so-called regional agencies. This consolidation and regionalization as proposed by the study was not supported by the academic or professional literature. Harader had not cited any academic, professional, or popular literature to support his consolidation and regional government concepts. As previously noted, the Gary agencies were doing well on their own, had no financial crises, and, unlike the South Shore railroad's 1980 petition for abandonment, the city of Gary was ready, willing, and able to continue provision of these services and to extend them to other areas of Lake County as well.[34]

On the other hand, I recommended in my memorandum that Mayor Hatcher strongly support many of the study recommendations, mostly those involving governmental cooperation and mutual assistance. Some of these included the following:

1. *A state-subsidized television station in Lake County.* Because of its central location, Gary would be an ideal site.

2. *A state office building in Lake County.* Again, because of locational factors, downtown Gary would be an ideal site.

3. *Expand use of fees and charges to reduce the reliance on the property tax.* Gary and other municipalities could charge a 1 percent franchise fee to the privately-owned electric and water companies.

4. *Provision of a regional law enforcement training facility.*

5. *Provision of a computerized bookkeeping system for all units of Lake County.*

6. *Establishment of a county morgue and a medical examiner's office for Lake County.* I advised that it be placed in the Lake County Government Center in Crown Point. I was amused at Harader's suggestion in the study that it should be in "the northern part of the county because it originates there."

7. *A standardized 911 emergency number for the entire county.*

8. *A state-sponsored fully-equipped forensic lab.*

9. *Cooperation in the training of fire personnel, a county-wide program to be coordinated through the Gary Fire Department.* Gary had the best trained and equipped fire department in the region. Gary fire insurance rates were lower in 1986 than they were in Merrillville.

10. *Adoption of the Assistance to Families with Dependent Children with the Unemployed Parent option (AFDC-UP).* This is an option available in Illinois and many other states; adoption in Indiana would do much to strengthen families.

11. *A universal application form for the Department of Public Welfare.*

12. *Eliminate work disincentives from social programs.*

13. *Workfare or job training programs for individuals and families not eligible for AFDC or AFDC-UP.*

14. *Consolidate the environmental/pollution control departments of Lake County local governments into a single county-wide organization.*

15. *Centralize and standardize the purchase of materials on a county-wide basis.* We would gain economies of scale in purchasing and reduction of duplication of services in inventory and warehouse operations.

16. *Examine the increased use of intergovernmental contracts and joint service agreements.*

In all, I recommended to Mayor Hatcher that the city of Gary endorse forty-six of the seventy-six recommendations. Seven were questionable, and I objected to twenty-three, mostly those in the areas of metropolitan consolidation and regional governments in the form of new special districts.[35] Mayor Hatcher agreed generally with my observations. In a press conference on Wednesday, October 8, Mayor Hatcher informed the media that, after reviewing the Lake County Government Study and conferring with city staff and consultants, he agreed with more than half of the study recommendations and was willing to discuss all others with mayors in Lake County, espcially those in Hammond, East Chicago, Whiting, Hobart, and Merrillville, in a public forum. "This way," stated Mayor Hatcher, "people will become better informed." Hatcher said that, although he was firmly opposed to consolidation, he did favor cooperation between cities as a means of eliminating duplication of services, improving efficiency, and lowering costs.

The next day, there was no mention in the *Post-Tribune* of Hatcher's remarks. In a staff meeting that I attended the day after the conference, Hatcher was downcast: "No matter what I say, the *Post-Tribune* is bound to paint me as an old stick in the mud who won't go along with their program. We must find a way to get a message out to the people of Gary. Most of them have only heard a little bit about the Metrolake consolidation. They don't realize that the same whites who ran away from Gary when I became mayor now want to steal our airport, transportation center, bus line, library system, and sanitary system."

Charlene Crowell, the mayor's press secretary, then spoke up, "Dr. Catlin, why don't you and Dr. Harader debate Metrolake. You're a better speaker than he is, and your paper on the literature tells me you know at least as much about government as he does." Before I could respond, the mayor's entire staff was saying, "Yes, Catlin, you can do it. Dr. Catlin will kick Harader's behind." With all of these morale boosters, I had no choice but to agree.

The Debates with Dr. Harader

Within twenty-four hours of Mayor Hatcher's staff meeting, all the arrangements had been made. Dr. Harader and I would debate the relative merits of Metrolake at the Genesis Convention Center in downtown Gary on Thursday, October 16. Mayor Hatcher would serve as mediator. There would be an initial presentation by Dr. Harader followed by my rebuttal. We would each answer questions directed to us by the audience and be given the opportunity to comment on the other's answer. The entire debate was to last no more than one and one-half hours.

The press was notified about our debate, and Patricia Carlisle's Office of Neighborhood Conservation publicized the event throughout the city in order to obtain a maximum turnout. Knowing that some of Mayor Hatcher's supporters were a bit overzealous, I was concerned that, unless the debate format was carefully planned, things could turn into a circus or worse. On Monday, October 13, I called Dr. Harader. He was not in, but minutes later he returned my call. I found him easy to talk with, and we spent almost an hour lamenting how President Reagan had devastated our cities with his cutbacks on housing, transportation, community development, education, and social services. We quickly agreed that our debate would be civil and factual.

About a half hour before the debate was to start, I drove to the Genesis Convention Center to find people already streaming into the building's assembly hall. I parked in the adjacent garage and went to the backstage area where Dr. Harader and Mayor Hatcher were waiting. Bill Harader was a slender, tense man in his late forties with a rural "Hoosier" manner, and, as we shook hands, it seemed to me that he was a nice guy. Mayor Hatcher then stood between us much like a referee between two boxers before a title match. That day, a *Post-Tribune* article by Rich James had predicted "fireworks" between Harader and me as we had both taken strong stands on either side of the Metrolake issue. Mayor Hatcher said, "The *Post-Tribune* is trying to start a fight, but we can't let them have the pleasure of selling papers at our expense. The entire purpose of this meeting is to have a forum where citizens can hear both points of view and then decide for themselves." That was all both Harader and I needed to hear. We were going to have a discussion as academics and not act like two wrestlers in a steel cage match.

The three of us then walked into the assembly hall to the cheers of over two thousand citizens. Most were from Gary, but, judging by the number of whites in attendance, there was a sizable contingent from Merrillville and the other south Lake County suburbs as well. Mayor Hatcher stood at a lectern at the center of the stage. I was to his right and Harader to his left, both at individual lecterns with microphones. As we stood in our respective spots, the cheering died down and was replaced by a tense silence.

Mayor Hatcher began by saying that this event was not a fight, not even a debate, but a discussion about Metrolake by two faculty members from local universities, both political scientists, both capable of discussing the pros and cons of this issue from an academic perspective. Joked Mayor Hatcher, "I told both Dr. Harader and Dr. Catlin they must use words we can all understand." The audience began to laugh, and the tension was broken.

Dr. Harader made the first presentation. He began by saying, "People want a large city, one they can be proud of, one that has efficient and effective services. The Metrogov consolidation, if adopted, will go a long way to bring this about." He then went on to detail his proposal, discussing at some length the borough system, the legislative council, and how Metrolake would avoid a catastrophic default if a steel mill such as Inland in East Chicago should close, leaving sixteen thousand workers without jobs. He talked about the savings from having sewage, transportation, and libraries on a regional level. He closed by saying, "It's up to you folks as to whether or not this happens." The audience gave Dr. Harader a quiet round of polite applause.

It was my turn to reply. "Yes, people want a large city they can be proud of. Yes, we all want to maximize efficiency and effectiveness in local government. But this proposal doesn't do it. If you look at the consolidations that have taken place in our nation since World War II—Nashville, Tennessee, Jacksonville, Florida, and Indianapolis—all three involved combining the central city with the county, which was largely rural. Metrolake does not do that. It is only a partial consolidation. It leaves out Merrillville, Crown Point, and other parts of south Lake County, and that is where all of the new development is occurring. Why did my colleague at the other end of the stage *not* propose a consolidation of all Lake County? That would have made more sense. Actually, a consolidation of Lake and Porter counties into a single government would have made even more sense. Talk about a large city—that type of consolidation would have 640,000 people under one government instead of only 405,000 with Metrolake. Talk about making the area less susceptible to economic devastation—spreading the possible loss over an additional 230,000 people and $300 million worth of additional assessed value makes more sense, doesn't it? What does Metrolake accomplish anyway? It certainly doesn't maximize efficiency and effectiveness. The same way a total Lake-Porter consolidation would.

"But, my friends and neighbors, this is what Metrolake does. It eliminates black political power. Gary would get the same amount of representation on the executive council as cities one-fourth its size. Now is that fair? I don't think so. This borough system proposed by my good friend over there is an anachronism of the nineteenth century. Do you want this kind of system for the twenty-first century? Of course you don't!"

By now the audience was cheering, and it was time for the punch line. "At first, this consolidation probably included just Gary, East Chicago, and Hammond, our region's three older central cities. But that configuration had a black and Hispanic majority, so they added Hobart. This made it 50 percent white and 50 percent black and Hispanic. This wasn't good enough, so Munster and Highland were added. The black and Hispanic population percentage then dropped to 40 percent. Then they didn't need Merrillville. That's why Merrillville and the others were left out. *What Metrolake does is simply to round up enough white folks to put Gary out of business.*"

At that point, the audience was on their feet cheering and shouting, "No Metrolake! No Metrolake!" Mayor Hatcher calmed the crowd, and it was time for questions. The first, directed to Dr. Harader, was "Do you think Unigov in Indianapolis has worked?" Harader smiled and then spent about five minutes extolling the virtues of Unigov: the economic boom, major league sports, tax savings, new museums, and so forth. When my turn came to rebut, I simply held up some sheets of paper and said, "Yes, Indianapolis is booming, but for whom?" I then recited from the census study that showed Gary blacks outpacing Indianapolis blacks in seven of ten categories including the most important, median income both in 1970 before consolidation and in 1980 after consolidation had been in place for five years. "Indianapolis is booming, but blacks don't seem to be getting a piece of the rock. We're better off in Gary even though we don't have Market Square Arena, the Hoosier Dome and Union Station." I added, "As for taxes, Owens and Wilburn, in their study of Indianapolis after Unigov, found that taxes went up, not down, and Indianapolis's per person tax load is higher than Gary's!" Turning to Harader, I added, "It's interesting that Owens and Wilburn's book didn't appear in the study's bibliography. In fact, I see virtually no literature about consolidation referenced in your study. Why?" Harader responded, "We certainly did review the literature." I replied, "It's not in the bibliography, nor is it cited anywhere in the study."

Harader said, "It's not there because it wasn't an academic report." I replied, "Dr. Harader, come on now, you have 31 citations on taxation, 38 on personnel administration, over 40 on budgeting, but—" I waved a copy of the study. "—no citations, nothing about consolidation."

Mayor Hatcher then quieted the crowd, which was beginning to boo Harader. The next question was directed at me. "We have real problems here in Gary. Is there anything that can be done to resolve them other than consolidation?" I replied, "Yes there is always cooperation between municipalities." I then cited the Ostrum and Tiebout quote on mutual cooperation and discussed the South Suburban Accord, whereby forty suburbs of Chicago, right on Indiana's border, pool purchasing and maintenance contracts to save money. Harader's reply, to my surprise, was "Cooperation has a lot going for it, but it doesn't expand the economic base."

The next question was posed to Dr. Harader: "Why was Merrillville left out of the proposed consolidation?" Harader's reply was "It did not make sense to include Merrillville since it is not part of the industrial base." My response was "Come on now, Bill, it's not part of the industrial base, but it sure as hell is part of the economic base. Merrillville and the Route 30 strip you left out of Metrolake has the region's largest shopping center, largest hotel complex, largest auto dealer strip, largest everything, and $300 million of assessed value that could help anyone's tax base." The audience was laughing. "Again, Dr. Harader," someone asked, "why was Merrill-ville left out?" Harader, by then completely flustered, shouted, "Because they didn't want to be included."

The crowd was by then seething with rage and booing lustily. Things were beginning to get out of control, as people in the audience shouted, "We don't want to be included either! No one asked our opinion!" But the crowd's outrage was understandable. I choose to define racism as "The notion that because one's own race is superior, the inferior race deserves to be subordinated by any and all possible means." Though Harader might have been a nice person, his answer was definitely racist. White people in Merrillville, the so-called superior group, didn't want to be part of Metro-lake, and their opinion counted. They were left out of Metrolake and were permitted to retain self-determination. Black people in Gary, the inferior group, were not even given the courtesy of being asked in the interview portion of the study whether or not they favored consolidation. Their opinion did not count anyway; thus, it was all right to assign them to Metrolake and the loss of self-determination.

After a few more questions and responses, Gladys Wise of Gary asked a final question. Shouted Wise, "Where is Chester Dobis? Dobis should be here because it seems Harader can't answer a lot of questions."

When it was time to sum up, Mayor Hatcher said that he hoped that the mayors of East Chicago and Hammond could join him in another public forum to discuss the pros and cons of consolidation. "I think the more public forums we have, the better informed people will be," said Hatcher. Harader summed up first, saying only that it was "up to you to decide which of these recommendations have merit and which should be adopted to make life better in Lake County." Harader, quite subdued, thanked the crowd for their attention and then sat down to polite applause.

At that point, having been involved day and night for almost a month with Metrolake and disappointed with Harader's lack of articulation and commitment to his own study, I decided to speak out without restraint. I started by saying, "Metrolake promises us good government, lower taxes, a safety net in case of a mill shutdown, and a nice, clean city. However, it does none of these things. This consolidation is unlike all others that have occurred in twentieth-century America. It takes in half a county, while all others included the entire urban area. By taking only half of the urban area, Metrolake leaves out the newer growth areas that could provide the tax base which in turn would fulfill the promises of lower taxes, a safety net, and a high level of municipal services, giving us this nice clean city. Metrolake does not provide for affirmative action and equitable representation. It leaves us with nothing but a promise of better times. If you look at Indianapolis and Jacksonville and Nashville, taxes have not gone down, they have actually increased, but blacks are certainly locked out of political and economic power. The study has some good points, actually more good recommendations than bad ones. But Metrolake is a bad recommendation. The academic literature is not supportive of consolidation, and I still want to know what my good colleague was thinking about when he failed to include the consolidation literature in his study. Bill, was it because the literature does not tend to favor consolidation?

"The recommendation about folding our city's district, airport, bus company, and library system into so-called regional agencies not yet created or identified doesn't square with the literature. The literature tells us that special districts are fine for creating new services or taking up services another unit of government no longer wants to provide. But our services are all right. They are performing well, there are no bankruptcies, no major scandals. Why should we simply give them away to some so-called regional agency that doesn't even exist and one that Gary will have no control over and very little influence in?"

I had the audience's complete attention, and it was time to come to the point.

I said, almost shouting, "When this proposal is held up to the light of academic literature and the realities of Gary and northwest Indiana, I must conclude that the advocates of Metrolake are more interested in eliminating Gary as a political, economic, and social force in northwest Indiana than in streamlining government. Metrolake is really the wolf of racism barely camouflaged by the sheep's clothing of good government. Don't be fooled by it."

I sat down to thunderous applause and cheers. Mayor Hatcher called the meeting to a close. People rushed up to shake my hand, and I was warmly embraced by friends, students, associates, faculty colleagues, and neighbors. Despite Harader's intransigence and refusal to answer several key questions, members of the audience were quick to come up, shake hands, and thank him for coming out to "enemy" territory to debate. The next day, Barry Saunders of the *Post-Tribune* tried to make a hero out of Harader, stating that "his biggest ovation was at the end of the two hour debate." "The applause seemed to be more an acknowledgement of survival than anything else."[36] The rest of the article read as if the debate was a draw. I was furious and called Saunders that day saying, "Barry, that article was all wrong. You were at the debate, you know that I verbally kicked his ass. Why didn't you write it the way it was?" Saunders defensively said, "I did, Doc, I really did, but the editor changed it."

Harader and I had another debate, this time at Harvard. Gary State Senator Carolyn B. Mosby was in residence at Harvard's JFK School of Government. The JFK school hosts an orientation program every two years for newly elected state legislators, and Senator Mosby was serving in the fall semester as an adjunct professor with that program. She also taught an undergraduate honors course in applied government. Having seen a tape of the debate, she felt that if Dr. Harader and I could have another debate in her class it would be perfect because her current topic was metropolitan government. Harvard would pay all expenses plus a nice stipend; all we had to do was show up.

The debate was set for Monday, November 3, at 8:00 P.M., Senator Mosby's class time. I flew into Boston that Sunday afternoon. Senator Mosby had arranged for me to stay in the Kennedy Suite located in one of the Harvard College dormitories. This was the room occupied by John Kennedy when he was a Harvard undergraduate in the late 1930s. Senator Mosby picked me up at the airport and dropped me off at the Kennedy Suite where I was to settle in and change for dinner later that evening. The suite was a bit old and delicately worn. It consisted of a bedroom, a sitting room with refrigerator and hot plate, and a private bath. It was furnished just as it was when young Kennedy was its occupant, with photographs and portraits of him all around. I cannot describe the sense of history I felt just being in that space. It was an experience I never had before and one I will always cherish. I was even more overwhelmed when, at dinner with three new legislators, two from California, and one from Iowa, Senator Mosby informed me that other recent occupants of the Kennedy Suite housed there when giving lectures at the JFK school included Bayard Rustin, Dean Rusk, Joseph Califano, and Benjamin Hooks.

The debate was held as scheduled. To my surprise, Harader had no new material for the assembled class of about twenty students. He used the same arguments and approaches that he had in Gary, and I responded the same way as I had at the first debate, although much less emotionally. The key moment came when a young white student, son of a Louisville, Kentucky, banker and a pre-law major got up and lectured Harader for his failure to present any literature to support consolidation, to include the entire county, and to include schools in consolidation to provide for racial integration. "In Louisville, we have one school district for the city and county and cross-town bussing in order to achieve integration. I went to integrated schools all of my life, and that experience has prepared me well for adulthood." Harader had nothing to say in reply, and, for the first time, I actually felt sorry for him.

Back home in Gary the following day, I met with Mayor Hatcher and his staff. I agreed to speak at two additional community forums on Metrolake. Neighborhood Conservation was to conduct a public referendum on Metrolake Saturday, November 22, using their eight citywide offices as polling places. The ballot was simple: yes or no on Metrolake. The forums were well attended, and I spoke on several local radio talk shows. The message was kept simple. Metrolake is no good because all it does is eliminate black power with no guaranteed advantage in its place. Also,

Metrolake is not supported by the academic literature. On "election day" 11,205 ballots were cast. Ninety-two percent were against Metrolake. The citizens of Gary had spoken, and now no one—not even Chester A. Dobis or Jerome J. Reppa—was about to push Metrolake and its related consolidations on Gary.[37]

Evaluating Metrolake

By January 1987, Metrolake was dead. No bills were introduced and brought to the legislature floor for its enactment, partly because Mayor Hatcher quietly got word out to the state house and senate leadership that if Metrolake and/or the related consolidations ever got to the floor he would personally lead a march from Gary to Indianapolis, one that could draw national media attention. Metrolake was quietly buried, and Hatcher's enemies then concentrated their efforts on defeating him in the May 1987 primary.

This case raises the following questions:

1. Was Metrolake a carefully contrived plot to eliminate black political power, or was it no more than the brainstorm of a naive academician?

2. Why did consolidation fail in northwest Indiana when it took place quickly in Indianapolis ten years before?

3. What is the relationship of consolidation to urban and regional planning?

4. What is the relationship between metropolitan consolidation and black governance?

5. Given the thinly veiled hidden agenda of the Indiana Legislative Council, why did a reputable academic establishment like Indiana State University take on this assignment?

A Contrived Effort or Isolated Incident?   In answering the first question, one must understand that it is a serious mistake to view Metrolake as an isolated incident brought on by the region's economic decline because of cutbacks in the steel industry. Had there not been a series of attempts on the part of white leadership elites to regain power after Hatcher's surprising upset win in the 1967 mayoral primary, the view of Metrolake as a response to a declining economy might have prevailed. But since 1967, white leaders had tried to rig an election, deannex the southern portion of Gary, supported a moderate surrogate-white black for mayor (Dr. Alexander Williams), created the town of Merrillville as an alternative power base in violation of the Indiana buffer zone law, and supported another black moderate, Thomas Crump, for mayor in 1983. The two principal leaders in the movement to create the Indiana Legislative Council and fund the Lake

Table 10. Population Breakdown by Race/Ethnic Group:
Proposed Metrolake Boroughs

Constituent City (Borough)	Total Population (1986 Estimate)	% Black	% Hispanic
Gary[1]	143,000	71	7
Hammond	92,000	6	6
Hobart/Lake Station	65,000	1	3
Highland, Munster, Griffith[2]	62,000	1	5
East Chicago/Whiting	43,000	30	35
Total	405,000	30	10

Source: Estimates were taken from the Northwest Indiana Regional Planning Commission data.

[1] Excludes Black Oak neighborhood.

[2] Includes Black Oak neighborhood.

County Government Study were Chester Dobis and Jerome Reppa. Dobis had led the successful fight to incorporate Merrillville, and Reppa was one of the twenty-five defendants named by Hatcher in 1967 in his successful lawsuit to prevent election tampering.

I have taken pains to point out that Metrolake was unlike any of the fifty or so city/county consolidations proposed between 1950 and 1985. But Metrolake was not an amateurish exercise in crafting a new governmental arrangement. Its conception in terms of foreclosing minority group political power was actually brilliant. By combining the three northern townships into one city (see figure 4), not only did it create an entity with a total population of 405,000 (30 percent of which was black and about 10 percent Hispanic), but the "borough" system made certain that blacks and Hispanics would *never* have more than two of the seven seats on the all-important executive council. With a 60 percent white majority in Metrolake, the mayor and controller elected citywide would most likely be white and, given the racial divisiveness in the region, would be responsive primarily to the needs of the elite majority. A glance at the racial compositions as shown in table 10 the five "constituent cities" or "boroughs" would quickly give an indication as to what group would dominate.

Given these racial breakdowns, only one city, Gary, could elect a black mayor. East Chicago could conceivably develop a Hispanic/black coalition and elect a minority person, but, over the years, Robert Pastrick, East Chicago's white ethnic mayor, had already developed a white/Hispanic coalition that dominated East Chicago politics. The Hispanics in East Chicago were mainly Mexican-Americans who considered themselves of Spaniard-Indian (Native American) heritage rather than the Spaniard-African heritage of Puerto-Ricans.[38]

Another stroke of brilliance shown by Metrolake's planners was that its configuration would empower, once again, the Lake County Democratic machine as the dominant political force in northwest Indiana. The machine had been weakened ever since Hatcher's 1967 election as mayor when he created his own submachine. Leaving out affluent areas such as Crown Point, St. John's Township, and even Merrillville was a plus for the machine, as these areas were seeing a steady influx of white-collar Republican voters who commute to jobs in Chicago. Even though Highland and Munster, which were proposed as part of Metrolake, are populated with a slight majority of white-collar Republican types, North Township, which includes these two cities, was in 1986 controlled by Horace Mamala, the township trustee and a major player in the Lake County Democratic party machine.

When all these factors are considered, it logically follows that Metrolake was not an isolated response to prolonged economic decline but a coldly calculated effort, part of a series of attempts by white elites not only to regain control of Gary, the region's central city, but to retain control in perpetuity. The regionalization of Gary's airport, transit system, sanitary district, and library was actually an initial short-term objective. Metrolake was the long-term goal.

Why Metrolake Failed.   Metrolake's planners failed because they underestimated the Hatcher administration's ability to mobilize widespread citizen outrange against consolidation and to raise logical academic arguments as to its weaknesses. In an interview with State Senator Carolyn B. Mosby in 1987 after Metrolake was no longer an issue, Senator Mosby said to me: "Mayor Hatcher's response took Dobis, Reppa, and that group by surprise. They also thought that so-called 'responsible' black leaders would come forward and endorse Metrolake. But you and Mayor Hatcher made it impossible for people like Dozier Allen and Tom Barnes to endorse it even if they wanted to. You had the academic arguments, and Mayor Hatcher had the political rhetoric. If you two hadn't spoken up, we would now be fighting for our lives in the legislature."[39]

Once we made the academic argument against Metrolake—it was only a partial consolidation, not capable of lowering taxes or acting as a safety net if one of the mills closed, and it did not have support from the academic literature—not one political scientist from the state's universities (Indiana University, Purdue, Notre Dame, Ball State, or Evansville) came forward to back Metrolake. Metrolake's political and academic supporters were painted into a corner essentially by a two-pronged attack from the Hatcher administration.

Consolidation and Urban/Regional Planning.   The educated enlightened layperson might wonder what a political consolidation case study has to do with urban and regional planning? The planning literature in recent years deals mainly with issues such as growth management, conservation of natural resources, urban revitalization (especially that of downtowns and neighborhoods), infrastructure provision, and computer applications such as Geographic Information Systems. However, planning implementation is a very political process. The form of government is a major determinant as to where scarce resources in the areas of community development, assisted housing, and infrastructure projects will be allocated. Governmental sensitivity to local neighborhoods is a major determinant as to where planners locate obvious "not in my backyard" or NIMBY land uses such as sanitary landfills, toxic waste sites, correctional facilities, and polluting industries. If Metrolake came into existence, there was good reason on the part of minority groups to fear that the white majority government would disproportionally site economic development, assisted middle-income housing, and "clean" infrastructure projects in white neighborhoods and place NIMBYs in Gary and the minority communities in East Chicago and Hammond.

Consolidation and Black Governance.   Clearly, unless an urban county is majority black—in 1980 only Fulton County (Atlanta) was in this category—metropolitan consolidation spells the end of black governance. But the issues surrounding this reality are not always clear-cut. In Rust Belt metropolises such as Gary, Detroit, and Newark, declining economics give rise to desperate leaders in black and white communities who think that it just might be worthwhile for blacks to trade in political power and whites to trade in local autonomy for the promise of an enhanced economy. That is one of the reasons Thomas M. McDermott, the mayor of Hammond, spoke of a consolidated Lake County as beneficial from "the standpoint of the size it would give us, the tax base it could give us, and from the standpoint of going after museums and sports franchises." Actually, if Metrolake's planners hadn't been so parochial and self-serving, they could have advocated a total consolidation of Lake and Porter counties with an urban service district in the northern higher-density residential, commercial, and industrial areas and a rural service area in the farmlands to the south. This would have produced a city of 640,000 residents, covering the entire lakefront from Chicago to Michigan City and all of the northwest Indiana steel mills. With an elected mayor and about fifteen council members elected from single-member districts, a reasonable configuration would result in the election of three blacks from Gary and perhaps one Hispanic from East Chicago. With a strong affirmative action program and an enactment by popular referendum, it would have been difficult to attack politically and academically. It could very well be that a consolidation of this type will be proposed for northwest Indiana and elsewhere in the United States, and if one could empirically show tax savings, it would be extremely difficult to resist.

Also, black and other minority communities are less able in the 1990s to deal effectively with consolidation than they were in the 1970s or early 1980s. The exodus of the black middle class to the suburbs has weakened leadership in majority-black central cities. Also, by 1992, blacks have largely forgotten the bitter struggles of the 1960s for open occupancy and access to public facilities and nondiscrimination in employment. In 1992, a thirty-five-year-old black professional was only ten years old in 1967 and probably more interested in riding a bicycle and shooting baskets in the playground than in civil rights activism. An entire generation of young, black, educated middle-class adults has grown up taking legally mandated equality for granted. Even the older generation tends to forget past struggles and the need to maintain vigilance at all times. In 1989, I interviewed Richard Comer, Gary's deputy mayor in the Barnes Administration. Comer, who upon graduation from Purdue University's College of Engineering became, in his words, "the first black to get a salaried position at U.S. Steel," chided the Hatcher administration for being "political" about Metrolake. I had to remind Mr. Comer that if Mayor Hatcher and I hadn't spoken out against Metrolake, there would be no Gary as we now know it and he wouldn't be deputy mayor over much of anything.[40]

Indiana State University and Metrolake.   Why would Dr. William Harader and the Center for Governmental Services at Indiana State University come up with a study well researched in budgeting, taxation, and personnel administration but with no mention of consolidation literature and then not only make consolidation a major recommendation but allow the press to run with it as the only issue for debate? I never got a clear response from the center on that one, but two conversations are worthy of note, as they shed some light on this issue.

After our debate at Harvard University, Harader and I shared a cab ride to the airport. I asked him, "Bill, why would you and the center propose Metrolake without strong literature to back it up?" He thought for a while and then said, "Bob, you know about the cutbacks. It's very difficult to get money for graduate students these days. You do what you have to do. That's all I want to say about it."

On October 12, 1990, I talked to Dr. Manindra K. Mohapatra, chairman of the political science department at Indiana State University and director of the Center for Governmental Services. I asked if any of the major consolidation recommendations had been followed up on by individual members of the legislature, and he told me that no follow-up occurred since the study was released in 1986. When I asked him what he thought of the study now that four years had passed, he said, "We are proud of the study. It was well funded by the legislature, it was the largest grant the center has ever received, and we'd love to get another contract of that size."[41]

By 1990, some of the study's recommendations had been enacted. A television station was opened in Merrillville to serve northwest Indiana with a programming consisting mainly of local news, sports, and features. Though a state office building hadn't been built, the state of Indiana was actively negotiating with the city of Gary to rent space in the Gainer Bank building on Fifth Avenue and Broadway, Gary's major downtown intersections. As to why Metrolake was crafted, we might never find out the entire story. Bill Harader was an amateur airplane pilot, and he flew his own private plane to our debates in Gary and Cambridge. In 1988, while renewing his pilot's license, he attempted a routine maneuver, crashed, and was killed instantly.

7

Changing Pilots During Takeoff

In 1956, Martin Meyerson, in an address to the American Institute of Certified Planners, introduced to the profession a new concept known as "mid range planning." At that time, planners' work consisted of either preparing twenty-five-year comprehensive or general plans at one end of the spectrum and, at the other end, making decisions on "immediate actions" such as zone change proposals, subdivision plats, public acquisitions, or even proposals for restructuring local governments as in metropolitan consolidation. Meyerson's mid-range proposal was designed to fill the gap between the two extremes. Elements of his mid-range proposal included ongoing research and analysis, policy clarification, monitoring and evaluation of program and project activities, and, most important, the detailed development plan. The development plan would have no more than a ten-year timespan, and, as Meyerson stated, "Long range comprehensive plans commonly reveal a desired state of affairs. They rarely specify the detailed courses of action needed to achieve that desired state. By their long range nature, they cannot do so. The development plan, in contrast, will indicate the specific changes in land use programmed for each year, the rate of new growth, the public facilities to be built, the structures to be removed, the private investment required, the extent and sources of public funds to be raised, the tax and other local incentives to encourage private behavior requisite to the plan."[1]

Part II of the Gary Comprehensive Plan of 1986 consisted of thirteen neighborhood schemes and was modeled as a set of development plans according to Meyerson's specifications. Other examples of mid-range development plans are "system" plans such as those for fire stations, marinas, utilities, and airports. This case study involves a system plan for Gary's municipal airport, and a brief chronology in terms of its outcome by 1992 is in order.

The Gary airport was built by the U.S. Army Air Corps in World War II and turned over to the city of Gary in 1950. Serving as northwest Indiana's largest general aviation field, it remained somewhat obscure until 1977 when the Hatcher administration proposed a $32 million development program with a goal of scheduled airline service for the 1.2 million residents of northwest Indiana and the Chicago south suburbs. The development program was approved by federal agencies. By 1983 a new terminal building was completed, but construction slowed down because of the reluctance of Gary's white suburbs and state government to assist in the airport's development and because of cutbacks in federal aid by the Reagan administration.

In 1986, the Federal Aviation Administration (FAA) commissioned a study to find a new airport for the Chicago area. A joint Indiana-Illinois blue ribbon committee with four representatives from each state was selected to choose the new site. Sensing an opportunity for Gary's airport to be selected, Mayor Hatcher joined forces with the major economic development group in northwest Indiana to pick a seventeen-member airport development commission, which I chaired. The commission issued its plans for airport expansion in April 1987, but the very next month, Hatcher was defeated in the mayoral primary by archrival Thomas V. Barnes. Between May 1987 and January 1988 when Barnes took office, there was no communication between the two, and the airport development commission's work was for naught. To make matters worse, when Barnes took office, he named a new airport board, but the old Hatcher board refused to quit. In February 1988, consultants for the FAA recommended Gary as their top choice for further study, but the State of Indiana government refused to support the Gary site unless, in the words of Lieutenant Governor John Mutz, the "proper oversight agency" was created to manage the airport's development.

By early 1990, the courts essentially ruled in favor of Barnes appointees, and his airport board was finally seated. But earlier in April 1989, Richard M. Daley was elected mayor of Chicago and moved quickly to propose the new airport on Chicago's far South Side. He also maneuvered to add three of his representatives to the eight-member selection committee. By late 1990, Indiana state officials and the northwest Indiana business community, realizing that steel industry employment was never going to rise to 1970s levels and that their only hope for renewed economic development was the new airport, began to back the Gary site. However, Daley now controlled the selection process, and on February 24, 1992, the Chicago site was chosen for the new airport.

The major question here is was the Chicago site selected over Gary because of the political skills of Daley, or did Indiana's state government and the northwest Indiana business community snatch defeat from the jaws of victory because of white racism? The key players in this drama are Gary mayors Hatcher and Barnes, Mayor Daley of Chicago, Governors Robert Orr and Evan Bayh of Indiana, Indiana U.S. Senators Richard Lugar and Dan Quayle, the two groups of airport consultants, and U.S. Department of Transportation Secretary Sam Skinner.

The Airport's Background

The Gary airport was opened on January 5, 1950, as a municipal facility. It was built on land donated by the United States government to the city of Gary. During the 1950s, the Gary Municipal Airport served as a general aviation facility for private aircraft and limited commercial freight operations. By 1960, it had the largest traffic volume of all airports in northwest Indiana. With the opening of the Chicago Skyway and the Indiana Toll Road in 1958, the Gary airport took on new importance as it was now linked to downtown Chicago by expressway with travel times at nonpeak hours averaging just under forty-five minutes.[2]

However, Gary's city government overlooked the potential of their own airport. Midway Airport on Chicago's South Side was the nation's largest facility in terms of passenger enplanements and served northwest Indiana as well. The Chicago Skyway placed this airport only forty-five minutes from downtown Gary. However, in 1961, Chicago opened O'Hare International Airport on the city's northwest side. O'Hare, an ultramodern state-of-the-art facility, was closer to downtown Chicago than Midway in terms of travel time and had exactly what Midway lacked: room for expansion and, at that time, avoidance of conflict with residential areas. Midway was surrounded with housing and industry on all four sides, and its runways could not be expanded to safely handle the new 707 and 727 jet airliners coming off the production lines at Boeing Aircraft Company in Seattle and Douglass Aircraft in southern California. By 1962, only one year after the new airport opened, Midway was just a shell of its former self, as all major airlines transferred operation to O'Hare. Residents of Gary and northwest Indiana then faced a 90-minute journey to O'Hare in order to utilize national or even regional passenger air service. Gary's provincial, narrow-minded government failed to cash in on this new opportunity. Dramatic increases in air travel demand was forecasted for the period of 1960-1985 nationally and in the midwest United States.[3] The Gary airport was only forty-five minutes to downtown Chicago, and it could serve not only the 600,000 residents of Lake and Porter counties in Indiana but some 500,000 residents of south suburban Chicago, many of whom lived in upscale communities such as Park Forest, Homewood, and Flossmoor, and were natural targets for promotion by airlines. The combined 1.1 million population of northwest Indiana and south suburban Chicago lived no more than a thirty-minute drive to the Gary airport. More important, the Gary airport was situated away from populated areas, and approaches and take-offs could be situated over Lake Michigan. The runways were long enough to accommodate Boeing 727 aircrafts.

However, the governments of Gary and other communities in north-west Indiana dropped the ball. The Gary Comprehensive Plan of 1964 only spoke of maintaining the airport as a general aviation facility, missing altogether its potential for commercial passenger service even though the plan's goal date was 1985. Actually, on the future land use map, the airport was shown as a regional park.

The 1970s brought greater airline passenger volume to O'Hare airport, and carriers began to search for alternatives. Although O'Hare was ex-panded, with new terminal facilities planned in the early 1970s, and was built ten to fifteen years later, previously constructed homes, offices, and industrial parks prevented runway expansion, and the noise from the constantly increasing number of flights began to interfere with everyday life. In 1980, a new company, Midway Airlines, opened at the then deserted Midway Airport, using smaller Boeing 737 jets. The company was ex-tremely successful, even surviving the 1979-1983 recession that ultimately wiped out other new upstart carriers such as Air Florida and People's Express. In 1976, the Indiana State Department of highways proposed a bypass on the Indiana Toll Road in the Gary-East Chicago area, known as the Cline Avenue Connector. It was planned as an alternate route for workers and deliverers at the East Chicago steel mills, enabling them to avoid conflict with interstate movement of passengers and goods to and from Chicago on the toll road. The Cline Avenue Connector had the additional advantage of reducing travel time from Chicago to the Gary airport by fifteen minutes. With these developments taking place, the Hatcher administration in 1976 began preparation of the Gary Municipal Airport Development Program.

The Gary Municipal Airport Development Program of 1977-1978

By the mid-1970s, the administration of Gary Mayor Richard G. Hatcher faced a pressing dilemma. On one hand, the administration was secure, as landslide victories in the mayoral primaries of 1971 and 1975 had placed Mayor Hatcher in a commanding position politically with no strong chal-lenger in sight. The election of Jimmy Carter as president in 1976 meant that federal funds would come to Gary in record amounts for the rest of the decade. Hatcher's influence was national. He was vice-chairman of the U.S. Conference of Mayors and a leading member of the Democratic

National Committee. The local economy was strong, as U.S. Steel employed between 25,000 and 27,000 workers during the boom years of 1975-1979 and employment at the other northwest Indiana mills was at all-time highs. Wages at the mills were the highest they would ever be up through 1992, with adjustments for inflation considered. On the other hand, downtown Gary had been deserted by business and professional people who headed south to Merrillville. There was virtually no communication between the Hatcher administration and the south Lake County business community. Though the Lake County Democratic party machine couldn't topple Hatcher, they certainly were not about to do anything that would help him retain office.

As pointed out in previous chapters, Hatcher's plans to revitalize downtown Gary rested upon the Negotiated Investment Strategy (NIS). NIS called for a series of projects, developed with public funds, which, when complete, would spur private development. The same strategy was used for the Gary Municipal Airport. If public money could be used to revitalize the airport, private spinoffs in the form of industrial parks, hotels, motels, and restaurants would take place. The administration was well aware of increasing airline passenger demand in the Chicago area. The fact that, by 1976, 1.2 million people in the south suburbs of Chicago and in northwest Indiana were ninety minutes from O'Hare Airport and that there was a thirty-minute travel time between downtown Chicago and the Gary airport once the Cline Avenue Connector was completed meant an additional advantage for Gary.

Having been reelected twice, Hatcher was able to place individuals on city boards and commissions to the point that he controlled every local governing body. The Gary Airport Board of Authority, by virtue of Indiana law, consisted of four members, two Democrats and two Republicans. By 1977, the board consisted of Elizabeth Williamson, a Hatcher supporter and Democrat, George Williams, the Gary Director of Planning and Development and, of course, a Hatcher supporter and Democrat, James H. Stump, a white Republican businessman, and Lawrence Rice, a Republican. Williamson was president, Stump was vice-president, Williams was treasurer, and Rice served as secretary. In 1977, this board hired Dr. A. William Douglas as executive director of the Gary Municipal Airport Authority District. Douglas was born in Gary and graduated from Gary's all-black Roosevelt High School in 1952. After service in the U.S. Air Force and a stint as an aviation radar technician for the Federal Aviation Administration, he attended Illinois Institute of Technology (IIT). He received his bachelor's degree in civil engineering in 1963, his master's degree in civil engineering in 1964, and a Ph.D. in engineering sciences awarded in 1967, all from IIT. Before coming to the Gary Municipal Airport Authority District as executive director, Dr. Douglas worked between 1967 and 1977 as an engineer at Inland Steel's East Chicago plant. He also served on the

Gary Airport Board from 1967 to 1977 and was president of that board from 1974 to 1977. He was clearly well qualified on technical grounds.

During 1976 and 1977, work progressed on the Gary Municipal Airport Development Program, and in November 1977 it was ready for unveiling. The program contained four elements, briefly described as follows:

1. *Land Acquisition and Railroad/Highway Relocation.* The Gary airport's original runways were actually longer than Midway's in Chicago, but in order to extend them to accommodate the newer 757 and 767 passenger and freight aircraft, 275 acres of land had to be acquired and the railroads now occupying them relocated. Once the land was acquired and the railroads and highways relocated, the runways, then 7,000 feet wide and 3,600 feet long, could be extended to 8,300 and 5,000 feet respectively.

2. *Site Preparation and Paving.* Runways, taxiways, ramps, and access roads built in the early 1940s were in need of major repairs. The cost was minimal, and the improvements could be completed quickly.

3. *Buildings and Other Structures.* In 1978, the terminal building consisted of a worn-out quonset hut of World War II surplus vintage. The hangars were old, inadequate, and unsafe, and fuel facilities were also inadequate. These elements called for a new passenger terminal building to accommodate three ticket counters, three luggage ramp areas, two rental car stations, a small restaurant and lounge, waiting areas, and administrative headquarters for the airport authority staff. Other buildings would include a crash/rescue/police facility, a cargo handling facility, additional hangars, and a fuel facility.

4. *Airport Industrial Park.* Studies undertaken by the Gary Municipal Airport Authority District from 1975 to 1978 indicated that the airport's expansion as planned would create demand for the development of 500 acres of office, storage-warehousing, and light industrial activity by 1980, 700 acres by 1990, and over 1,000 acres by 2000. The land was available just north of the airport's property line. It was estimated that airport expansion and the industrial park development would produce over 10,000 jobs by 1980 (if improvements could be completed by then), 11,700 in 1990, and 16,506 in 2000.[4]

In order to implement this four-part program, a detailed Capital Improvement Program (CIP) was prepared as part of the Development Program. Highlights of this CIP are in table 11.

The game plan on the part of the airport authority was to utilize available federal grants for airport development and make up the local share with a combination of special federal grants from the Economic Development Administration (EDA), the Community Development Block Grant Program (CDBG), the Urban Development Action Grant Program (UDAG), and revenue bonds with, as a last resort, general obligation

Table 11. Gary Municipal Airport Development Program, 1978

Project/Element	Date to be Completed	Total Share	Federal/State Share	Local Share
A. Land Acquisition and Relocation				
1. E.J.E. Railroad Relocation	1979	$9,000,000	$7,200,000	$1,800,000
2. Extension of Runway #1 from 7,000 to 8,300 ft.	1980	2,000,000	1,600,000	400,000
3. Relocation of Commercial and Industrial Uses	1982	4,000,000	3,200,000	800,000
4. Extension of Runway #2 from 3,600 to 5,000 ft.	1982	1,000,000	900,000	100,000
B. New Buildings and Facilities				
1. New T-Hangars	1979	800,000	800,000	—
2. Crash/Fire/Rescue/Police Facility	1979	700,000	530,000	170,000
3. Landscaping/Drainage	1979	600,000	540,000	60,000
4. Passenger Terminal	1980	5,000,000	2,500,000	2,500,000
C. Site Preparation				
1. Glide Slope Facility	1979	400,000	400,000	—
2. Air Cargo Apron	1982	500,000	500,000	—
D. Airport Industrial Park				
1. Land Acquisition, Utilities, and Site Preparation	1979	8,000,000	7,200,000	800,000
Total Cost		32,000,000	25,370,000	6,630,000

bonds. The development program was endorsed by all necessary federal and state regulatory agencies, and work began in early 1979.

However, just as things were beginning to move forward, Ronald Reagan was elected president. Federal funds were now in short supply, and, after 1981, no new federal monies were allocated for airport expansion. The defeat of Indiana Senator Birch Bayh in 1980 by Dan Quayle, a young political unknown, also dealt a major blow to the airport expansion. Adam Benjamin continued to work for the airport's development, viewing it as a regional dynamic rather than a "Gary" project. However, his untimely death in 1982 brought these efforts to a halt as his replacement Katie Hall lacked the seniority necessary to push through projects of that type. Hall's May 1984 primary defeat labeled her as a lame duck, and, by the time Peter Visclosky entered the Congress in January 1985, he had to climb the seniority ladder and learn the political ropes. Also, Visclosky viewed the airport as a Gary project (not one serving the region) as long as the city of Gary retained control of the facility.

By 1985, only the T-hangars, the glide slope facility, the crash/fire/

rescue/police facility, and the passenger facility were completed. The T-hangars were completed in 1980, the glide slope and landscaping efforts were finished in 1983, and the crash/fire/rescue/police facility and the passenger terminal were completed in 1984. With these improvements in place, the Federal Aviation Administration designated the Gary Airport as a reliever for O'Hare and Midway in 1984. Of the $32 million construction package, only $7.5 million worth was complete. No new grants were available, and, though the airport authority was working on about $3 million worth of old grants, future prospects seemed very dim. Mayor Hatcher had initially sought, without success, support for the airport expansion program in 1975 from south Lake County business groups, politicians, and regional governmental agencies. He continued to seek support through 1985 from these same groups, but they refused it unless the airport was handed over to a new regional agency. As Mayor Hatcher told me during an informal conversation in 1983 on the revised Gary Comprehensive Plan: "We were really moving with the airport until Reagan came along. Losing Birch Bayh didn't help either. Our silent enemy is the white power structure of Lake County. They ran from Gary when I became mayor but still want to control the city, especially our airport. They see the potential; anyone can, but they won't help us unless they have total control. I keep asking them, if we gave you control of the airport, what could you offer us? Their response was 'our expertise.' What expertise? None of them had run an airport the size of Gary's!"[5]

Hatcher's Overtures to State and Local Governments

After Katie Hall's defeat in the 1984 Democratic party primary, Mayor Hatcher realized that it was time to win friends and influence people among Indiana state government, local governments in Lake County, and the metropolitan area's business community. Negotiations began with the U.S. Steel Corporation on their purchasing an urban redevelopment site on Fifth Avenue and Broadway as well as selling part of their lakefront site to the city of Gary for use as a marina. In an effort to get state government to commit more money for road improvements on state-assisted highways within Gary and to open up lines of communication in general, Mayor Hatcher hosted a reception for all Indiana legislators at the beginning of the 1985 Assembly in Indianapolis. The reception was well attended and many legislators who were Republicans from rural areas and small towns remarked that they found Hatcher to be "a warm and gracious fellow once you got to meet him."[6]

Hatcher's new-found openness extended to matters involving the airport as well. The new passenger terminal had opened, and the runways were already capable of handling aircraft up to the size of Boeing 727 and 737 jets. Airline deregulation had created a number of regional passenger "hubs" across the nation, including nearby Indianapolis, and with commuter aircraft flying between the hubs and smaller towns, the Gary airport was ripe for the initiation of passenger service. First, Hatcher changed the name from Gary Municipal Airport to Gary Regional Airport. Working with the business community, Hatcher was able to get Britt Airlines, a commuter service, to provide flights from the airport to the nearest regional hub of Indianapolis. Britt Airlines opened this service in April 1985. Although business was initially brisk, Britt had to cancel service on July 31, 1985, because of low passenger volume and lack of a state subsidy. Britt blamed lack of passengers, Hatcher claimed that Britt failed to use adequate advertising, and State Senator Carolyn B. Mosby said that the service should have begun in January, when the legislature was in session and the weather was cold and hazardous for driving. Mosby believed that if Britt had given the city an eight- to nine-month trial period, service could have been made profitable. At any rate, Gary's airport had scheduled airline service for the first time, and the venture could be described as at least partially successful. Commuter aircraft could in fact take off and land from the airport, the fire/crash/rescue squad had realistic training operations, and the terminal was found to be quite usable.

In September 1985, the Northwest Indiana Forum was founded. This group was limited to the region's top 100 business, institutional, civic, and governmental leaders. Included in this membership was Mayor Hatcher and six other Gary residents, including myself. The forum's agenda was to promote northwest Indiana's economic development by advertising the region's assets; mutual cooperation among the various cities and Lake and Porter County governments; and involvement of major industries, including the four major steel corporations (U.S. Steel in Gary, Inland and LTV in East Chicago, and Bethlehem in Portage) and the Northwest Indiana Public Service Company (NIPSCO), the region's only Fortune 500 corporation located in Hammond. Richard Griebel was hired as president and chief executive. Griebel, a former oil company executive in New York, headed up various corporate urban affairs divisions and played a major role in upgrading northern New Jersey from an industrial wasteland to a respectable neighbor of New York City. In his initial speech upon coming to Indiana to head the forum, he compared northwest Indiana with its relationship to Chicago to Newark and northern New Jersey and its relationship with New York: "When we started in Newark back in the late 1960s, we had a background of decay, race riots, and hopelessness. When we left in 1980, we had built Meadowlands Stadium, the Brendan Byrne Arena, and the racetrack. We upgraded the Newark Airport to where it is now among the top ten passenger carriers in the nation. We built skyscrapers, new universities, a medical school, and new housing in Newark, all with the help of a black mayor, Kenneth Gibson. We can do that here if we work together. In order to do this we must include Gary and Mayor Hatcher in from the beginning. We can't do it without the region's largest city!"

The Gary contingent—Mayor Hatcher, Deputy Mayor Jim Holland, Director of Physical and Economic Development Bob Farag, and I—couldn't believe what we were hearing. Finally, a white leader was willing to work with and not against Gary and Mayor Hatcher to improve the region. The business people from the region's suburbs couldn't believe what they were hearing either. At the end of his address, Griebel received a standing ovation, and the new energy created by his remarks filled the room. He talked about the region making great strides: attracting the White Sox from Chicago to play in a new northwest Indiana stadium and upgrading the Gary airport to a position where it would function as the third airport in the Chicago area after O'Hare and Midway. He talked of attracting new steel-related specialized industries to the region in order to take advantage of the skilled but largely idled work force available. His entire message was one of hope, not despair, pettiness, rancor, jealousy, or other negatives.

Griebel proved to be true to his word when, almost one year after his arrival, the Metrolake controversy arose. South Lake County interests attempted to push Griebel into getting the forum to endorse Metrolake. Griebel's private response to Mayor Hatcher and the south Lake County individuals was "Hell no. This thing is divisive and unecessary." Publicly, he had no comment.

Griebel was extremely interested in getting the Gary airport moving again. After touring the terminal facilities with Mayor Hatcher and a group including myself, he remarked, "What a waste. You have this nice new terminal and it's just sitting here." Another reason for newfound interest in the Gary airport was that, in June 1986, the Federal Aviation Administration commissioned a $2 million study to determine if a third major airport was needed in the Chicago area to relieve O'Hare and Midway. Depending on study results, the third airport could be the present Gary site. After several discussions with Mayor Hatcher and south Lake County interests during the fall of 1986, Griebel and Hatcher decided to form a seventeen-member regional commission to develop a strategic plan for the airport's development. Griebel would name eight members from south Lake and Porter counties; Hatcher would name eight members from Gary. Both Hatcher and Griebel wanted to name the chairman for this group. Hatcher insisted that because the airport was in Gary the group chairman should be someone of his choice. Griebel relented, and Mayor Hatcher asked me to chair this new group. I agreed to do so, and the Gary Airport Promotion and Development Commission was launched.

The commission consisted of Gary members A. William Douglas,

executive director of the Gary Regional Airport; Douglas Grimes, formerly
Gary city attorney and a close associate of Mayor Hatcher; James Holland, the Gary deputy mayor; Donald Thompson, Gary tourism director;
Dharathula (Dollie) Millender, Gary city councilwoman at large; Dr. Phil-
lip Rutledge, director of the School of Public and Environmental Affairs at
Indiana University Northwest; Dr. Randall Morgan, Sr., a prominent civic
leader; and Mayor Hatcher himself. Griebel named himself to the commission and Reverend William Booth of First Baptist Church in Gary; Steve
Braver, manager of the *Post-Tribune*; Phillip Coote, manager of the Water
Department of Valparaiso in Porter County; Richard Gardner of Calumet
Construction Corporation in Hammond; Jim Ranfrantz, the deputy director
of the Northwestern Indiana Regional Naming Commission; James Sudlack, senior vice president of Mercantile National Bank in Hammond; and
Bill Wellman, a developer from Merrillville. We would hold all of our
meetings at the airport's administrative offices located in the passenger
terminal building. The airport staff would supply necessary secretarial
services. Our first meeting was set for Tuesday, December 16, 1986.

The Commission's Report

At the time of the commission's first meeting, there were at least two
general directions for the group. On one hand, talk was all around about the
need for a third Chicago airport. Preliminary reports from the firm of Peat,
Marwick and Mitchell, consultants to the Illinois Department of Transportation and to the Bistate Study Commission, which consisted of four
individuals from Illinois and a like number from Indiana, showed that by
the year 2000 there would be at least 2.5 million annual enplanements that
could not be met by O'Hare and Midway even given the expansion plans for
both airports. This consultant group had included the Gary Airport as one of
four alternate sites for the third Chicago airport, the other three being
Aurora, Rockford, and Milwaukee's Mitchell Field. The possible benefits
were tremendous: 20,000 to 30,000 new jobs in adjacent industrial parks,
hotels, motels, restaurants, and offices; national identity and a boost in
corporate office location potential; increased property tax receipts from new
construction. The other direction was a much more modest one: upgrade the
airport to reestablish first commuter air service, then limited passenger
service, using 737 aircraft on existing runways.

After discussing the matter with Mayor Hatcher, Richard Griebel, Jim
Ranfrantz from the regional planning commission, and me, the group
decided that it would be best to go with the low expectation goal of restoring
commuter air service first and then, within a matter of one to two years,
establish Gary as one alternate to Midway, using 737 and 727 jet aircraft

flights to places such as Detroit, Pittsburgh, New York City, Washington, D.C., Atlanta, and Florida cities. After the second milestone was reached, the airport could compete for third Chicago airport designation, a choice that, according to Peat, Marwick and Mitchell, would not be made until at least 1990. This direction satisfied everyone. Richard Griebel simply wanted to get air service restored. The only problem with that was that to make air service restoration the only goal we could find ourselves foreclosing other possibilities needlessly. Mayor Hatcher wanted to push exclusively for third airport designation. The problem with this approach was that to put all of our eggs in one basket could be disastrous if another airport was selected, at which time we could be left with nothing to show for years of effort.

We decided, at my request, to form four subcommittees: (1) urban planning and development; (2) program development; (3) promotion and marketing; and (4) finance. I agreed to chair urban planning and development, and my cochair was Jim Ranfrantz of the Northwestern Indiana Regional Planning Commission (NIRPC), who promised staff assistance for us. Program development was to be chaired by Donald Thompson, who had considerable experience in this area. Bill Wellman, who successfully marketed the Merrillville Holiday Inn when it was built in the mid-1970s, agreed to chair the promotion and marketing subcommittee. Phillip Coote agreed to chair the finance subcommittee, and Jim Sudlack of Mercantile National Bank in Hammond agreed to serve as cochair of that group. We agreed to submit a report to Mayor Hatcher and Richard Griebel no later than March 31, 1987.

Between January and the end of March, we had biweekly meetings either with subcommittees or in general sessions. In January, we spent most of our time discussing broad goals and objectives. By the end of February, some basic proposals were emerging. By mid-March, our subcommittees had prepared initial reports, and by the end of March, our draft report was finalized, all on schedule.

The report's goal was "to prepare a set of recommendations that will enable the Gary Regional Airport to become at least the third major facility in the Greater Chicago Area."

Objectives were to (1) reestablish air passenger and freight service as early as late spring 1987, (2) work toward becoming competitive with Chicago's Midway Airport as early as 1989, using the existing passenger terminal to full capacity, and (3) plan strategies to compete successfully with other locations for designation as the Greater Chicago third major airport facility. These three objectives were viewed as a continuum, the first, short-range; the second, mid-range; and the third, long-range.

Each of the four subcommittees developed broad objectives. The urban planning and design subcommittee's objectives were to prepare a series of recommendations that would maximize the physical potential of the Gary Regional Airport and to guide further physical growth and development in the northwest Indiana region. The program development subcommittee aimed to measure and quantify the airport's present and future capabilities, especially as they related to number of flights and passengers, freight tonnage, and parking capacity, and to develop an action program including all steps necessary to prepare the airport for meeting its immediate action, mid-range, and long-range goals. The promotion and marketing subcommittee planned to prepare an action program that would enable the airport to "sell" itself to potential customers within its defined market area. And the finance subcommittee's objective was to prepare a financial management program that would identify and monitor costs to be incurred under urban planning and development, program development, and promotion/marketing.

What the plan attempted to accomplish was to link the long-range goal, the third airport designation, to the short-range goal of immediate commuter airline passenger service by a mid-range goal, improving the runways to accommodate the full range of present and projected aircraft (such as the new fuel-efficient mid-sized airlines being constructed by Boeing, Douglas, and Lockheed) and developing an initial industrial park. This way, even if Gary did not get the third airport designation, at least regional passenger service would be established and in place by the year 2000, which is the earliest time a third airport would be available.

The only stumbling block was our finance subcommittee. Phil Coote, instead of preparing drafts and discussing them with the full body as all other subcommittees did, repeatedly pointed out that A. William Douglas, the airport executive director would not turn over to them financial records going back ten years. An audit report released on February 4, 1987, by the State of Indiana Board of Accountants (which by law monitors all local governmental agencies, especially special districts like the Airport Authority District) was highly critical of the airport's handling of its finances. Though there were no charges of theft, misappropriation of funds, or other major fiduciary deficiencies, the agency was cited for what amounted to sloppy bookkeeping. Rather than prepare a long-range financial plan featuring the kind of revenue mix that would be needed to pay for proposed short- and mid-range improvements, the finance committee of Phillip Coote, Jim Sudlack, and Bill Wellman chose to sit on their hands and prepared a weak statement that only identified current resources held by the Gary Airport Board of Authority.

On Thursday, April 16, 1987, the Gary Airport Promotion and Development Commission met to adopt its strategic plan of action. In attendance were most commission members, the airport staff, and the media. I called for the subcommittee chairs to make their reports. As planning chair, I talked about the need to expand the airport's service area to take in the Chicago south suburbs and part of Chicago's South Side. I also talked about our specific plan recommendations for needed improvements in the short-run (cost: $120,000), mid-range part I ($12,700,000), mid-range part II ($18,000,000), and long range (no set figures calculated).

Our program subcommittee discussed existing facilities and their plans to upgrade security maintenance and operation. The promotion and market-ing committee proposed an ambitious strategy to advertise the airport to potential users. The finance committee could only say they couldn't do anything because "Douglas won't give us any information." They failed to provide a financing plan for the $31 million in short- and mid-range projects costed out by the planning subcommittee, even though it was their subcom-mittee charge to do so, Mayor Hatcher and Richard Griebel repeatedly asked them to do so, and I gave them the improvement cost breakdown in detail in late February. With the majority of this subcommittee being from south Lake County and Porter County, the other commission members and I had good reason to feel that they were attempting to sabotage our group effort because it was a given that, with the failure of Metrolake, the airport would remain under control of the city of Gary.

The commission voted unanimously to accept the report. The *Post-Tribune* and the *Hammond Times* both ran articles on the commission's ac-tion the next day. If one read both accounts, he would think that two differ-ent meetings had taken place. The reporters for both papers had attended every commission meeting and several of the subcommittee meetings as well. Both reporters were thoroughly familiar with the commission's work. The *Post-Tribune*'s article was the usual anti-Hatcher, anti-Gary variety; the *Hammond Times* article was factual.

The *Post-Tribune* article was by Nancy Winkley but carried no byline. It read:

LACK OF FINANCIAL REPORT STYMIES AIRPORT PROPOSAL

A plan to make Gary Regional Airport the Chicago area's third major airport was made public Thursday, but the report says the airport director withheld financial information making it impossible to take the first step.

The report is being presented by the Airport Promotion and Development Commit-tee to Mayor Richard G. Hatcher and Northwest Indiana Forum Director Richard H. Griebel. Hatcher and Griebel appointed the committee, chaired by Robert A. Catlin.

The 25-page report, released at a committee meeting Thursday, spells out how Gary could compete with Chicago's O'Hare International Airport and Midway Airport, and what changes would be needed at and around the airport.

But a report by the finance subcommittee said no real plans can be made, including any talks with state leaders about money, because no one knows where the airport stands financially.

Catlin said the committee can't get to step one because airport Director A. William

Douglas and his staff won't give them the financial information they need. Catlin, an Indiana University Northwest professor and city planner, said, "Regardless of numerous requests for this detailed information, the only financial data that the committee has received from the staff at the airport are unsubstantiated projections of future budgets.

"The committee has no answers to such questions: What it is costing to run the airport; what the sources and amount of its income are; what its outstanding debts are; what outside agencies have claims against it; what legal actions are pending; and any number of other such important questions," he said.

Without the information, the report said, the committee cannot "accomplish this first and most vital step."

Douglas was out of town and did not attend the meeting.

The committee wants year-end reports for the last five years showing financial operations at the airport. It also asked for copies of the latest State Board of Accounts audit of the airport released in Indianapolis last week.

"The audit by Indiana's fiscal watchdog agency criticized airport management for failing to keep track of income, granting extra vacation to employees and excessive spending.

Douglas responded that the airport had problems with bookkeeping in the past but was now "In 100 percent compliance" with state demands.

The *Post-Tribune* reporter wrongly attributed the finance subcommittee statements directly to me. Phillip Coote read these remarks aloud at the presentation, and reporters from both papers were there. The *Post-Tribune* article was nothing more than a cheap shot at the Hatcher administration.

The *Hammond Times* article by Phillip Wieland read:

PROMOTIONAL PANEL ADOPTS PLAN FOR GARY AIRPORT

A plan to develop the Gary Regional Airport into a major aviation facility has been adopted and plans now will begin for implementing it, said Robert Catlin.

Catlin, chairman of the Gary Regional Airport Promotion and Development Commission, said the report adopted by the commission Thursday "is not a static thing. It could change over time as we get input from consultants and other interested parties."

The commission has been meeting since January to come up with recommendations from bringing passenger and freight service to the facility and for developing the area around the airport. Development of the airport is expected to create thousands of jobs and to be a vital step in the revitalization of the region.

Recommendations include immediate changes to encourage greater use of the airport and long-range plans to make the airport the third major airport in the Chicago area, after O'Hare International Airport and Midway Airport.

Catlin said the study differed from past airport studies in that the commission recognized that the market area for the airport is not confined to Northwest Indiana but includes downtown Chicago, the south suburbs of Cook County and areas east of Interstate 57 in Illinois.

This expansion of the market area would add about 2.5 million persons and about half-a-million jobs that could benefit by using the airport.

The commission endorsed the airport master plan, calling for the extension of the crosswind runway. Extension of the runway is needed to accommodate larger aircraft and is considered essential to any efforts to make the airport the third major airport.

The report also recognizes that implementation of the plan will have to involve cooperation between Gary and officials from Lake, Porter, and LaPorte counties, the Northwest Indiana Forum, the Northwestern Indiana Regional Planning Commission, Chicago, chambers of commerce in Northwest Indiana and the South suburbs, mayors and other officials in the airport's market area. . . .

The commission will meet again May 14 to begin developing a strategy for implementing the report's recommendations. Catlin said he did not know how long it would take.

Public response to the commission's report was positive; several letters were sent to the *Post-Tribune* and to the airport offices expressing support for the plan. Actually, the mid-range proposals were mainly those recommended by the airport district's 1978 development program. We scheduled the next meeting for May 14, 1987, only a few days after the Gary Democratic mayoral primary.

The Election of Thomas Barnes

By 1986, conditions in Gary could best be described as serious, almost desperate. U.S. Steel's Gary Works, which employed as many as thirty thousand workers in the 1970s, was down to only six thousand employees. Unemployment in Gary was 15 percent compared with 8 percent in the region and 6 percent nationwide. Although residences, for the most part, were in good to excellent condition, commercial areas were shoddy. The city had no movie theaters, full-service restaurants, hotels, or motels and few supermarkets. City services were in disarray as equipment wore out and there were no funds for replacement parts. Conditions had been steadily declining since the late 1970s, and there was no upturn in sight. Federal funds that helped prop up the Hatcher administration were dwindling to a trickle with the Reaganomics cutbacks, and federal revenue sharing was being phased out. U.S. Steel continued to file taxpayer's suits every time the city proposed to raise taxes to meet their growing obligations. State government wasn't helpful either, despite Hatcher's positive overtures in 1985 and 1986.

Since 1980, the number of Hatcher's critics and political enemies had been growing. Thomas Crump ran against Hatcher in the 1983 mayoral primary, and though he lost, he still managed to win 46 percent of the vote, the best showing against the mayor since he won the Democratic Party primary in 1967. This win was possible mainly because of support by Dozier Allen, the Calumet Township trustee and Hatcher's 1975 opponent in the mayoral primary. After the elections, Allen became once more an opponent of the mayor. He was joined in that category by Thomas Crump; Earline Rogers, a Gary state representative; Dr. Vernon Smith, a Gary city councilman; Gary City Judge Charles Graddick; and Thomas Barnes, the township assessor. This informal group dubbed themselves the "No Names." Their agenda was to hold a series of private meetings and develop a consensus as to which one was best prepared to challenge Hatcher in the 1987 mayoral primary. This group met informally during 1985 and 1986. Toward the spring of 1986 it seemed that Thomas Barnes, Earline Rogers, Charles Graddick, and Vernon Smith had the best chance against Hatcher because they had not previously run against him for mayor and therefore were essentially fresh faces.

Before the "No Names" could reach consensus, two events took place in Gary that significantly changed the 1987 mayoral race outlook. In early 1986, Mayor Hatcher was voted out as head of the Gary democratic party by dissident precinct committee members led by followers of Thomas Barnes. In retaliation, the Hatcher followers ran their own candidate against Barnes in the May 1986 democratic party primary for Calumet Township assessor. Barnes trounced the Hatcher-backed candidate, winning the primary with over 70 percent of the total vote. Strengthened by this turn of events, Thomas Barnes announced on June 6, 1986, that he was running against Hatcher for mayor. The other "No Names" were surprised by Barnes's announcement but quietly agreed to back him because (1) he had the momentum, having been behind the ouster of Hatcher as Gary Democratic party chairman and just coming off a very strong primary victory against a Hatcher-supported opponent, and (2) he had not run against Hatcher before as Crump and Allen had and therefore was not tagged with a "loser" image.

Thomas Barnes was born in 1936 in rural Arkansas and moved to Gary with his family when he was only six months old. Graduating from Roosevelt High School in 1954, he enrolled in Purdue University and received a bachelor of science degree in engineering in 1958. He also was commissioned as a second lieutenant in the U.S. Army through Purdue's ROTC program and served two years on active duty.[7] After returning to Gary in 1960, Barnes found that racial discrimination in employment prevented him from finding work as an engineer with the local mills or with the city of Gary. Therefore, he took over the family business, Barnes Washing Machine Repair. He also worked for a time as a social caseworker for the local department of public welfare, one of the few job categories opened to black college degree holders at that time. He studied law at night at Chicago's DePaul University and received his J.D. degree in 1972. After developing a successful law practice, he ran for Calumet Township assessor with backing from the Hatcher political organization.[8] With Calumet Township approaching a black majority for the first time, Barnes squared off against a longtime solidly entrenched member of the Lake County Democratic party machine. Barnes won an upset victory with 52 percent of the vote and then won the assessor's post in the fall general election with token Republican opposition. With his training in engineering and law, Barnes proved to be an excellent assessor. He was reelected in 1982 with only token opposition as he was able to show that he was running a clean, efficient operation with no scandals or investigations coming from federal, state, or county governments.

Supported by the Hatcher organization since 1978, Barnes then broke with Hatcher over the issue of police car replacements in 1984. The city's police vehicle fleet consisted of units purchased in 1978 and 1979 when the local economy was strong and federal funds were in ample supply. By 1983, the fleet was rusting and worn out. With Gary's rising crime rate, coupled with inadequate resources to fight crime, public opinion demanded that new vehicles be purchased by whatever means possible. The Hatcher administration proposed that a ten-year bond issue in the amount of $2.2 million be used to finance the purchase of 110 fully equipped police vehicles and spare parts. Barnes correctly noted that the city would be paying for these vehicles seven or eight years after their useful life had expired. Barnes asked "who would sign a ten-year car note for something that is going to last only two or three years?"[9] Barnes, according to public administration and urban planning theory, was right. Capital improvements financed by longterm general obligation bonds should at least have a useful life equal to the bond repayment period. At 10.5 percent interest, the going rate for a city with an "A" rating such as Gary,[10] the interest costs over a ten-year period would be an additional $2 million, making the cost for each vehicle about $40,000, the price of the 1984 top-of-the-line Mercedes Benz automobile. Barnes filed a taxpayer's suit against the city of Gary and effectively blocked the bond issue. Hatcher bitterly remarked that the city had no other option than to enter into a lease purchase agreement with a five-year term. This lease purchase plan, according to Hatcher, would cost the city over $500,000 more than the bond issue and would result in heavier than anticipated annual cash-outlays, and, he said, with the city strapped for funds, additional employees would have to be laid off.[11] The battle lines between Barnes and Hatcher were clearly drawn.

The mayoral campaign began as soon as the 1986 November general elections were over. The Hatcher forces were initially confident of victory. They still had over nine hundred employees, almost half of whom were patronage workers who could be called upon for "volunteer" work during the campaign. The mayor's staff consisted of people who had worked in Gary city government and in political campaigns for up to twenty years and had learned by trial and error not only how to run city government but how to run winning political campaigns as well. The recently constructed Adam Benjamin Transportation Center and the Parks and Recreation Administration Building and Fitness Center were proof that, despite the cutback of federal funds, the city was still able to build striking and attractive public works. Barnes would be able to mount a strong campaign too. His assessor's office contained over one hundred patronage employees and, coupled with patronage workers from his allies—the Calumet Township trustee, the city judge's office, and even volunteers from the Lake County Democratic Organization—Barnes had as many, if not more, troops as Hatcher.

Mayor Hatcher entered this race with more negatives than ever before. The local economy had not recovered to the same extent as that for the nation and the state of Indiana. Although the transportation center opened in 1985 and the Parks and Recreation Administration and Fitness Center in 1986, their relative successes were canceled out by the failure of the Sheraton Hotel, which closed in 1985. The Genesis Convention Center, Hatcher's showpiece, was still losing money; the restrooms were inadequate; and kitchen facilities for banquets still had not been installed. Hatcher had tried to develop a two-block area just south of the convention center in cooperation with Gainer Bank, but that arrangement fell through in 1986 because Gainer insisted that the proposed development—including a budget hotel, cinema complex, and fast-food restaurant center—be built around their drive-up bank, which, because of its location in the middle of the site, precluded development of much of anything else.[12] Also, by 1987, residents were tired of public works as a substitute for more meaningful progress such as jobs, improved city services, and substantial reductions in crime.

For the first time, the Hatcher campaign would be marred by tragedy and scandal. In October 1986, Barbara Leek Wesson, the Gary city clerk and one of Hatcher's chief political operatives, died of heart failure. In February, Rosemary Jackson, a Gary precinct committeewoman and Hatcher's chief grass-roots political organizer, was killed in an automobile accident just blocks from her West Side home. The loss of these two key organizers deprived the campaign of much of its spirit as well as structure. Also, both women were "morale boosters" for Mayor Hatcher, who over the years always had the words of encouragement and assurance every politician needs when going through a tough election campaign.

Since his election as mayor in 1967, Hatcher had run the city free from graft, corruption, or scandal, with the city always being under the watchful eye of federal, state, and county prosecutors waiting for the first infraction to take place. Hatcher did not smoke, drink, or gamble, nor was he a womanizer. For almost twenty years, the newspapers and state law enforcement officials had tried without success to get something on him. But in 1985, federal prosecutors started a major investigation of northwest Indiana politicians, including members of the Lake County Democratic machine and those in Mayor Hatcher's organization. In early January of 1987, indictments were brought against seven members of the Hatcher administration's leadership team, the most significant person being Ronald Sullivan, the mayor's manpower chief and director of the Department of General Services, which included the sanitation department. Sullivan was accused of embezzling of public funds, lying to a grand jury, income tax evasion, and several minor counts. The trials of Hatcher's administrators were not held until after the election, and Sullivan was found guilty of all major counts and sentenced to federal prison. These indictments tarnished the previously untouched administration and took away Hatcher's ability to claim that he was running an efficient and clean government free of graft and corruption.

The campaign was lackluster and without major issues. Barnes's theme was simply "it's time for a change." He offered few details and no specifics as to what changes would be forthcoming if he won the election. Hatcher ran on his record, and his campaign themes were almost identical to those used in the 1983 primary: new construction downtown and a promise of better times as evidenced by such innovations as having a sector of the city designated as an enterprise zone, plans for the marina, expansion of the city's airport, and adoption of the comprehensive plan of 1986. A poll taken in January 1987 by the *Gary* INFO, the city's longstanding black newspaper, showed that 45 percent of all respondents stated they didn't care who was elected and another 20 percent didn't even know who was running against Mayor Hatcher.[13]

Going into the final week of the campaign, the *Post-Tribune* gave Barnes a slight lead, while both candidates' polls showed their leader to be ahead. The *Post-Tribune* had a strong endorsement for Barnes. The election was held on Tuesday, May 7, 1987, a day marked by cloudy, rainy weather, a typical spring day in northwest Indiana. When the results came in, the winner was Thomas V. Barnes with 24,450 votes compared to only 18,409 votes for Mayor Hatcher. Barnes won with 58 percent of all votes cast, and Hatcher's total was his lowest ever, lower than even in the three-way primary against Katz and Konrady in 1967 when he won with 20,272 votes. More telling was the fact that, among Gary's 75,000 registered voters, fewer than 43,000 showed up at the polls, only 57 percent in contrast with a 60 percent turnout for Katie Hall's 1982 general election triumph and 68 percent for the 1983 primary featuring Hatcher and Crump. Barnes's winning total was short of the total votes Hatcher received in past primaries (see table 12). If anything, apathy was the real winner in that election. In this case, the less lethargic campaign won out. But a win is still a win. Barnes was assured election in the fall as Democrats in 1987 outnumbered Republicans by over forty to one in Gary. In the days following the election, the *Post-Tribune* remarked in an editorial that "Hatcher's place is assured in history, but Barnes's election promises a new day and better times ahead." It seemed that their attitude about Gary had turned 180 degrees after Hatcher was defeated.

Table 12. Richard G. Hatcher's Primary Election Results, 1967-1987

Year	Incumbent	# Votes Incumbent Won	% Incumbent Won	Major Opponent	# Votes Opponent Won	% Opponent Won	Remarks
1967	Martin Katz	17,910	34.4	Richard Hatcher	20,272	39.8	Konrady took third place with 14,151 votes
1971	Richard Hatcher	34,742	62.5	Andrew Williams	20,842	37.5	Williams had the business community's support
1975	Richard Hatcher	30,377	58.2	Dozier Allen	22,844	41.8	Allen was formerly a staunch supporter of Hatcher
1979	Richard Hatcher	24,832	60.1	Jesse Bell	16,463	39.9	Bell was seriously underfunded
1983	Richard Hatcher	27,835	54.7	Thomas Crump	23,150	45.3	Hatcher allied with Dozier Allen
1987	Richard Hatcher	18,409	42.0	Thomas Barnes	24,450	58.0	Hatcher's enemies united against him

Between the Primary Victory and Barnes's Inauguration

Even with Barnes's win in the primary, the Hatcher administration still had almost eight months before it went out of office. The only question pondered by Hatcher staffers was whether or not the administration would put itself on hold and simply ride out the remaining months as a lame duck or continue to take an activist stance until the very end. That question was settled on Monday, May 13, 1987, when Hatcher met with his executive staff.

Looking relaxed and confident as if *he* had won the election, Mayor Hatcher stated, "We're fighting right to the end. When history is written no one will be able to say that we didn't discharge our responsibilities to the citizens of Gary. We're not sitting on our hands; instead, we're going to work harder than ever." After detailing his expectations for the high-profile departments—police, fire, sanitation, parks and recreation—he got around to planning. The planning department would as its first priority continue to work on details for the marina. Taghi Arsharmi was given the additional responsibility of preparing a detailed site plan for the expanded airport. I was asked to continue as chair of the Airport Promotion and Development Commission and hold monthly meetings to implement the plan agreed to by that group in April.

When the Promotion and Development Commission convened at the airport terminal the next day, the Lake County contingent was jubilant. Somewhat tentative and reserved during the months we deliberated prior to adopting our proposal, that group was now relaxed and completely in their element now that Hatcher had lost. Boomed Jim Sudlack, "Now that Barnes will be mayor we'll *really* have a regional airport now." I had to remind Sudlack that, first of all, Barnes was not mayor now and wouldn't be until January and, second, Barnes might fool them once in office. I said, "Barnes did what he had to do to get support from people like you in order to get elected, but he could turn out to be more militant than Mayor Hatcher."

The consultants to the Illinois Department of Transportation, Peat, Marwick and Mitchell, were now in the process of conducting public hearings on the third airport question. The airports under consideration for expansion to third Chicago airport designation included these in Gary; Milwaukee; Aurora, Illinois; and Rockford, Illinois. The Rockford hearing was set for June. Gary's was for June 2, Aurora's for June 3, and Milwaukee's for June 4.

The hearings in Rockford proved to be negative. Speaker after speaker, mostly citizens, got up and repeatedly stated that they didn't want a "jetport" in their back yard. One elderly resident stated, "Dammit, I moved from around O'Hare just to get away from all the noise and now you guys want to put this thing right next to me."[14] By the end of the evening, even

Peat, Marwick and Mitchell were convinced that Rockford should be eliminated from the airport sweepstakes.

The public hearing was scheduled for Gary on Tuesday, June 2. That day, a *Post-Tribune* article appeared entitled "FAA Study ruled out Gary as Third Airport Site." The story stated that the Federal Aviation Administration had found that a major increase in flight operations at the Gary Airport would interfere with flight patterns at O'Hare and Midway.[15] This had come up during the commission's deliberations, and we were told by Peat, Marwick and Mitchell that the O'Hare and Midway flight patterns could be redesigned. Griebel had repeatedly stated that when the Newark Airport expanded flight operations, the New York City airspace was redesigned so that no conflict with La Guardia or Kennedy would be present. That day as the mayor and I talked about the hearing to be held that evening, we discussed the *Post-Tribune* article, and Hatcher simply remarked, "The *Post-Tribune* is at it again."

The meeting was to be held at the airport passenger terminal. We decided to use the waiting room area for the meeting itself and ordered six hundred folding chairs to accommodate residents. The restaurant space was reserved for a public exhibit of the aviation authority's master plan and related photographs. The administrative offices were quickly converted to a VIP lounge as Lieutenant Governor John Mutz and Lane Ralph, a representative of Indiana senators Richard Lugar and Dan Quayle, were to speak.

The hearing was to begin at 8:00 P.M., but by 7:00 P.M. the waiting room was filled to capacity. Gary's Lew Wallace High School Marching Band was on hand to play a medley of John Phillip Sousa tunes to keep the crowd pepped up and in good spirits. By 8:00 P.M., twenty-five speakers had signed up, and the hearing started on time to a standing-room-only crowd, about half from Gary and the other half from nearby northwest Indiana communities. Mayor Hatcher, the first speaker, discussed the advantages of the Gary airport and the fact that the public supported expansion of the facility. Hatcher stated at the end of his remarks, "The entire region is behind this development effort, for it will mean regional economic development and regional job opportunity on a scale that could never be accomplished with any other project. Only the development of a third jetport could have the potential of replacing all of those jobs that have been lost as a result of the economic decline in our area."

Similar statements were read by Elizabeth Williamson, president of the Gary Airport Board of Authority, Gary State Representative Charlie Brown, and Dr. A. William Douglas, the airport board executive director. But what really got the crowd excited were statements by Senators Richard Lugar and Dan Quayle and a personal address by Lieutenant Governor John Mutz. The joint statement by Lugar and Quayle was read aloud by Lane Ralph, a senatorial aide to Lugar, based in Indianapolis:

Joint Statement
of U.S. Senators Richard G. Lugar and Dan Quayle (Both R-IN)
on Expansion of the Gary Regional Airport
and the Chicago Airport Capacity Study
June 2, 1987

We appreciate the opportunity to submit a statement on behalf of the Gary Regional Airport at the public information meeting about the Chicago Airport Capacity Study that Peat, Marwick, Mitchell, & Co. has organized here this evening.

The purpose of the Chicago Airport Capacity Study, which was initiated by the Federal Aviation Administration, is to determine whether there is a need for an additional major airport facility in the greater Chicago region to accommodate the significant volume of passenger and other aircraft traffic now using the facilities and services of O'Hare International Airport, as well as the growth in that traffic projected in the future.

We have little doubt that this study will conclude that there is indeed a need for an additional major airport in this area.

We also believe that, when the study turns to consider where such a new facility should be located, it will recommend an existing airport as the most viable site for economic, financial and environmental reasons.

In our opinion, that site should be the Gary Regional Airport.

In making this recommendation, we note the important consensus that has developed in Northwest Indiana that the Gary Regional Airport merits the consideration of the Chicago Airport Capacity Study. We are pleased to support the efforts of the many governmental entities, economic development agencies and private citizens in Northwest Indiana who, for sound reasons, maintain that Gary Regional Airport is ideally suited to become the third major facility in the Chicago region.

We believe the Gary Regional Airport deserves favorable consideration for the following reasons:

1. The Gary Regional Airport's existing facilities and equipment provide an excellent foundation for future development.

2. Land is currently available adjacent to the Gary Regional Airport for its future development and expansion.

3. The Gary Regional Airport is well situated. Given the location of the two existing primary airports in the Chicago region—O'Hare to the northwest of the city and the more central Midway Airport—expanding Gary Regional Airport to the southeast would geographically balance the major air transport facilities relative to the population of the Chicago region. Currently, business and private travelers in the densely populated areas of south suburban Illinois and Northwest Indiana are without a convenient airport facility.

4. The Gary Regional Airport is *already* served by an extensive surface transportation infrastructure. The South Shore Railroad, the Indiana Toll Road, Interstate 80/94 and many other east/west highways will permit the movement of people and freight to and from the Gary Regional Airport with limited disruption *and* limited additional capital outlays. The Airport's close proximity to Burns International Harbor and the Port of Chicago should also be noted.

The siting of a third major Chicago airport will be followed by considerable economic development for the selected city and its surrounding communities. We believe this positive economic impact should be acknowledged, and that the economic needs of the candidate communities should be actively considered as one of the criteria for determining a site. As we all know, the communities of Northwest Indiana and south suburban Illinois have been hard hit by plant closings and the decline of heavy industry in the region. The economic impact of expanding and further developing the Gary Regional Airport would do much to foster an economic recovery in the area.

For all these reasons, we believe the Gary Regional Airport should be chosen as the site for the Chicago region's third major airport.

As Peat Marwick proceeds with the Chicago Airport Capacity Study, we urge you to consider carefully our statement and the comments from Northwest Indiana leaders that follow ours here tonight.

As soon as the aide finished reading the statement, over eight hundred spectators rose to their feet, cheering. Now that Senators Lugar and Quayle had endorsed the Gary site as the best location for third airport status, the airport plans were ready to take off. This was a marked departure from their previous stance of neutrality. The statement was the result of months of quiet negotiations among Mayor Hatcher, Richard Griebel, and the senator's offices. Now the airport authority could move forward with plans for air service. The FAA grants suspended earlier in the year because of poor bookkeeping on Douglas's part would be restored because of the influence of Lugar and Quayle.

Lieutenant Governor John Mutz then took the stand. As the crowd cheered, Mutz announced that the Indiana Transportation Coordinating Board had just that very day approved an application for $9 million in Federal Matching Funds for the Gary airport. The award would need matching grants of $450,000 each from the airport authority and the state. Mutz promised that would be no problem: "You will get the money from the state. All you need to do is float bonds for the remaining monies."

When the meeting closed at 10:45 P.M., over thirty politicians, business persons, and citizens had spoken. Every one was in favor of airport expansion. The next day, Tom Knightly of the *Post-Tribune* ran a front-page article entitled "Gary Jetport Plan Gets Wide Support." Unlike previous *Post-Tribune* articles on Gary, this one was accurate and informative.[16] The only mistake was the size of the crowd. The *Post-Tribune* put it at 450, whereas the Gary fire marshall estimated over 800 in attendance and actually had to shut the doors to keep additional people out for fire safety reasons.

The next evening, the Peat, Marwick and Mitchell team held a public hearing on the proposed site in Aurora, Illinois. Aurora, a southwest Chicago suburb, was well located, just forty minutes from downtown Chicago by expressway, and, because the airport was located in a rural area, it seemed to be a good candidate. However, two hundred angry residents turned out, and everyone who spoke was against the airport. In a local newspaper, Dan Wheat wrote, in an article entitled "Airport Growth Plan Finds No Happy Landings":

Talking at the podium at Waubinsee Community College Wednesday, explaining his consulting firm's airport study, Dan Haney appeared to be flying solo.

By the time the audience of more than 200 area residents was through giving instruction he relayed the message; I read you loud and clear.

And he said he thinks he is convinced the Aurora Municipal Airport near Sugar Grove should be removed from consideration for becoming the Chicago area's third major airport.[17]

The meeting in Milwaukee was not even held because of citizen protests. In a cryptic note by Dan Haney to his bosses in San Francisco, Haney said: "We regret that the June 4, 1987 Public Information Meeting concerning the possible expansion of General Mitchell International Airport as part of the Chicago Airport Capacity Study has been cancelled. We hope that this will not cause any inconvenience."[18]

On July 17, 1987, Peat, Marwick and Mitchell presented its initial report to the Illinois Department of Transportation recommending further investigation of the Gary site. It ruled out Aurora because of public opposition and Rockford and Milwaukee because of public opposition and because they were too far away from Chicago. But jubilation in Gary was short-lived: because of political pressure from Illinois Governor James Thompson, Peat, Marwick and Mitchell decided to add at least three new sites, two in Illinois and one on the Indiana-Illinois border, for further study. The new Peat, Marwick and Mitchell report was set for release in February 1988. When it came out, Gary was still ranked number one, but the report called for "further study."

As the summer of 1987 came and went, we in the Promotion and Development Commission put all of our efforts into attracting a commuter airline that could provide service to Indianapolis, Detroit, and perhaps Cleveland and Pittsburgh as well. We were still enthusiastic about the possibility of being designated as the site for the third Chicago area airport. Gary was Peat, Marwick and Mitchell's top choice because of the lowest construction bid (estimated by us at $1 billion), public support, and accessibility to Chicago via an interchange on the Indiana Toll Road just south of the airport, facilitating travel to downtown Chicago in just thirty minutes. While the FAA was still concerned about airspace conflict between Gary and the two existing Chicago airports, on July 17, in a letter to newly named FAA administrator T. Allan McArtor, Senators Lugar and Quayle urged the FAA to reconsider their airspace design patterns to accommodate Gary. They wrote that any airport that would be reasonably close to Chicago would be likely to have an adverse impact upon O'Hare flight patterns and added that flight paths in New York City and Los Angeles appear to be more crowded than those in Chicago.[19]

As fall 1987 came, we had every reason to believe that by the first of the year not only would commuter air service be in place but we would receive the third airport designation as well. Peat, Marwick and Mitchell had ranked Gary as number one, we had strong support from Senators Lugar and Quayle, and, with Thomas Barnes about to take over as mayor, at least we had neutrality if not outright support from the *Post-Tribune* and suburban northwest Indiana leaders. By October, T. Allan McArtor, FAA administrator had officially ruled that the airspace could be redesigned so that Gary would not conflict with O'Hare and Midway. However, there were still problems. The 1985-1987 audit finding the airport authority guilty of lax bookkeeping methods didn't help as it gave the impression that with local leadership in control the Gary airport couldn't possibly handle expansion. In an *Indianapolis Star* news article, Lieutenant Governor John Mutz suggested regional control of the Gary airport, stating that "Indiana would assist in any way it can in seeing that either Gary's airport is developed or a new site comes to northwest Indiana." He said, "Legislation of some sort would probably be needed to create the proper oversight agency."[20] The same article noted in closing, "There is an implication that Gary with its high unemployment and crime rate and its rust belt image doesn't have enough charm to serve as a major link in America's air service network."

We had heard this before. Griebel's standard response was "That hasn't stopped Newark from using its proximity to New York City to develop its airport." Still, the Promotion and Development Commission went on with its work. We contacted every commuter airline in the Midwest regarding initiation of service from Gary. Negotiations were started with a few interested airlines, but by November we seemed to be running into an invisible stone wall. Then we heard from a city employee: "Barnes has put the word out that no agreements are to be made with the Hatcher administration on anything; the marina, airport, landfill, anything."[21] We wanted not to believe this highly reliable source and in any event with Barnes taking over as mayor in January we felt that he would quickly review our work, approve what we had done, and then move forward.

Just after Thanksgiving, rumors surfaced that soon-to-be-mayor Barnes would scrap everything connected with the Hatcher administration and start from the beginning. This included the Promotion and Development Commission's work as well as plans for the marina and the Fire Station Development Program that I had just prepared. Those of us who were appointed to the commission by Mayor Hatcher didn't want to believe that, but we were getting the cold shoulder from our commission counterparts who had been appointed by the Northwest Indiana Forum and Richard Griebel.

Our last meeting was held on Friday, December 11, 1987. The Gary Regional Airport Promotion and Development Commission was scheduled to go out of business on December 31 unless Barnes chose to continue the group's work. By the time of the meeting there was no word from the

Barnes camp as to whether or not he wanted the group to continue either with the present membership or with members of his choice. On the agenda was a presentation by Taghi Arsharmi, the assistant planning director for the city of Gary, of the department's Renaissance 2000 airport site plan. The plan called for an airport district of 3,500 acres bounded by Fifth Avenue on the south, Cline Avenue on the west, and Lake Michigan on the north. Arsharmi, assisted by Carla Grigsby, a recent graduate of the architecture program at Tuskeegee University, had worked hard on preparing a first-rate design scheme showing a new 345,000-square-foot terminal, new runways conforming to Peat, Marwick and Mitchell's third airport requirements, 6,000 parking spaces, a "traveler's park" with motels, restaurants, and a small convention center all interconnected by skywalks, an industrial park with over 10,000 jobs, and a transit connection at the terminal to the South Shore Commuter Railroad. The existing terminal would be used as a general aviation center. After Arsharmi's presentation, Jim Ranfrantz of NIRPC derisively remarked that his design was "Buck Rogers planning." I responded that it was Neil Armstrong planning, and just as Neil Armstrong landed on the moon we can eventually land the third Chicago area airport if we stick together. In closing remarks, Griebel and I stated that it was of the utmost importance for the incoming administration first to focus on getting air service started and then move quickly, adding jet DC-9 and 737 service, essentially phase II of our plan. The third airport designation was the least important task. Our final recommendation was that the new administration hire a consulting firm to take our place.

Barnes Deals with the Airport Issue

As mentioned earlier, by October 1987, things were going extremely well for the Gary airport. Peat, Marwick and Mitchell had ranked Gary first among the four sites for third Chicago area airport designation. Indiana's two prominent Republican senators, Richard G. Lugar and Dan Quayle, were solidly behind the Gary airport and had prevailed upon T. Allan McArtor, Federal Aviation Administration head, to move aside the problem of airspace conflict between an expanded Gary airport and O'Hare and Midway.[22] Our Promotion and Development Commission was working to line up commuter companies to provide air service initially to Indianapolis and Detroit. Gary's mayor-to-be, Thomas Barnes, enjoyed the support of the south Lake County business community and the *Post-Tribune*, as, among other things, they felt that he would be receptive to regional control of the airport.

But Thomas Barnes proved them wrong. At a political rally at his campaign headquarters on Saturday, October 10, Barnes reported to his followers on his meeting with Lieutenant Governor John Mutz and other state officials regarding the airport. When asked if he indicated at the meeting or in any other meeting that he was willing to consider regional control, he emphatically stated, "No!" "What we need at this point is cooperation from other entities, and that's the posture others are taking as well," stated Barnes, sounding now just like Richard Hatcher when he was confronted exactly one year before with Metrolake.[23]

I could not help but shove the newspaper article about Barnes's refusal of regional control under the nose of Jim Sudlack and the other Lake County members of the Promotion and Development Commission at our meeting three days later. "What do you think of Barnes now?" I asked in a friendly taunt. Sudlack and his cronies did not know what to say. They had counted on Barnes turning over the airport—and the entire city of Gary as well—to them. But they didn't know Mayor Barnes. Here was a man who paid his dues by scraping together just enough money to attend Purdue University and graduating with a degree in engineering and who, after serving in the U.S. Army as an officer, could not find a job in his field because of racism. Barnes was not naive. He knew that the city of Gary had operated the airport for almost forty years without any help when it was just another general aviation field. He knew the difficulty faced by the Hatcher administration, of which he was a part until 1984, in obtaining federal grants in the late 1970s to upgrade the runways and build the passenger terminal. Only a fool would turn the airport over to a group of outsiders who had never run an airport themselves after all the time and effort Gary had spent on improving that facility.

Though Barnes had made his intentions clear about regional control, there was still no indication on how he intended to operate the airport. The fate of Dr. A. William Douglas was unclear. Douglas was a Hatcher man, but he had attended Roosevelt High School with Thomas Barnes and, as they were in the same age group, they had similar experiences of once being young, black, college-educated men unable simply because of employment discrimination to find work in fields for which they were well prepared. A clue came on Tuesday, October 13, when the *Post-Tribune* ran an article on page one of the local section detailing that Douglas was upset at not being invited to a meeting held by Lieutenant Governor Mutz and attended by Barnes. At that meeting, Mutz gave Barnes assurances that Gary would control the airport if it was chosen as the third major airport for the Chicago area.[24] Airport board members Elizabeth Williamson and Victor Thornton agreed that Douglas should have been invited. Douglas said, "The Lieutenant Governor made the decision not to invite anyone from Mayor Richard Hatcher's administration but he made an error in not evaluating how the city of Gary would feel. There's talking about cooperation but that's no way to create it. I don't understand what he [Barnes] was saying or even if he was saying anything. Who controls the airport should not even be an issue. Gary controls the airport . . . there is no need for Gary to lose control of the airport. Most of the people who use O'Hare are from other places but you don't hear people saying Chicago should not run it."[25]

It was reported that Barnes took Dr. Douglas's statements as a personal insult. "Who does Douglas think he is?" fumed Barnes. "I'll show him."[26] Between October and December 31, no one from the incoming Barnes administration bothered to contact either Dr. Douglas or myself about the airport. I was expecting someone from Barnes's staff to contact me not only about the airport but about the 1986 Comprehensive Plan and the Fire Station Development Program. But no calls came to Taghi Arsharmi, Arlene Colvin, or me. This was unfortunate because we were all prepared to share information on planning and development issues with the new administration.

Mayor Barnes Picks a New Aviation Authority Board

When Mayor Barnes took office, the Gary Airport Board of Authority consisted of four Hatcher appointees. Mayor Barnes immediately undertook a policy to purge members of the city's boards and commissions whom he viewed as loyal to the former administration. On February 8, 1988, he terminated all members of the aviation board and announced four new appointments. The old board, led by Elizabeth Williamson, filed suit in federal court charging that their ouster was illegal and politically motivated. While the matter weaved its way through the court, the old board and new board worked simultaneously. The new board met during the day, then locked up the administrative offices and conference room at the close of the business day, forcing the old board to meet evenings in the nearby public library. In a temporary arrangement worked out by attorneys for both boards, all matters requiring signatures, such as purchase orders, payroll certifications, and correspondence with state and federal auditors, were received and signed off on by both boards. Dr. A. William Douglas and his staff reported to both boards.

With all the confusion of dual boards meeting, passing conflicting resolutions and giving conflicting orders to staff, the immediate task of obtaining air passenger service was put on hold. The new board asked Douglas to resign in December 1988. He decided to comply, noting the frustration of having to work for two masters moving in different directions, and his last day was February 28, 1989. In an interview with me, Douglas stated,

With Peat Marwick's ranking of our facility as best suited for third Chicago area airport designation, strong, unanimous citizen support for Gary Airport expansion all over northwest Indiana as contrasted with opposition at all the Illinois sites, support from Lugar and Quayle who worked out the airspace conflict, we had a beautiful window of opportunity. We should have started commuter service no later than June 1988. Lugar was getting our grant suspension by the FAA lifted, and we could have started expansion of the runways by early 1989. But with this mess of having two boards operating at the same time, we lost momentum. I think the window of opportunity has closed.[28]

After Douglas left, the new board conducted a nationwide search for a replacement. The search resulted in the appointment of Dennis W. Sparks of Richmond, Virginia, who came on board in August 1989. Sparks was a former airline pilot with an M.B.A. who had specialized in marketing for the Richmond Airport Board. However, Sparks quit after only ten weeks amid reports that he couldn't get along with airport board members.[29] The new board then appealed to the state to help find a new director. The state agreed to do so and to supplement the new director's salary, but in return the director would report not to the Gary Airport Board but to the Indiana State Department of Transportation's Division of Aeronautics headed now by Richard H. Griebel, former coleader of the old Promotion and Development Commission and president of the Northwest Indiana Forum. Sensing a connection to the former Hatcher administration as well as loss of control of the airport, Mayor Barnes directed his board to squash that move. Finally, in November of 1989, Lavel Gatewood, deputy executive director of the Gary airport since 1982 and a veteran Gary civil servant, was appointed acting executive director in charge of day-to-day operations. On January 27, 1990, the new board chose the firm of R.W. Armstrong and Associates, an Indianapolis group of aviation marketing consultants, to handle promotion and development for the airport. R.W. Armstrong had twenty years of experience working for airports and worked for thirty-five airports in Indiana and Ohio, including the highly regarded airports in Indianapolis and Columbus, Ohio.[30]

In February 1990, the court case was finally settled and the new board officially seated.[31] The fight between the old and new boards was costly, divisive, and time-consuming. Two years had passed since Barnes's inauguration, and still there was no commuter air service from Gary's airport. Gary was still the preferred third Chicago area airport site by Governor Evan Bayh, Senator Lugar, and Senator Dan Coates, who replaced Dan Quayle upon his election as vice president. Most northwest Indiana business leaders and governmental officials were also supportive of expansion of the Gary airport. However, there was now a new player coming in off the bench. His name was Richard M. Daley, the recently elected mayor of Chicago.

Daley Enters Third Chicago Area Airport Race

When we began our work on the Promotion and Development Commission in early 1987, Harold Washington was mayor of Chicago. His position on the airport issue was that no new facility was needed; O'Hare could meet all area needs until at least the year 2000 and, if additional capacity was needed, another runway could be added to O'Hare. After Washington died in November 1987, his replacement as mayor, Eugene Sawyer, took the same position on the airport issue. Both men were friendly to Gary Mayors Hatcher and Barnes and were quietly supportive of Gary expanding their airport and adding flights so long as it didn't cut into O'Hare or Midway's business.

In 1988, Richard M. Daley, son of the famous Chicago mayor, announced that he would run in a special spring 1989 primary and general election called in order to finish Washington's four-year term that began in April 1987. Richard M. Daley had lost to Washington in the 1983 Democratic party primary, finishing third behind Washington and former Chicago Mayor Jane Byrne and winning 30 percent of the total vote. After Washington's death, Daley collected the remains of his father's old machine and was soon ready to challenge Eugene Sawyer, who was picked to succeed Washington by a coalition of black moderate and old-line Daley machine aldermen. Daley won the primary, beating Sawyer easily, and then won the general election over Chicago Alderman Timothy Evans, inheritor of the remnants of Harold Washington's old organization, in April 1989.

Chicago had lost almost 300,000 industrial jobs between 1960 and 1985, and though 220,000 service sector jobs had been added during the same period, there was still a net loss of employment.[32] Although the downtown or Loop was still vibrant with over 500,000 workers and visitors entering each day, and the city's magnificent lakefront still drew visitors from around the world to its cultural and sports attractions, Daley knew that in order to be a credible candidate in the 1991 Chicago mayoral elections he had to accomplish something of major significance. Daley knew that if he could reverse Chicago's economic losses over the past thirty years, he would finally come out of his father's shadow, become his own man, and, of course, win easily in the mayoral primaries and general elections of 1991. The third Chicago airport offered that possibility.

Originally, the Bistate Aviation Commission, consisting of four representatives from Illinois and four from Indiana and headed by both states' lieutenant governors, had hired Peat, Marwick and Mitchell to study the need for a third major airport in the Chicago area. When Peat, Marwick and Mitchell came out in July 1987 with then preliminary recommendation of expansion of the Gary airport as their first choice, the Illinois representatives were angry. After Peat, Marwick and Mitchell turned in their final report in February 1988, making Gary the first choice with an expansion of Milwaukee's airport to handle overflow flights that would have gone to O'Hare, the Illinois Bistate Commission called for a new study, and the Indiana members didn't object. This would later turn out to be a fatal mistake on their part.[33] By early 1989, a new firm was on board, the TAMS group out of Arlington, Virginia. This group, backed by over $1 million in Federal Aviation Administration grant monies, reviewed the Peat, Marwick and Mitchell work and settled on four sites for further evaluation. One was the Gary Regional Airport, the second was in Kankakee, Illinois, the third was in southern Will County, Illinois, and the fourth was a site straddling the Indiana-Illinois border about twenty miles south of Gary and fifty miles south of Chicago. The three Illinois and bistate sites were in rural undeveloped areas. The TAMS consultants then found that, instead of 65 million enplanements in the Chicago area by 2010 as projected by Peat, Marwick and Mitchell, 90 million enplanements would occur, necessitating an airport site of at least ten thousand acres.[34] The Indiana Department of Transportation after reviewing this data calculated that expansion of the Gary airport to meet these new requirements would take at least twelve thousand homes and cause the relocation of over thirty thousand residents, half from Gary, the other half from East Chicago and Hammond.[35]

On December 14, 1989, Mayor Daley announced plans for a new third Chicago area airport within the city limits. (See figure 5.) Located in the Lake Calumet area, a region on Chicago's far south side consisting of abandoned steel mills, toxic waste sites, and landfills, the airport would take about nine thousand acres of land, uproot eight thousand homes and forty-seven businesses, and reroute the Grant Calumet River, which flows from Lake Calumet to Lake Michigan through Gary. The benefits would be tremendous. Daley's planners, after spending over $1 million on their own study, estimated that the Lake Calumet Airport would generate 200,000 new permanent jobs and produce a $1.6 billion annual payroll. The site, adjacent to Interstate Highway 94, was only twenty minutes from downtown Chicago, closer than Gary's site and closer than both O'Hare and Midway. Daley immediately applied for a $5 million planning grant for detailed development schemes from the Federal Aviation Administration. U.S. Transportation Secretary Sam Skinner proposed that instead of a separate study it would be better to include the Lake Calumet site along with the other four. With Daley's onslaught, Indiana's Democratic Governor Evan Bayh, elected in 1988 in an upset victory, weakened on his previously

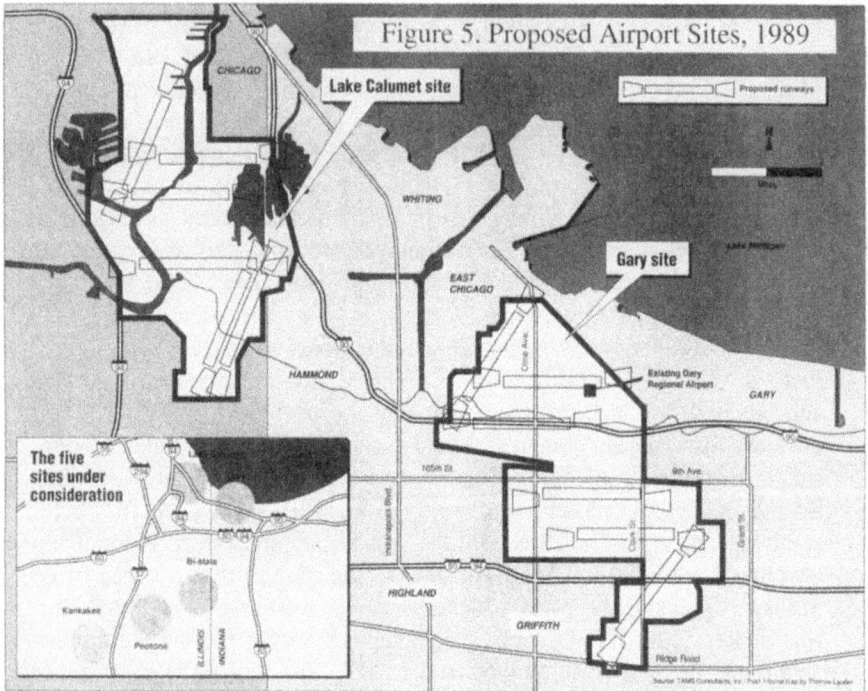

Figure 5. Proposed Airport Sites, 1989

strong support for the Gary airport expansion, citing that the potential dislocation of four thousand to twelve thousand homes and a portion of U.S. Steel's Gary Works was "something we have to weigh in the equation." Gary leaders were angered at Bayh's retreat because Gary and northwest Indiana voters had provided him with just enough votes to win the governorship. Barnes lashed out at Bayh, stating, "I think it inconceivable the state would bail out before the bistate study is completed." Bayh immediately retracted his statement and vowed support for the Gary airport.[36] Daley adroitly agreed to drop his $5 million request for planning money if the bistate commission was expanded from eight to eleven members, with three coming from Chicago. Over repeated objections by Indiana Governor Bayh, Mayor Barnes of Gary and Mayor Thomas McDermott of Hammond, whose proposed marina could be scuttled by a Lake Calumet airport, the "deal" was approved by Secretary Skinner in July 1990. Frank Luerssen, chairman of Inland Steel Company headquartered in Chicago, was chosen as chairman of the new eleven-member bistate commission on August 28, 1990.[37] On October 2, Daley selected his representatives, which included his brother William M. Daley, a savings and loan executive; Robert M. Healy, president of the Chicago Federation of Labor and Industrial Union Council; and James Compton, president and chief executive officer of the Chicago Urban League and a major leader of Chicago's 1.2 million-strong black community.[38] As a consolation prize to Indiana Governor Bayh and Mayor Barnes of Gary, the Gary airport was awarded $2.5 million for runway improvements. This was not new money. The Federal Aviation Administration simply expedited Gary's request for funding in exchange for not fighting Chicago's addition to the airport race.[39]

Still Sam Skinner's deal left Gary with a major setback in the third airport race. Daley's addition of three members to the site selection committee gave Illinois a 7 to 4 advantage. Daley's Lake Calumet site or even an expanded O'Hare choice received a major boost on October 27, 1990, when Congress, over the objections of Indiana Governor Evan Bayh and Senators Richard Lugar and Dan Coates, passed legislation allowing Chicago to charge up to three dollars per passenger departure from O'Hare and Midway for airport construction. Daley's planners estimated that this new departure tax would generate $2 billion for Chicago by 2010. Gary cannot use this legislation because they don't have a large passenger operation.[40] In November 1990, Illinois Republican Governor James Thompson's hand-picked replacement, Secretary of State Jim Edgar, narrowly defeated Neil Hartigan, a Daley machine Democrat for governor. This breathed some new life in Gary's effort for third airport designation because, had Hartigan won, Daley would have a 7 to 4 majority on the selection board and the Lake Calumet airport site would have won in a walk.

Citizen objection to the rural Illinois and the bistate site was considerable in 1990. On January 9, 1990, residents of areas around the three Kankakee and Will County sites objected strenuously to a new jetport in their area.[41] Citizens in the Lake Calumet area met on September 18, 1990, to protest the airport in that location, but because the majority of them were longtime supporters of Daley's archrival former Chicago Alderman Edward Vrdolyak, Mayor Daley could ignore their protests.[42] And in the November 1990 general elections, in the Lake Calumet area of Chicago, Will County, and Kankakee County, where four of the five sites were located, over 60 percent of the voters voted against the new jetport in ballot referendums.[43]

The Gary Airport Status in 1991

By the end of 1990, the Gary airport had made considerable progress. Direct Air, a commuter carrier, began service on June 11, 1990, to Pittsburgh and Detroit with two flights to each daily. The firm of R.W. Armstrong developed a $17.5 million improvement plan, which was adopted by the board on March 28, 1990. This plan, similar to portions of the 1978 Gary Airport Board Development Program and almost identical to the Mid-

Range Part I Program adopted by the Promotion and Development Commission on April 16, 1987, was a major step forward. R.W. Armstrong recommended an immediate application to the FAA for $3.2 million to upgrade the runways.[44] As stated earlier, $2.5 million was appropriated by the U.S. Department of Transportation's Secretary Sam Skinner for this very purpose as part of the deal requiring Mayor Barnes and Governor Bayh to keep quiet about the addition of Chicago Mayor Richard M. Daley's Lake Calumet site for third airport consideration and of three members of his choice to the eight member bistate site election committee. This grant would certainly help Barnes in his reelection bid in May 1991, but one could argue that it came two years later than it should have.

As the year 1991 began, the Census Bureau had bad news for Gary. Their preliminary figures released on January 19, 1991, showed that Gary's population had decreased from 151,953 in 1980 to only 116,646 in 1990, a 23 percent drop. Although Hammond and East Chicago also lost population, their decreases were minuscule compared with Gary's. Gary now had fewer residents than at any time since 1940. Actually, the entire northwest Indiana region lost population. Lake County's population dropped from 522,564 to only 475,594, a 9 percent decrease. Porter County had a slight increase—from 119,476 to 128,932, an 8 percent boost—but the entire two-county SMSA still lost almost 40,000 people between 1980 and 1990. The reason for the regional population decline was the loss of almost 50,000 jobs in manufacturing, mostly steel and steel-related, between 1980 and 1990.

For the first time since its founding in 1906, Gary's black community lost population. In 1980, there were 107,000 black Garyites, but that figure dropped to only 94,000 in 1990, a 12.1 percent decrease. The Lake-Porter Metropolitan Statistical Area's black population decreased from 126,000 in 1980 to 117,000 in 1990, a 7.1 percent drop. Even though some 3,500 blacks moved from Gary, Hammond, and East Chicago to Lake and Porter County's suburbs between 1980 and 1990, nine thousand blacks left the region altogether (see table 13). In 1980, 99.5 percent of the region's black population was confined to the central cities of Gary, East Chicago, and Hammond. By 1990, 96.9 percent of all blacks resided in these cities. So while a few middle-class blacks found their way to the suburbs, nineteen of twenty blacks were still confined to central-city ghettos.

The Gary mayoral primary began to take shape as soon as the new year began. Mayor Barnes announced he was running for reelection and was quickly joined in the race by former mayor Richard G. Hatcher, Dozier Allen, and Scott King, a young white attorney and political newcomer. Barnes ran on his record of success in working with the region's business establishment and state government, claiming that he needed four more years to undo the 20 years of damage wrought by his predecessor. Hatcher accused Barnes of giving away the city with his $130 million tax abatement

Table 13. Distribution of Northwest Indiana's Black Population, 1980 and 1990
(Gary-Hammond-East Chicago MSA)

	1980			1990		
	Total Population	Black Population	% Black	Total Population	Black Population	% Black
Central Cities						
Gary	151,953	107,644	70.8	116,646	93,982	80.6
East Chicago	39,786	11,802	29.7	33,892	11,379	33.6
Hammond	93,714	5,995	6.4	84,236	7,743	9.2
Total	285,453	125,441	43.9	234,774	113,104	48.2
Suburbs						
Crown Point	16,455	158	1.0	17,728	259	1.5
Griffith	17,026	28	.2	17,916	434	2.4
Highland	25,935	29	.1	23,696	56	.2
Hobart	22,987	43	.2	21,822	48	.3
Lake Station	14,294	3	>.1	13,899	31	.2
Merrillville	27,677	36	.1	27,257	1,367	5.0
Munster	20,671	23	.1	19,949	87	.4
Schereville	13,209	36	.3	19,926	143	.7
Remainder— Lake County	79,258	254	.3	78,627	1,159	1.5
Portage	27,409	30	.1	29,060	117	.4
Valparaiso	22,247	177	.8	24,414	142	.6
Remainder— Porter County	70,160	92	.1	75,458	195	.3
Total	357,328	909	.3	369,752	4,038	1.1
Total—Lake County	522,965	126,051	24.1	475,594	116,688	24.5
Total—Porter County	119,816	299	.3	128,932	454	.4

Note: In 1980, 126,350 blacks resided in MSA. Of this number, 125,441 (99.5 percent) resided in central cities. In 1990, the total MSA black population dropped to 117,142, of which 113,104 (96.8 percent) resided in central cities.

over ten years to U.S. Steel in exchange for allowing a marina to be constructed on property they owned. Dozier Allen stressed his experience as township trustee and a longtime Democratic party political operative. Scott King, backed by an unlikely coalition of young blacks dissatisfied with all longterm Gary politicians, elderly whites who remained in Gary, and the Gary police and firefighter unions, insisted that a new face was needed to bring business and industry back to Gary and that he was that person.

The major issue in this campaign was the debate over casino gambling. In 1988, Indiana voters repealed a state constitutional ban on gambling of any kind and also approved a state lottery. Mayor Barnes petitioned the legislature to allow casino gambling in Gary to improve the city's economy. The casinos would be located at the abandoned U.S. Steel's Buffington Harbor on Lake Michigan's west end, a convenient thirty-minute drive for Chicagoans but physically separated from Gary's residential and commercial areas (see figure 4). Governor Bayh initially promised to consider the matter but then, after complaints from church groups, including some in Gary, shot the measure down by threatening a veto.

Barnes then decided that a nonbinding referendum in the November 1989 general election would send a signal to the legislature that Gary citizens were solidly behind casino gambling. He and State Senator Carolyn B. Mosby actively campaigned for the referendum to bring national attention to this issue.[45] The referendum passed by a four-to-one margin, and, three weeks later, Senator Mosby died of cancer at age 57. In the 1990 legislative session, both Bayh and Joe Hogsett, his secretary of state, campaigned against the referendum, and it was bottled up in committee. This angered Gary residents, and some younger dissidents within the city's Democratic party committee called for a boycott of Hogsett when he would come up for election in November 1990. However, Mayor Barnes and Gary's political establishment felt that a fight of that type would jeopardize the support needed from the Bayh administration for the Gary airport. In the fall of 1990, Mayor Barnes and Deputy Mayor Comer personally crushed a revolt by "young Turks" John Key and Keith Rogers, the son of Gary State Senator Earline Rogers and a former student of mine at IUN. In opposition to Hogsett because of his opposition to casinos, Key and Rogers organized a "Say No to Joe" rally on the steps of city hall on October 28, 1990. Only five people attended because Hogsett was given a strong endorsement by Mayor Barnes, Dozier Allen, Indiana Democratic Party Chairman Michael Pannos, and several precinct captains.[46]

In the 1991 legislative session, a new casino bill was prepared by Gary leaders and introduced in the legislature. It called for revenue distribution as follows: $45 million annually to be spent on Gary capital projects including health care facilities, schools, and police and fire equipment; $17 million annually to repay the bonds that would be used to build roads, sewers, and other infrastructure needs for the casinos; $16 million annually in property tax relief for Gary, 45 percent of which would go to U.S. Steel; and $65 million annually in revenue-sharing to cities throughout the state on a population basis. This bill was strongly supported by suburban business interests and elected officials, including Chester A. Dobis, the architect of

Metrolake. Hatcher blasted the bill, stating, "This bill is as anti-Gary as perhaps any piece of legislation I have seen introduced in the Indiana legislature." He was particularly chagrined about the revenue-sharing pro vision, which would give to Gary only $1.12 million of the $65 million distributed annually, and about U.S. Steel's property tax windfall of almost $8 million annually. Stated Hatcher, "I know our legislators drafted this bill, but I have a feeling the USX attorneys were in the room." Hatcher also stated that the composition of the two commissions that would control the casinos was poor because there was no requirement for minority group inclusion.[47] After almost three months of debate, the casino bill passed in the house but was bottled up in the Senate Finance Committe and died just before the legislature adjourned on April 30, 1991.[48]

On Sunday, May 5, the *Post-Tribune* gave Mayor Barnes a strong endorsement for reelection. Stated the *Post-Tribune*, "Gary Mayor Thomas V. Barnes deserves to be re-elected to a second term so that he can continue his work to improve Gary." The *Post-Tribune* dismissed the other candidates: Hatcher because he "has done little during the campaign to suggest that he has changed his attitudes or tactics," Dozier Allen because his plans for Gary were "sketchy and at best unworkable," and Scott King because he "lacks the management and organizational experience that would lead us to believe he can marshall the solutions."

On election day, 37,632 votes were cast; only 52 percent of all registered voters turned up at the polls. Mayor Barnes was reelected with 45 percent of the vote. Former Mayor Hatcher was a distant second with 25 percent, and newcomer Scott King received 23 percent of the vote to finish third. Dozier Allen was way behind in fourth place with only 5 percent of the vote.

Richard M. Daley was also a big winner in early 1991. In the February 27 primary he won 65 percent of all votes cast against only 29 percent for Cook County Commissioner Danny K. Davis, a former protégé of the late Harold Washington. Former Mayor Jane M. Bryne trailed badly with only 6 percent of the vote. Daley won 92 percent of the white vote and 12 percent of the black vote. Danny Davis won only 3 percent of the white vote and 84 percent of the black vote, but only 35 percent of black registrants turned out compared with over 60 percent of white registrants. Daley went on to win the April general election with 70 percent of the vote.

Finally, on February 24, 1992, the bistate commission voted 6-4-1 to build the third airport on the Lake Calumet site. All three Chicago representatives were joined by three Illinois members to provide the winning margin. The four Indiana representatives all voted for Gary. Illinois representative State Senator Aldo DeAngeles voted against both Lake Calumet and Gary, arguing that these sites would prove to be unbuildable because of environmental problems.[49] The Indiana contingent, led by D. William

Moreau, Governor Bayh's aide, put on their best face after the vote, with Moreau stating, "We came out of this process with Gary as the alternative site."[50]

Changing Pilots During Takeoff

When the Barnes administration took office on Janury 2, 1988, the future of Gary's airport was promising. Peat, Marwick and Mitchell had ranked the site tops among all contenders for third Chicago area airport designation. Indiana Senators Lugar and Quayle were not only supportive of Gary's airport as the third Chicago facility but they prevailed successfully on the Federal Aviation Administration to set aside its objection to Gary's expansion interfering with the Chicago aviation airspace. Support for Gary's airport expansion was widespread among northwest Indiana's business, political, institutional, and civic leadership even in communities such as Merrillville, Hammond, and Hobart, which traditionally had been hostile toward Gary. Mayor Barnes had the support of the *Post-Tribune*, a long-time Hatcher critic as that paper welcomed Barnes relatively low-keyed diplomatic approach as contrasted with Hatcher's strident rhetoric. The *Post-Tribune* continued to be supportive of Mayor Barnes even when he made it known that he would never accept regional control of the Gary airport.

However, this "window of opportunity," as phrased by former airport authority director Dr. A. William Douglas, all but closed in a bitter, divisive two-year battle between the new board appointed by Mayor Barnes and the old board who were Hatcher loyalists. As a result, no one had a hand on the cockpit controls until February 1990 when the courts, for all practical purposes, sided with Mayor Barnes, and his appointees were seated. During this two-year hiatus, much was lost or at least deferred. Commuter airline service, which could have started in 1988, didn't begin until 1990. The initial federal grants for airport expansion could have been awarded in 1988 but weren't allocated until October 1990. The third airport momentum was lost and by the time Gary's airport leadership was in place and speaking with one voice, Chicago and Mayor Richard M. Daley had entered the fray and all but taken over. Secretary Skinner's "deal" with Daley might not have taken place if the Promotion and Development Commission's Program had been pushed forward. If the Commission's recommendations had been vigorously endorsed by all participants by 1989, Gary would not only have had commuter airline service but would have been fielding a jet flight program to cities such as Detroit, Pittsburg, New York, Dallas, West Palm Beach, Tampa, Orlando, and Miami, and perhaps a route or two to the Caribbean or Mexico. With this level of activity *before* 1990, Gary could have presented a case so strong that with continued endorsement by Senators Lugar and Coates, Skinner could have forced Daley to back off. Whose fault was it for the struggle over the cockpit controls when the Gary Regional Airport was trying so hard to take off and fulfill its potential? After three years of reflection upon my experiences in Gary, I have concluded that the fault lies almost entirely with the former Hatcher administration.

A major rule in politics in a civilized society is that the loser congratulates the winner and then stands back and allows the victor to run their own operation without interference. Whe Mayor Hatcher lost in the May 1987 Democratic party primary, he did not endorse Barnes from the time of his defeat until he left office on December 31, 1987. The lack of an endorsement had a chilling effect on any potential exchange of ideas and information between Hatcher administration staffers and the Barnes organization. With virtually no transition, although there were eight months between May and January for it to take place, Mayor Hatcher did to Barnes almost the same thing that the embittered administration of Martin Katz did to Hatcher in 1967 after *they* lost the primary. There was no transition in 1967 either after the primary or the November election, and when Mayor Hatcher went to city hall on January 1, 1968, to start work, he found the doors to city hall chained shut. While Mayor Barnes didn't find the doors chained when he started work as mayor on January 1, 1988, there were still some invisible barriers present as the equally embittered Hatcher administration left office the evening before.

Certainly Mayor Barnes had the right to request resignation of Hatcher-appointed members to all city boards and commissions, including those on the Airport Board of Authority. Under Gary's strong mayor form of government, the mayor has the right to name and dismiss members of these boards, something the Federal Court of Appeals agreed with at least in principle. If Mayor Barnes had been able to proceed with his own board from the beginning, the Gary airport would have made substantially more progress than they were able to with the burden of dealing with dual leadership for two years.

Did white racism negatively impact Gary's chances for designation as the third Chicago area airport? Again, after reflection I conclude that to a certain extent it existed and did have a negative effect. When Peat, Marwick and Mitchell first indicated that Gary was its first choice, Indiana's Lieutenant Governor John Mutz's statement that "legislation of some sort probably would be needed to create the proper oversight agency" was unnecessary. Instead, Mutz and then Governor Robert Orr should have chided the state of Illinois for rejecting the Peat, Marwick and Mitchell study that recommended Gary as the first choice. As a Gary resident from 1982 to 1987 and a close observer of conditions there ever since, I felt that Mutz and Orr would have strongly denounced those who cast aspersions on Peat, Marwick and

Mitchell's study if the Gary Airport was run by a regional body. The other members of Indiana's component of the bistate commission dropped the Peat, Marwick and Mitchell report because they thought a new study would recommend an Indiana rural site. They were dead wrong. Also, Governor Bayh's premature questioning of Gary's viability for third airport designation because of preliminary consultant estimates of relocation needs was an indicator of soft support. The Governor's action would in all probability not have occurred had the airport been located in a city headed by a nonblack mayor. Also, on another issue, one wonders if Governor Bayh would have been so opposed to casino gambling in an Indiana city other than Gary.

While the previous paragraph is one of speculation, one must understand that in the 1990s racism is more subtle than ever but still present not only in Indiana but all over America. Governor Bayh is not going to make a statement to the effect that blacks cannot run an airport but, knowing that he is a knowledgeable and capable public official and that he is keenly aware of the history of strident and blatant racism against blacks in Gary and elsewhere in Indiana, one would be led to believe that he would be outspoken in support of the Gary airport expansion in order to remove all doubt about possible racial bias toward Gary. An example of the softness of Evan Bayh's administration to the Gary airport expansion was the lack of promotion for the Gary site compared to the all-out promotion of the Lake Calumet site by Mayor Daley of Chicago. By December 1990, Chicago had named a panel of corporate, civic, labor, and other community leaders to drum up support for Lake Calumet. Chicago had distributed a newsletter to communities that were to be affected. Included in the newsletter were messages from Daley, facts and figures on job creation and how airport-generated revenue would relocate people dislocated by the project. Understanding that because all five sites met the technical requirements the selection would be based on politics, Chicago felt that mobilizing public support would make the difference. Stated Robert Repel, an aide to Mayor Daley, "They [airports] are built because of political consensus and commitments to get things done."[51]

On the other hand, by the end of 1990, the Bayh administration had done no promotion work for the Gary airport except to commission an $80,000 public relations study by Cassidy Associates, a marketing consulting firm out of Washington, D.C., and to hire William Staehle, former Gary planning director and Indiana University Northwest administrator, as an "airport advocate" at $45,000 per year.[52] Cassidy and Associates completed their study in May 1990, but Indiana officials refused to release its recommendations, prompting the *Post-Tribune* to file suit in Lake County Superior Court for the study to be released. By the end of 1990, none of the recommendations of the Cassidy report had been acted upon.[53] When questioned about Indiana's lack of effort in promoting the Gary site, Bayh's top airport aide Thomas Koutsoumpas could only state, "The fact that they [Chicago] have started a bit ahead of us is not that important." [54] A *Post-Tribune* editorial on November 25 urged that work on the Gary airport expansion begin as soon as possible and chided the Bayh administration for "conflicting messages" on the Gary site. [55]

Finally, support for the Gary airport expansion from the state of Indiana and northwest Indiana's white business institutional and political community should have come in 1978. It need not have waited until 1991 when the latter group had the mayor of their choice seated in Gary and finally realized that the city's airport was their only option for the area's economic recovery. By waiting thirteen years to back airport expansion in Gary, northwest Indiana lost an opportunity to place itself in a commanding position for being designated as the third Chicago area airport. Support in 1978 would have by 1988 assured that Peat, Marwick and Mitchell's recommendation of Gary as the third airport site would have been implemented without serious opposition as the Indiana governor's office and both U.S. Senate seats were held by Republicans with close ties to the Reagan administration and the U.S. Department of Transportation. The refusal of prominent white leaders to endorse and support the airport authority's 1978 expansion plan hurt not only Gary but the entire region, and there was no reason for it other than thinly veiled racism.

In Atlanta, the city's airport board designed and constructed a $200 million terminal complex between 1975 and 1978 with state and federal funds despite attempts by some rural Georgia legislators to create a state agency to take over the city's airport. These "good ole boys" were rebuffed by Atlanta's corporate elites: Coca Cola, Delta Airlines, and Southern Bell, who felt that a takeover fight would be bad for business. In Gary, however, the attitude on the part of the white business elites was that they preferred no airport at all unless suburbanites of their choice would run it. That attitude made no sense. If the proposal was to create a bistate aviation authority like the Port Authority of New York, a compelling argument could have been made, as the operators of O'Hare and Midway airports would have brought "hands-on" technical expertise from a background of seventy years of running major aviation facilities. But this was never called for by the northwest Indiana leadership. They wanted a regional agency headed by themselves where the only northwest Indiana experience in running an airport designated as a reliever for O'Hare and Midway was in Gary. Where was their expertise, as Mayor Hatcher talked about in our initial conversation regarding the Gary airport in 1983? In the absence of any logical reason, one must conclude that racism guided their thoughts and that in doing so they hurt themselves more than anyone else.

At any rate, Bayh's lack of forceful commitment to the Gary airport for whatever reason created a situation in which, when eyeball to eyeball deals had to be made between Bayh, Daley, and U.S. Transportation Secretary Sam Skinner, Bayh was left without any real cards. All the other players knew Bayh's commitment was soft; therefore, all Bayh and Indiana Senators Lugar and Coates (if they cared) could bargain for was a $2.5 million grant for improving the Gary airport runways, one the Gary airport board had applied for beforehand and, based on merit, could have eventually received anyway. Mutz and Orr's refusal in 1988 to demand implementation of the Peat, Marwick and Mitchell recommendations, which favored Gary as the third airport site, and then Bayh's softness on the issue did the entire state of Indiana a disservice.

8

Implications of the Gary Experience

At the beginning of this book, I indicated that the purpose and direction here was essentially to utilize urban planning and development, which always takes place in a political context, as a "lens" to examine the much broader issue of the dynamics of black governance (i.e., a city headed by a black mayor with a majority-black legislative body that in most instances would be a city council). Not only would the three case studies presented here add to the body of knowledge concerning majority-black governance, but the experiences of Gary, which during the 1970s and early 1980s might have been unique to that city, are now transferable to many more urban places. In 1970, there were only 7 cities with populations of 50,000 or more that were majority black; that number rose to 15 in 1980 and 25 in 1990. There were only 153 cities in 1970 with population of 2,500 or more that were majority black, and, in 1980, this number had risen to 224, an increase of 46.4 percent.[1] The 1990 U.S. Census showed that 275 cities and places nationwide with populations of over 2,500 were majority black (see table 14), an increase of 79 percent since 1970. Therefore, lessons learned in Gary during the 1980s can be transferred, to some degree, to almost 300 urban places nationally in the 1990s.

Although I have not mentioned cities with Hispanic and Asian majorities, the experiences and accompanying lessons, though by no means identical to those with black majorities, are similar. In 1980, San Antonio, Texas, had a Hispanic majority, mostly Mexican-American (Chicano), while Miami and Dade County in Florida now have Hispanic majorities. Westminster and Garden Grove, California, now, according to estimates by the Orange County Planning Department, have Asian majorities mostly made up of recent immigrants from Vietnam and other Southeast Asian nations. These Hispanic and Asian majority cities are growing at a faster

Table 14. Changes in Black Population Dynamics in the United States

	Counties with a Black Population of 50,000 or more	Places with a Black Population of 50,000 or more	Places of 2,500 or more Total Population with a Black Population of 50% or more	Places of 1,000-2,500 Total Population with a Black Population of 50% or more
1970	74	48	153	88
1980	93	62	224	151
1990				
Northeast	23	11	21	1
Midwest	19	18	32	11
South	60	34	214	174
West	10	8	8	1
Total	112	71	275	187
% Change, 1970-1990	+51.4	+47.9	+79.7	+112.5

Sources: 1980 Census of Population: Summary Characteristics of the Black Population for States and Selected Counties and Places, issued January 1987; 1990 U.S. Census Preliminary Data PL-94-171.

rate than majority-black urban places in terms of numbers. Like majority-black cities, those with Hispanic and Asian majorities face discrimination on the part of local white business, institutional, civic, and political elites and those in surrounding cities and the region who resent having to share meager and constantly dwindling resources with these "new kids on the block."

Therefore, I postulate that the experiences of Gary during the 1980s have implications that are far-reaching. If those in positions of power can learn from the Gary experience, then perhaps the mistakes of Gary will not be repeated. These mistakes include but are not limited to white flight on the part of businesses and professions from the central core, refusal of white elites to respect Gary leaders as capable equals, and attempts by those elites to undermine the city and thereby, especially in the airport case, undermine themselves.

Types of Majority-Black Cities

In Chapter 1, we noted that in 1980 there were fifteen majority-black cities in the United States with populations over fifty thousand. We also discussed that all black mayors, even those in majority-black cities, could not be grouped together; there were significant differences in degrees of power for mayors depending on whether the governmental form was strong mayor, weak mayor, or council manager. Mayors in strong mayor governmental forms have the most power, and those in council manager forms have the least amount of power.

By 1990, after ten additional years in the evolution of majority-black (and other minority) cities, some additional differentiations may be noted. I classify majority-black cities in three distinct categories: Type I—large central cities with populations of 50,000 or more, significant presences of multiple Fortune 500 corporation headquarters, and/or at least one four-year university of 5,000 students or more, and/or health care centers with at least 1,000 patient beds each; Type II—other cities of 50,000 or more people without multiple Fortune 500 corporation headquarters and/or universities of 5,000 students or more; and Type III—cities with populations between 2,500 and 50,000. The figure of 50,000 minimum population is significant because it is one criterion by which the census bureau designated central cities or cities of the first order. It is also the minimum population level for designation by federal agencies as an "entitlement" city for automatic receipt of monies from programs such as the Community Development Block Grant from the U.S. Department of Housing and Urban Development.[2]

Type I cities (see table 15) are, in order of total 1990 population size, Detroit; Baltimore; Memphis; Washington, D.C.; New Orleans; Atlanta; Newark; Birmingham; Richmond, Virginia; Jackson, Mississippi; Savannah; Camden, New Jersey; Wilmington, Delaware; and Harrisburg, Pennsylvania. All these cities have Fortune 500 corporation headquarters or major universities, as previously defined, or at least one major health care institution with 1,000 patient beds each. The presence of corporate headquarters, universities, health care centers, and, in Jackson and Harrisburg, state capitols, is important because (1) they are placebound for the most part and therefore have long-term vested interests in the city, (2) the leadership is well educated, enlightened, and usually not wedded to old prejudices that preclude doing business with black mayors and majority black city councils, and (3) especially for those cities with major universities, there is a critical mass of scholars in a variety of disciplines that can provide direct assistance to city governments and a pool of recent and former graduates who have chosen to remain and enrich these cities' cultural, social, and civic life. The presence of these three elements means that Type I cities can reasonably expect to develop and maintain strong central business districts and at least one or two "upscale" neighborhoods with attractive physical environments, good schools and recreation facilities and adequate infrastructure. They will still have to fight major problems such as crime, a deteriorating physical plant, out-migration of the white *and* black middle class, loss of adequate jobs, and a declining tax base, making the provision of public services extremely difficult. And of course, all three types of cities

Table 15. Characteristics of Type I and II Majority-Black Cities (Ranked by Total 1990 Population Size)

City	Total Population	% Black	# Fortune 500 Corp. HQ's	# B.E. 100 HQ's	4-Year Universities (5000+ Students)	Total # of Students at 4-Yr. Univ. in 1988
Type I: Detroit	1,027,974	75.7	5	15	2	35,000
Baltimore	736,014	59.2	2	3	3	17,200
Memphis	610,337	54.8	2	1	1	31,500
Washington, D.C.	606,900	65.8	4	9	6	70,600
New Orleans	496,308	62.0	2	3	2	26,400
Atlanta	394,017	67.1	9	8	3a	40,400
Newark, N.J.	275,221	58.5	3	2	2	17,200
Birmingham, Ala.	265,968	63.3	0	0	1	24,300
Richmond, Va.	203,056	55.2	7	5	2	19,202
Jackson, Miss.	196,637	55.7	1	0	1	11,000
Savannah, Ga.	137,560	51.3	1	1	1	6,000
Camden, N.J.	87,492	56.4	1	0		5,000
Wilmington, Del.	71,529	52.4	3	0	1b	18,600
Harrisburg, Penn.	52,376	50.6	0	0	1	11,500
Type II: **Gary, Ind.**	**116,646**	**80.6**	**0**	**2**	**1**	**5,000**
Inglewood, Calif.	109,602	51.9	0	0	0	0
Macon, Ga.	106,612	52.2	0	0	0	3,800
Compton, Calif.	90,454	54.8	0	0	0	0
Albany, Ga.	78,122	55.0	0	0	0	2,100
East Orange, N.J.	73,552	90.0	0	1	0	3,100
Mt. Vernon, N.Y.	67,153	55.3	0	0	0	0
Irvington TWP, N.J.	61,018	70.0	0	0	0	0
Pine Bluff, Ark.	57,140	53.5	0	0	0	2,500
Monroe, La.	54,909	55.6	0	0	1	11,000

Sources: 1990 Rand McNally Marketing Guide; June 1990 *Black Enterprise Magazine*; U.S. Census, 1980 and 1990.

[a] The Atlanta University Center: six member colleges are counted as one university.

[b] The University of Delaware is located in Newark, ten miles from downtown Wilmington.

will have to deal with potentially hostile white elites in the local and regional business and institutional community.

Type II cities by 1990 included Gary; Albany and Macon, Georgia; Inglewood and Compton, California; East Orange and Irvington Township, New Jersey; Pine Bluff, Arkansas; Monroe, Louisiana; and Mount Vernon, New York. Though these cities do not have the attributes of corporate headquarters, major universities, and health care institutions present in Type I centers,[3] the critical mass of population alone creates a situation in which a variety of neighborhoods and housing types with varying degrees of quality for both are present. All these cities contain at least one neighborhood of attractive single-family detached homes with adequate community facilities. Of these, only Gary, Albany, Pine Bluff, Monroe, and Macon can be considered central cities. The others are actually large suburbs of even larger cities that became majority black because of ghetto expansion from the central city.[4] Also, the fact that, because of population size, these cities qualify for entitlement federal aid programs gives their leaders more flexibility than do mayors of Type III cities.

Type III cities are perhaps the most fragile. First of all, the term "city" is actually a misnomer, almost one-quarter are simply urban places, unincorporated county enclaves. These places must rely on the generosity of the county for maintenance of basic services, but county government has no political reason to do so. For example, Willowbrook is an unincorporated urban place in Los Angeles County just south of Los Angeles. Its 32,000 mostly black and Hispanic residents are governed essentially by a five-member board of supervisors in a county with over 8 million people, over 1 million of which reside in unincorporated urban county islands. Each supervisor represents over 1.6 million residents. Therefore, what impact can 30,000 people have on that supervisor, especially when they are poor and minority? (See table 16.)

Even for the three-quarters that are self governing, most are either suburban or rural entities surrounded and dominated by larger white cities and/or counties. Over two-thirds of these places or cities are located in the Deep South where until the late 1960s most blacks could not even vote. Even though today actual personal discrimination is no different in the South than in the Northeast or Midwest, longstanding attitudes present a silent, invisible barrier to social change in a way not present elsewhere in the nation.

Many cities, such as Belle Glade, Florida, despite having a black majority, are still controlled politically by whites who also control the local public school systems, health care institutions, and public social service networks. Examples of Type III cities include Harvey, Illinois, just south of Chicago; Riviera Beach, Florida, sixty miles north of Miami; Plainfield,

Table 16. Black-Owned Businesses in 1987
(Total Black Population 80,000 to 130,000)

City	Total Population	Black Population	% Black	# of Firms	1980 Sales	Per Capita Sales: City	Estimated MSA pop.	Per Capita Sales: MSA
Gary, Ind.	**151,953**	**107,644**	**70.8**	**1,302**	**$ 99,771,000**	**$656.59**	**624,300**	**$159.81**
Cincinnati, Oh.	385,457	130,467	33.9	2,752	123,249,000	319.75	1,442,700	85.47
Boston, Mass.	562,871	126,729	22.5	3,191	197,578,000	351.00	2,841,000	69.54
Columbus, Oh.	564,871	124,880	22.1	2,775	84,235,000	149.12	1,334,000	63.14
Kansas City, Mo.	448,159	122,699	27.4	3,039	160,584,000	358.45	1,567,700	102.41
Nashville, Tenn.	455,651	105,942	23.3	2,745	95,612,000	209.84	985,000	97.06
Pittsburgh, Penn.	423,938	101,813	24.0	1,970	99,867,000	235.56	2,109,100	47.35
Charlotte, N.C.	314,447	97,627	31.1	3,003	142,778,000	454.13	1,113,100	128.28
Jackson, Miss.	202,895	95,357	47.0	2,405	145,883,000	718.64	402,500	361.99
Buffalo, N.Y.	357,870	95,116	26.6	945	66,575,000	186.03	966,100	68.91
Norfolk, Va.	266,979	93,987	35.2	2,565	119,264,000	446.68	1,372,300	86.92
Ft. Worth, Tx.	385,164	87,723	22.8	2,467	65,641,000	170.42	1,277,800	51.40
San Francisco, Calif.	678,974	86,414	12.7	3,131	140,058,000	206.27	1,606,500	87.21
Shreveport, La.	205,820	84,627	41.1	1,270	36,351,000	176.53	362,700	100.14
Louisville, Ky.	298,451	84,080	28.2	1,851	62,030,000	207.84	968,300	64.09
Baton Rouge, La.	219,419	80,088	36.5	2,195	81,498,000	371.43	543,200	150.08

Source: 1987 Economic Census, Survey of Minority Owned Businesses, Black, MB87-1 U.S. Department of Commerce Bureau of the Census.

New Jersey; and East Cleveland, Ohio. All these cities are essentially suburbs of large cities with residential areas ranging from sound and attractive to deteriorating. Others, such as Belzoni and Holly Springs, Mississippi, and Eudora, Arkansas, in the Mississippi River Delta are extremely poor communities with dilapidated housing and with infrastructure and health conditions much like those of Third World countries.

Tables 14 and 15 show the various types of cities that are majority black and black governed. Given the three types of black-governed cities and places, the experiences of Gary are most transferable to its Type II sisters: Camden, New Jersey, and, perhaps to a lesser extent, Compton, California, and East Orange, New Jersey. However, there is some degree of transferability from Gary to the others who are bound together by being a majority-black city or urban place in a majority-white nation.

Comparing the Hatcher and Barnes Administrations

Chapters 2 through 6 examined the administration of Richard G. Hatcher, and Chapter 7 reflected on the accomplishments of Thomas V. Barnes as mayor. At this point, a comparison of the two administrations is in order. We must, of course, take into consideration that Hatcher's administration was in office for a twenty-year period but that, at this writing, the Barnes administration had completed just over four years in office.

The Hatcher Administration.   The fact that Richard Hatcher survived as mayor of Gary for twenty years, winning reelection four times by significant and, in all but one case, landslide majorities, is an accomplishment by itself. It is rare for mayors of cities with populations over 150,000 to last that long, and, in this nation during the twentieth century, only one other man, Richard J. Daley, mayor of Chicago from 1955 until his death in 1977, has done so. Thomas Bradley of Los Angeles and Coleman Young of Detroit will reach their twenty-year marks in 1993, but their situations are entirely different from that of Hatcher in Gary. Both were first elected in 1973 when, thanks to Hatcher, Carl Stokes, and Kenneth Gibson, black big-city mayors were no longer a novelty. Their campaigns were not tarnished by racism to anywhere near the degree Hatcher's was. In Los Angeles, Bradley has enjoyed the benefit of a robust Sun Belt economy that hardly rippled during the 1979-1982 recession. The city actually gained population between 1970 and 1990 (2.7 million in 1970 and 3.5 million in 1990), which is extremely rare for central cities, even those in the Sun Belt. Young's Detroit did experience severe economic decline in the 1970s and 1980s with downturns in the automobile industry,[5] but, with the Big Three automakers and ten other Fortune 500 corporations headquartered in Detroit or nearby suburbs,

Coleman Young was able to enlist their clout in obtaining new automobile plants in the city, a people-mover system for the downtown area, and the massive Renaissance Center on the Detroit waterfront, as well as modest increases in white-collar service-oriented employment, as Detroit is a financial and business center for almost all of Michigan, northeast Indiana, and northwest Ohio.[6] Hatcher had none of the pluses enjoyed by Bradley or Young. How then, did he manage to stay in office for so long?

First of all, Hatcher came on to the mayoral scene when federal aid to cities was at an all-time high in constant dollars. During 1968, Hatcher was able to obtain almost $100 million in commitments from the Johnson administration for a wide variety of projects, including housing, urban renewal, model cities, youth employment, and various public works. When Nixon came to the presidency in 1969, most of these programs were either firmly in place or committed, and the Nixon-Ford administration that governed through 1976 could not stop them. When Jimmy Carter came into office in 1977, the money for Gary began to flow once more in abundance, and, by 1980, the federal government had given over $300 million to the city of Gary. Though the majority of these funds were for "soft" programs such as social services, job training, and employment preparation, much was in new housing and other capital improvements. By 1983, the Hatcher administration had built 1,300 units of new public housing and 1,100 units of moderate income section 235 and 236 housing and had placed 500 units in the Section 8 subsidy program, all of which were either new or rehabilitated dwellings. The administration built four new major parks, all with swimming pools, and, by 1986, major public works had been added, including the Genesis Convention Center, Transportation Center, Sheraton Hotel, the Genesis Towers and Knights of Columbus Senior Citizens' housing and a parks administration/fitness center. Four new schools were added, including the 3,000-pupil capacity West Side High School with a 5,000-seat gymnasium, a must for basketball-crazed Indiana. The airport expansion plan of 1977 was well on its way to implementation with a new terminal hangar and maintenance facilities completed by the time Hatcher left office. The new housing created a reality of improved conditions for many, and the new public works at least gave an illusion of better times to come. For many more, certainly, the federal aid and the projects and programs that resulted from it helped Hatcher's popularity with the masses.

Second, Hatcher, upon taking office, quickly went to work to reverse the pattern of city jobs bias against blacks. In 1967, though Gary's population was 50 percent black, blacks held only 28 percent of all city jobs, and only 5 percent of the police were black. Of 26 departments, only 2 were headed by blacks. By 1980, the pattern had changed to 75 percent of the jobs being held by blacks. A black chief of police was first appointed in 1974, and, by 1980, 55 percent of the police officers were black. Two of the four division heads were black, and, of 29 operating departments, 21 were headed by blacks and 2 by Hispanics. Also, the city work force had increased between 1968 and 1980 by 400 employees, most of whom were hired by the new federally funded programs. This new addition to the city's work force, though prohibited by federal law from engaging in political activity, was able to "cover" for 300 to 500 employees paid directly from city coffers when the time came for them to engage in political campaigning. With this reserve army of "volunteers," the Hatcher machine was able to steamroller opponents in Gary elections and assist favored Democrats in state and national elections.

A third reason for Hatcher's success was that his outspoken manner touched a chord among Gary's black voters. Even those Garyites who were not on the city or federally funded payrolls and those who were not living in one of the 3,000 new housing units built or rehabilitated by the administration could rejoice when Hatcher attacked white business and political leaders. Hatcher refused to bite his tongue and was quick to denounce white opponents as racists. While these denouncements didn't endear him to the white business and institutional community, they won points among black Garyites. As one Gary minister put it, "Most blacks here work for whites. When their supervisors do them wrong they'd love to tell them off, but they can't. When Mayor Hatcher talks bad about white folks, it's just like he's telling off these people's bosses. He's saying just what these people want to say but can't." [7]

Hatcher has been criticized by scholars William Nelson and Phillip Meranto as not building a power base that could last past his tenure as mayor. [8] Their book was published in 1979 and prepared during the period from 1974 to 1978. That observation may have been true in the 1970s, but, by 1983, the Hatcher Gary submachine was at its height. Hatcher's followers occupied a majority of the city council seats, all city boards and commissions had a majority of members who were his appointees, and the Gary Democratic Party Committee was solidly controlled by him. The state senator and all state representatives from Gary were Hatcher people. He was able to engineer the election of Katie Hall to the U.S. Congress. The machine's base was the Gary Democratic Party Committee. As Indiana law provides for elective offices to be held by the party, not the individual, if a vacancy occurs for the state legislature, city council, or any other elective office in Gary such as city judge, city clerk, or county council, it is the *committee* that elects the replacement, who then serves until the next primary or general election. With this mechanism in place, once blacks gained control of the Gary Democratic Party Committee, they ran an extremely effective machine that was in a position to reward friends and punish enemies. Barnes now controls the Gary machine Hatcher built.

Hatcher's strengths turned out eventually to be his weaknesses. He took over the Gary Democratic Party Committee and by the early 1980s turned it into an invincible machine. His use of federal funds for housing, employment, and public works won allegiance from thousands of voters. His outspokenness on racial issues won the admiration of tens of thousands of black Garyites. However, when unemployment and mass layoffs came to Gary during the 1979-1982 recession, the machine could do nothing to help, and the machine's leader was blamed by angry citizens and opportunistic local politicians. When, thanks to Reaganomics, federal funding was cut back, there were no new public works projects or housing developments to be initiated. Layoffs of city employees took place in 1983. Again, it was Hatcher who was blamed for the lack of new projects and the layoffs. Because Hatcher was outspoken and quick to cry racism to an already hostile *Post-Tribune*, the newspaper retaliated with a never-ending barrage of bad publicity about Gary. After 1986, with no new projects for Hatcher to point to, the voters tired more of the *Post-Tribune*'s negative portrayal of Gary and its citizens than they rejoiced vicariously at Hatcher's successful confrontations with white leaders. Because Hatcher literally controlled every aspect of Gary's political governance, he could never point the finger at anyone else. He had exclusive power, but at the same time he found himself with absolute responsibility.

Several scholars have noted through the years Hatcher's difficulties with the *Post-Tribune*.[9] Greer notes that the *Post-Tribune* was negative against Hatcher's 1967 mayoral candidacy from the beginning and refers to an article published on February 8, 1967, saying, "Hatcher, a lawyer, is a Negro. He's been told the city is not ready for a Negro mayor." Nelson and Meranto characterized the *Post-Tribune* as being extraordinarily harsh in its coverage of the Hatcher administration, "playing up mistakes and underplaying important accomplishments." Levine noted in 1974 that "during his first term of office, he did not receive any support from the *Gary Post-Tribune*." I have noted in the Metrolake and airport case studies the biased coverage of the Hatcher administration by the *Post-Tribune* as contrasted with balanced coverage by the nearby *Hammond Times*.

Why was the *Post-Tribune* so hard on Hatcher? Was it because of racism alone or were there other factors? There must have been other reasons besides race for the *Post-Tribune*'s opposition to Hatcher because, when Barnes took over, the *Post-Tribune* did an about-face. They were even neutral when Barnes first announced his opposition to regional control of the Gary airport and again when he attacked Governor Evan Bayh for being soft on the state's commitment to the Gary airport.

The reason for the *Post-Tribune*'s strident opposition to Hatcher may go back as far as 1966. In an interview in the September 16, 1966, issue of the Black Muslim newspaper *Muhammad Speaks,* Hatcher is quoted as saying, "As far as I'm concerned, the white community's interpretation of black power is irrelevant. Before a white man can talk to me about this, he'll first have to talk about white power which has been exercised so ruthlessly against black people. When he explains that, I'll talk about black power. If a man bombs my home from a plane or any other way I would demand that he be tried. Why can't the North Vietnamese try men who are bombing their homes? In any event, the United States should certainly find a way to get out of Vietnam. It's getting worse instead of better and there's no way of winning against the huge forces of Asia."[10]

One has to understand the nation's overall mood in 1966 to analyze the impact of that quote on Gary's white leadership, for which the *Post-Tribune* serves as a mouthpiece, according to Greer. In 1966, Stokeley Carmichael had just coined the term "black power," and it was opposed not only by most whites but by black leaders such as Dr. Martin Luther King, Roy Wilkins of the NAACP, and Whitney Young of the Urban League, all of whom feared a white backlash. Hatcher's remarks on black power, though appropriate when viewed from a perspective of twenty-five years, certainly did not make any friends in Gary's white leadership group. But his remarks about the communists North Vietnamese show trials of captured American pilots really offended not only Gary's white leaders but the rank and file white ethnic steel workers and their families. In 1966, while there was significant opposition to the Vietnam War, the majority of Americans supported U.S. policy in Southeast Asia, believing President Johnson's promise that "the boys would be home by Christmas of 1967." Not until the Tet Offensive of February 1968 did public opinion shift against the war. In 1966, support for the war was strong among steel workers because the need for ships, tanks, armored cars, and other war material meant a need for steel and thus job enhancement. Also, support for what was then viewed as a winnable war was in line with the blue-collar "kick-ass" mentality of Gary's white ethnic working class even though, ironically, it was that group's young men who were drafted and sent off to fight and die in the Asian jungles, along with blacks and Hispanics. Hatcher's remarks, therefore, were viewed as almost treasonable by this group and their leaders. With quotes like the one from *Muhammad Speaks,* it's no wonder the *Post-Tribune* viewed Hatcher as a radical and a communist sympathizer and as someone they couldn't control. With his outspoken rhetoric, including head-on attacks against racism, which continued throughout his tenure as mayor, it is understandable why the *Post-Tribune* despised him.

However, I feel that Hatcher's strident rhetoric was justifiable given the level of institutional and individual racism in Gary during the 1960s and 1970s and even in the 1980s. In order to mobilize popular support, he had to speak out against injustices by U.S. Steel, the business community, and county and state government and take appropriate action against Methodist Hospital when they tried to desert the city in 1974. A quieter, more agreeable mayor would not have lasted more than one or two terms. If Hatcher had the benefits of Tom Bradley's sunny Los Angeles boom economy or Coleman Young's tycoons like Henry Ford II, then perhaps he could have been more diplomatic. He did what he felt was right, and it happened to be expedient. Twenty years in office, $300 million in federal aid, thousands of city jobs for Gary blacks who had been excluded from them before 1968, 3,000 units of affordable new and rehabilitated housing and significant public works: these are his legacies. It will be another twenty years before one can determine if Gary's present and future mayors did better.

Hatcher's only shortcoming, in my opinion, was his failure to endorse Barnes after his May 1987 primary victory and work toward developing a dialogue and, as an outcome, a smooth transition. Had Hatcher done so, the two-year delay in making progress on the airport's expansion plan and the marina construction delay, among others, may have been avoided.

The Barnes Administration.   Two months before taking office, Thomas V. Barnes gave an indication as to his leadership style when after being asked whether he favored regional control of the Gary airport he replied, "No . . . what we need at this point is cooperation from other entities . . . we want an airport that works." [11] The statement was firm and to the point, avoiding the strident rhetoric of former mayor Hatcher. Barnes, once in office, repeated this posture on at least two other occasions. Once, when Bayh wavered on support for the Gary airport, Barnes said, "I don't want our own team to quit on us before the race is over. I can't abide insensitivity from the governor's office." On another occasion, Barnes, in a face-to-face meeting with Mayor Daley of Chicago, refused to back down on his contention that the Gary airport site was the best location for the third Chicago area airport. So in Barnes's four years in office he has cultivated an image as someone who wants to cooperate with county and state government as well as business leaders but who will still staunchly defend Gary's interests. The *Post-Tribune*'s response has been one of either neutrality or support for the Barnes administration. Gary voters spoke in May 1991 when Barnes defeated Dozier Allen, the Calumet township trustee, former Mayor Hatcher, and Scott King in the Democratic mayoral primary.

But after four full years in office, Mayor Barnes cannot point to any clear accomplishments. The airport is not much further along than it was in 1985 when Britt Airlines offered commuter flight service. The marina is still on the drawing board even though Barnes accommodated U.S. Steel with a ten-year $130 million tax abatement on the *expectation* that the steel giant will sell or lease enough of its vacant Lake Michigan property to facilitate marina construction. The city's landfill has reached capacity, and an alternate site has not been found. No new industry has come to town. The

Barnes administration put all its cards on casino gambling but, after four years of trying, still has not won a round. Gary's black middle class has started to move south to the suburbs of Merrillville, Crown Point, and even Valparaiso in order to be closer to shopping and take advantage of better schools and relatively crime-free environments.

But when all factors are considered, Mayor Barnes is doing as well as can be expected. Hatcher's refusal to support and endorse him after Barnes won the 1987 primary resulted in at least a two-year delay on several projects, including the airport and the marina. The Rust Belt economy is soft even for cities such as Chicago, Detroit, Cleveland, and Milwaukee. The state of Indiana, while saying all the correct things, was soft on pushing the Gary airport for expansion, which *would* have improved not only Gary's economy but that of the entire northwest Indiana region as well. Dwindling federal funding because of continued military buildups, the savings and loan scandal, and a $300 billion budget deficit for 1990 means that Mayor Barnes will probably never enjoy the luxury of federal monies available to Hatcher when he was mayor.

In short, both Hatcher and Barnes were right for their times. Given the racial climate in the late 1960s and 1970s, Hatcher's strident rhetoric was needed to prevent white elites from taking advantage of Gary and to mobilize Gary's voters into a strong, singleminded bloc that totalled over 85,000 registrations by 1984. Even as late as 1986, Hatcher's forceful manner was needed to crush Metrolake. However, by 1991, things were different. Northwest Indiana's leaders are finally reconciled to a Gary they cannot control and must do business with. With almost 400 black mayors nationally, 33 of which govern cities of 50,000 people or more, including 2 of the 4 largest, mayors of color are no longer a new and untested phenomenon. In 1990, the times call for a person of Mayor Barnes's temperament and leadership style. There is no reason not to believe that, in the years of 1991 to 2000, Gary will continue to do as well as it possibly can, given its circumstances.

Myths and Realities

Myths such as (1) blacks cannot manage or govern, (2) political empowerment is not transferable to economic empowerment, and (3) whites will be fair toward blacks if it is in their self-interest to do so, are difficult to pinpoint, identify, and then clarify. Very little is written about these matters, but they still exist. Wilber C. Rich states that "one of the widely held and rarely articulated issues during the Detroit People Mover Construction was in fact whether blacks were ready to manage and govern multimillion dollar corporations—The City of Detroit." [12] Eisenger, while not directly coming out and saying there is no transferability between blacks political empowerment and economic enhancement other than municipal jobs and contracts, tends to give one that opinion.[13] And the notion of doing what it takes to enhance one's self-interest is a basic societal value that needs no reference.

The experience of Gary, Indiana, and other majority-black cities especially during the 1980s cast new light on these concepts. Basically, that experience can be summed up as follows:

Myth: Blacks Cannot Manage or Govern
Reality: In the first place, black mayors who came on the scene in the late 1960s through the present time are extremely well educated. Both Hatcher and Barnes are attorneys as are Thomas Bradley in Los Angeles, Kurt Schomoke in Baltimore, and the late Harold Washington of Chicago. One, Dr. Lionel Arrington in Birmingham, Alabama, holds a Ph.D. Among the 35 blacks who hold the office of mayor in cities of 50,000 or more population, only one does not hold at least a bachelor's degree. Black mayors are at least as well educated as their white counterparts.

In both the Hatcher and Barnes administrations, top staffers were all suitably educated for the positions that they held. When I came to Gary in 1982, I had twenty-one years of professional experience as an urban planner working in Minneapolis, Los Angeles, Baltimore, Washington, D.C., New York City, Atlanta, and Tampa. During this time I had numerous opportunities to observe firsthand the detailed operations of city government: public hearings, staff conferences, one-to-one meetings and day-to-day working relationships. My work also took me to smaller towns such as San Bernardino, Oxnard, and Riverside, California; Plainfield, New Jersey; Albany and Batavia, New York; College Park, Macon, and St. Mary's, Georgia; and Opelika, Alabama. By 1987, as I left Gary, I could honestly say that the city's work force from the mayor to entry level professionals were, if anything, more competent than those in comparable white-led cities such as San Bernardino, Riverside, and Oxnard, California, and almost equal in competence to those in much larger cities. The major problem was poor equipment and overwork because of staff shortages caused by layoffs. Even with these handicaps, the city staff in Gary is quite capable.

When it comes to urban planning, black-majority cities have, if anything, more capable staffs than those of white majority-white-led counterpart cities. First of all, since the early 1980s, graduate schools of planning have been enrolling and graduating blacks at a rate of 8-10 percent of the total.[14] Blacks represent about 6 percent of all urban and regional planners in the nation compared to only 3 percent of lawyers and doctors, 4 percent of business managers, and 2 percent of engineers. Many of these planners after working in white cities or consulting firms find themselves "at home" in a black setting where racism is no longer a barrier to professional advancement.

Any problems black majority city mayors and their staffs have is not owing to incompetence. *Blacks can manage and govern.* The problems in managing and governing as shown in the Gary case studies, are caused by lack of financial resources to hire adequate numbers of staff and purchase equipment and lack of sincere cooperation on the part of the local and regional business community and suburban, county, and state governments.

Another troublesome aspect of this myth is the widely held notion that everything was fine in northeastern and midwestern U.S. cities, but when blacks took over city halls, decline set in. We discussed in Chapter 2, Gary's decline in terms of retail and service jobs between 1950 and 1965 and the drop in the rate of new construction in this city during the same time. Edward Greer in *Big Steel, Black Politics and Corporate Power in Gary, Indiana* details this phenomena, which of course took place *before* Richard Gordon Hatcher became Gary's mayor in 1968. Jeanne Lowe in *Cities in a Race with Time* details the same picture of decline for almost *all* U.S. cities between 1945 and 1965. After World War II, upwardly mobile white middle-class residents began to leave the cities for suburbia as soon as the Levittown Long Islands, and Park Forest, Illinois, were built for them. These suburban developments began to attract the new auto-oriented shopping centers such as Old Orchard and Evergreen Park outside of Chicago and Northland and Eastland just outside of Detroit, for example, as early as the mid-1950s, and they immediately took retail trade dollars from the city's downtowns. These older shopping centers evolved into the suburban edge cities of today such as Chicago's Schaumberg and Washington, D.C.'s Tyson's Corners, Virginia, and all of the billions of public and private monies invested in central business districts between 1960 and 1990 has failed to turn this tide.

The decline of central cities *before* the period of black mayoral victories between 1967 and the present is well known. To perpetuate the myth that black mayors equal initial decline is nothing more than an exercise in a racist interpretation of American urban history.

Myth: Political Empowerment Does Not Transfer to Economic Empowerment
Reality: First of all, this is a dangerous notion because it implies that as political empowerment only helps a few; elected officials and city job holders, blacks are just as well off with white led governments. Following this, if cities are white led, then businesses will feel more comfortable moving to that city or remaining there. When the Metrolake proposal came out in 1986, many black Garyites whom I encountered in the grocery stores,

barber shops, or just on the street said that with a white mayor, jobs and businesses would come to town and things would be better.

What tends to be overlooked is the reality that black political empowerment does result in enhancement of black-owned business. Of the top one hundred industrial/service businesses and the top one hundred automobile dealerships cited by the 1991 issue of *Black Enterprise* magazine, fifty, or 25 percent, were located in the twenty-four majority-black, black-led cities of 50,000 people or more, although the black population residing in these cities only accounted for 11 percent of the nation's total blacks. Another measure is shown by table 16. The U.S. Census report "Minority Owned Businesses, Black," published in 1989 with 1987 data shows the sales dollar volume of black businesses by SMSA. When Gary is compared to fifteen cities with similar sized black populations, we find that the sales volume of black businesses exceeded or equalled eight of the fifteen comparison cities. When one considers that these cities that surpassed Gary were either major regional business centers such as Boston, Cincinnati, Kansas City, Charlotte, and San Francisco; a major military center with plenty of Section 8.A minority assistance contracts such as Norfolk, Virginia; or a city such as Jackson, Mississippi, the state capital, a majority-black city by 1990, and home of a stable black business community that has been in place since the Civil War, Gary's accomplishments are even more notable as it has none of these attributes and is located in the declining Rust Belt Midwest. But when one looks at per capita sales in the SMSA, Gary leads all fifteen comparison cities except Jackson, Mississippi. Though this is not a definitive observation, it does indicate that some transferability to the black economic sector takes place when blacks are politically empowered.

Black businesses are certainly enhanced in terms of contracts and vendor services when black mayors are in power. For example, Georgia in 1980 had a black population of 1,465,181. Florida's 1980 black population was 1,342,688, almost the same. The 1990 Census showed Florida's black population at 1.7 million and Georgia's at 1.65 million. However, Georgia has a total of ten *Black Enterprise* top 100 firms, nine of which are located in Atlanta or its adjacent suburbs of Decatur, East Point, and College Park. Florida only had two *BE* 100 firms both located outside of the major Florida urban black population centers of Miami, Jacksonville, and Tampa. Florida, of course, has no large majority-black cities like Atlanta.

In Gary, the presence of black political domination since the mid-1970s has certainly paid off for black-owned business. In 1991, Gary had two *Black Enterprise* 100 companies: Powers and Sons Construction Company and Tom Gillespie Ford Automobile Dealer. Powers and Sons built many of the downtown public works projects during the Hatcher administration and based on that experience can now compete for jobs in the suburbs. Gillespie supplies the city of Gary with police cars. Both Mamon Powers, Jr., and

Tom Gillespie, Jr., acknowledged that being in a majority-black city makes a difference.

Myth: Whites Will Be Fair If It Is in Their Self-Interest to Do So
Reality: In Gary we found that white leadership elites would rather damage themselves than work with a black mayor for mutual benefit. The desertion of downtown Gary by the white business and professional class after Hatcher's 1971 reelection was expensive, divisive, and ultimately hurt the regional economy. The abandonment of downtown Gary by the two largest banks, the savings and loans, and related enterprises for Merrillville ten miles south and twenty minutes further from Chicago's Loop or downtown area meant longer travel times for executives when they had to visit Chicago's financial and business center. The two hospitals, Methodist and St. Mary's, chose to build brand new full-service facilities in the suburbs during the late 1970s even though the region's total population was declining and there was already a surplus of beds in their older headquarters.[15]

The airport is another case in point as it showed that whites would rather have no airport at all than support the expansion of Gary's airport unless they could control it. Their rationale for control was bankrupt, they had no expertise to offer, the airport was built and developed by the city of Gary, and they did not even show an interest in it until the late 1970s when air travel demand rose to a point where additional enplanement capacity was needed and expressway expansion made the Gary airport only a thirty-minute drive from downtown Chicago. State and county government, along with the northwest Indiana business community, steadfastly refused to support the Gary airport's 1977 expansion plan even though the airport expansion would have been a boon to the region's economy. When Barnes became mayor and the push for the third Chicago airport was initiated, soft, weak lip-service support from Indiana Governor Evan Bayh hurt Gary's chances of obtaining that designation and the economic development deliverables that would come for Chicago.

This phenomenon is not limited to Gary. Riviera Beach, Florida, is a majority-black city in the booming southeast Florida region. Its city water department, founded in 1914, has provided service to Riviera Beach residents for almost eighty years. The facilities are constantly updated and in recent memory there have been no instances of water main breaks or pollution that would of course disrupt service. In 1988, Seacoast, a private utility company that supplied water to an unincorporated area adjacent to Riviera Beach, decided to go out of business. Riviera Beach bid for the service along with Palm Beach Gardens, a consortium of other small recently incorporated municipalities and Palm Beach County. Riviera Beach had the lowest proposed rates lines adjacent to those of Seacoast and familiarity with operating details of the private utility's system. Still, the mostly white voters of the area served by Seacoast opted to go with the consortium and its higher rates and impersonal service because, in the words of one exit-poll respondent, "I don't want anything to do with those people" in Riviera Beach.[16]

Usually, well-educated and worldly elites such as Henry Ford II in Detroit and the CEOs of Prudential and Mutual Benefit Life Insurance companies in Newark, New Jersey, rise above petty racism and make decisions based on what is best for their corporation, knowing that the welfare of their corporation is directly tied to the welfare of the cities in which they are located. However, in our Type II and III cities (Gary and Riviera Beach), which lack the presence of major corporate headquarters, too often racism and ignorance defeat business decision dynamics and common sense.

Planning and the Black Community in Majority and Minority Environments

The experiences of preparing Gary's comprehensive plan provide valuable lessons for the almost three hundred majority-black incorporated municipalities and Census Designated Places (CDPs). These lessons apply in varying degrees to the enhancement of black neighborhoods and communities all over this nation. The experience of developing the Gary Comprehensive Plan of 1986 showed that in majority-black communities, long-range comprehensive planning must have no longer than a fifteen-year time frame in order for its goals, objectives, and policies to be embraced by resident leaders. With the poverty level among blacks at least three times that for whites, black communities are too beset with the problems of trying to exist from day to day for them to accept the typical twenty- to twenty-five-year time horizon of most comprehensive plans. Other cities have recognized this reality. In the late 1970s, Atlanta under Mayor Maynard Jackson initiated a 15-5-1 process. Long-range planning covered a fifteen-year time period, mid-range development plans were set with a five-year implementation period, and the immediate action decisions on *project* implementation—zone changes CDBG initiation, capital budget formulation—were of course covered by the one-year period. In 1981, Camden, New Jersey, took the same stand in terms of the long-range/mid-range/ immediate action continuum. Looking at the *reality* of mid-range implementation in Camden, Atlanta, and other cities that tried that method, I found that program implementation such as new housing, fire stations, schools, or street widening *never* takes less than five years from project conception to ribbon cutting. Instead, a 7- to 10-year period is required. Therefore, we adopted a 5- to 10-year period for the mid-range plan to be implemented, which is exactly what Meyerson called for in 1956 and Friedmann recommended in 1965 and in later publications.[17]

We found in Gary that, to most residents, the long-range plan had no meaning unless it was tied to more tangible realities shown by mid-range and immediate action plans. We found people listless, inattentive, and even dozing off when we droned on about goals, objectives, and policies "the way Gary was going to be." But when we connected those policies to program objectives such as the new fire station completed in year four of the neighborhood development plan and site selection next year in the immediate action plan, it got people's attention. In 1990, all 461 local governments in Florida were rushing to complete plans mandated by the state's Growth Management Act of 1985. Without new funds from the state to prepare those plans, not only are most communities preparing only the long-range plan elements required by the law but no one is doing mid-range plans concurrently with the long-range plan as we did in Gary. This is unfortunate because if both long-range and mid-range plans were prepared in concert with each other not only would one set become a test of the other but the combination would make for a much higher level of citizen support and, therefore, political support as well.

The problems faced by majority-black/minority communities and those for low-income white enclaves have been studied and restudied over time. These problems include poverty, deteriorating housing and infrastructure, inadequate public schools and recreational facilities, outmigration of the upwardly mobile middle class, and disinvestment by business elites and the accompanying loss of jobs, both primary or export and secondary or import positions.[18] However, a new problem has arisen to challenge these communities: LULUs (Locally Unwanted Land Uses) and NIMBYs (Not in my Back Yard) such as landfills, toxic waste dumps, halfway houses, and correctional facilities are beginning to find their way into lower-income communities as the nation creates more garbage and hazardous wastes and sends more convicted men and women to prisons while, at the same time, the overall environment is becoming more developed and more urbanized, making placement of these unwanted facilities in unpopulated areas more and more difficult. Robert Bullard among others has published several articles on the impact of LULUs and NIMBYs on black communities that have no self-determination at all, are only elements within white city or county governance, or are in towns so small and weak they can be imposed upon by county and state governments.[19] One might think that black-controlled cities, especially larger ones of 50,000 or more people, could successfully resist these LULUs and NIM-BYs. However, no matter how offensive these may be, to cities that are struggling financially, inducements can be made that would be difficult for communities to reject. A regional landfill with dumping charges payable to the city in which it is located can be an attractive inducement despite possible long-term negative health and related environmental consequences. A prison can create thousands of new permanent jobs, but it can also hurt a city by discouraging other potential employers from locating in the city. Even now, Gary is attempting to attract a NIMBY, casino gambling. Although the casinos will be located miles from populated areas, their presence will not add much to a city already stigmatized by its dirty steel mills and a past history of wide-open illegal gambling, after-hours drinking, and prostitution.

The role planners play in the siting of LULUs and NIMBYs are critical as their siting depends on land use, transportation, and environmental quality, all under the purview of planning standards and criteria. In the past, planners have tended to play it "safe," opting to protect middle-income predominantly white neighborhoods at the expense of lower-income predominantly black communities. As noted by Robert D. Bullard,

Zoning, deed restrictions, and other 'protectionist' devices have failed to effectively segregate industrial uses from residential uses in many black and lower income communities. The various social classes with or without land use controls, are unequally able to protect their environmental interests. Rich neighborhoods are able to leverage their economic and political clout into fending off unwanted uses while residents of poor neighborhoods have to put up with all kinds of unwanted neighbors including noxious facilities. Public opposition has been more vocal in middle and upper income groups on the issue of noxious facility citing. The NIMBY syndrome has been the usual reaction in these communities. As affluent communities become more active in opposing a certain facility, the citing effort shifts to a more powerless community as opposition groups call for the facility to be cited "somewhere else." The Somewhere Else, USA often ends up in poor powerless minority communities.[20]

If urban planning is to be relevant to black and other low-income communities, planners must respond to this new danger just as they did in the old days of urban renewal, or "Negro Removal," with new and innovative techniques such as "checkerboarding." Checkerboarding is a staged redevelopment process where first a nonresidential site is selected, cleared, and occupied with new housing, with residents from a designated block having preference for the new housing. Then, when all residents are relocated from the designated block, the block is cleared, new housing is built, and the process is repeated.

Unfortunately, though planning schools are enrolling and graduating minority and women students at a rate comparable to their national population percentage, the coursework does not, as a rule, lend itself to the concept of social justice. From the late 1960s through the late 1970s, planning schools introduced and maintained courses and even concentrations in social policy. As early as the mid-1970s the Nixon administration began to emphasize planning and management systems as a first priority of the HUD 701 program. Coupled with a changing national mood away from equity planning, this forced a shift away from social policy to "hard" skills in quantitative analysis and computer applications in order to better prepare students for the emerging job market. The shift was so pronounced that a 1975 newsletter of the National Association of Planners, a group representing black professional planners, urged creation of continuing education short courses sponsored by the American Institute of Certified Planners to "retrofit black and other planners trained in social policy with quantitative skills for the new job market." The number of planning faculty with specializations in social planning, social policy, minority group communities, planning and women, and planning for multiple publics decreased from 136 in 1979 to only 81 in 1990 according to the *Guide to Graduate Education in Urban and Regional Planning*. With poverty, homelessness, inadequate housing, disappearing jobs, crumbling infrastructures, and continued emphasis on a military buildup, despite the end of the Cold War, we must go back and balance quantitative skills with the *qualitative* skills of sensitivity, insight, openness, and a breadth and depth of the social sciences, especially those involving and relating to the culture of blacks and other North American minority groups.

Planning Strategies for Majority-Black Cities

In a work such as this, the temptation will always be to try to devise some grand strategy to ameliorate the multiple problems of these cities. There is no grand strategy. Every city presents a separate, individual, and unique case. Planners must be sensitive and creative, as well as knowledgeable on issues, resources, and planning/implementation techniques.

In Gary, we found that proximity to the Chicago area job market coupled with a stock of standard, affordable, and relatively attractive housing led to the strategy of marketing Gary as a bedroom community to upwardly mobile working-class families living in Chicago. However, that was a Gary situation. The strategies that are appropriate for Atlanta; Baltimore; Camden, New Jersey; East St. Louis, Illinois; and Riviera Beach, Florida, will have to be conceptualized, tested, enacted, and implemented by planners working in those cities.

If there is an overall approach to a solution for problems besetting all three hundred majority-black cities and urban places in America it is to bring federal and state assistance to the cities back to where it was in the late 1960s and early 1970s in terms of constant dollars. Several proposals have been mentioned in recent years by groups such as the U.S. Conference of Mayors, the National Urban League, and, most recently, the Center for

Community Change. All call for packages of $30 billion to $50 billion per year for five to ten years for housing, infrastructure, education, job training, health care, and social services with most going to urban areas and "places" of 2,500 or more population. The U.S. Conference of Mayors in 1987 called for a shift of $30 billion per year for five years from defense to domestic needs, their "priorities resolution" called for one million new housing units, mass transit improvements, 30,000 new health care workers, and funds for improved social service programs. The National Urban League in January 1990 called for a "freedom budget" of $50 billion per year for five years for urban and rural areas because, with the end of the Cold War, a "peace dividend" would mean new monies available for reprogramming even with the need for deficit reduction. However, that hope was decimated by the $500 billion savings and loan bailout by the end of 1990. The Center for Community Change, a twenty-year-old nonprofit organization out of Washington, D.C., that assists low-income groups, stated that despite the savings and loan bailout and the budget deficit there was a need to address what they called the "third deficit": deferred maintenance on our urban areas and rural places in terms of housing infrastructure, health care, social services, and economic development. They called for $130 billion for housing, infrastructure, and social services. The Center for Community Change proposes that their program, unlike others proposed, would be financed by changes in income tax laws, mainly in terms of increased taxes for the rich who, under the pre-1978 system, would have paid $93 billion more by 1990 than they did.[21] Even though these voices for change were silenced by the December 1989 invasion of Panama, which cost $2 billion, and Operation Desert Storm in 1990 and 1991, which will cost at least $15 billion to U.S. taxpayers when all bills are in, our domestic needs *still* must be addressed. Only by pressing for change will change come, whether it is by lobbying elected officials, electing more sensitive ones, or demonstrating.

The Involvement of State Government

Majority-black cities can move forward if a strong commitment on the part of state government is provided. In Chapter 7, I showed how indifferent attitudes on the part of Indiana state government between 1988 and 1990 hurt Gary's chances to land the third Chicago area airport. However there is at least one example of how strong state support can assist in a city's turnaround.

Camden, New Jersey, located just across the Delaware River from Philadelphia, is very similar to Gary. A prominent center of diversified manufacturing until the 1960s, Camden lost industry and witnessed white flight of residents and businesses during the 1970s and 1980s. But Campbell Soup decided to retain their Fortune 500 headquarters in the city and construct a new office complex on Camden's Delaware River waterfront. Then, in 1989, this city, led by black mayor Aaron Thompson, convinced the state legislature to place the new state aquarium on the waterfront next to the Campbell Soup site. The aquarium built at a cost of $55 million was completed in February 1992, and, by July 1992, over twelve thousand schoolchildren from all over the state had visited the facility. The New Jersey state aquarium has generated plans for the Delaware River Port Authority Headquarters, the South Jersey Performing Arts Center, a hotel and convention center, a waterfront visitors center and shopping complex, and market income housing all adjacent to the aquarium. Camden, which actually had a population increase between 1980 and 1990 (from 84,910 to 87,492), is on its way back, thanks in part to the proactive stance of its state government.

Gary, Northwest Indiana, and the Twenty-First Century

At the 1988 Democratic Party Convention, the Reverend Jesse L. Jackson took to the podium and stated, "Some of us came over on slave ships. Some of us came over on passenger ships. But whatever ship we came here on, we're all in the same boat now." Those same words can be applied to the plight of Gary and the Northwest Indiana Primary Metropolitan Statistical Area, which consists of Lake and Porter counties. Mainly as a result of the loss of over 50,000 industrial jobs between 1975 and 1990,[22] the entire region's population shrank from 643,000 in 1980 to just 604,526 in 1990, a 6 percent decline and 38,000 in overall numbers. Among twenty-three metropolitan areas in the East North Central District (Illinois, Indiana, Michigan, Ohio and Wisconsin), only seven others *lost* population during the decade. Only Peoria and Youngstown had a greater population percentage loss, both 7.3 percent (see table 17).

The three central cities were the big losers. Gary's population dropped by 23 percent, East Chicago by 14 percent, and Hammond by 9 percent. But this was not the city to suburb shift seen nationwide since World War II. This time, almost 40,000 people left the region altogether. For the first time, the region's black population dropped, by up to 9,000. This time, the region's suburbs lost population when natural increase is factored in. There was virtually no change in the total population of Lake County outside of the three central cities. Porter County's "growth" was only 7 percent, and, when natural increase is factored in, this represents virtually no growth at all.

The problems, once restricted to Gary and, to a lesser extent, East

Table 17. Population Change from 1980 to 1990 in the East North Central
Census District

City	Central City			MSA or PMSA[1]		
	1980	1990	% Change	1980	1990	% Change
Illinois						
Chicago	3,005,072	2,783,726	−7.4	6,060,401	6,070,577	0.2
Peoria	124,160	113,504	−8.6	365,864	339,107	−7.3
Rockford	139,712	139,426	−0.2	279,514	283,719	1.5
Springfield	100,033	105,511	5.5	187,770	189,550	1.0
Indiana						
Evansville	130,496	126,272	−3.2	276,253	278,990	1.0
Ft. Wayne	172,391	173,072	0.4	354,156	363,811	2.7
Gary	**151,968**	**116,646**	**−23.2**	**642,733**	**604,526**	**−6.0**
Indianapolis	700,807	741,592	5.8	1,166,575	1,249,822	7.1
South Bend	109,727	105,511	−3.8	241,617	247,052	2.3
Michigan						
Ann Arbor	107,969	109,592	1.5	264,740	282,973	6.9
Detroit	1,203,369	1,027,974	−14.6	4,488,024	4,382,299	−2.4
Flint	159,611	140,761	−11.8	450,449	430,459	−4.4
Grand						
Rapids	181,843	189,126	4.0	601,680	688,399	14.4
Lansing	130,414	127,321	−2.4	419,750	432,669	3.1
Ohio						
Akron	293,092	223,019	−23.9	660,328	657,759	−0.4
Cincinnati	385,410	363,040	−5.5	1,401,471	1,465,049	4.5
Cleveland	573,822	505,614	−11.9	1,898,825	1,831,122	−3.6
Columbus	565,052	632,270	11.9	1,243,827	1,377,419	10.7
Dayton	193,549	182,044	−5.9	942,083	951,280	1.0
Toledo	380,363	332,943	−12.5	616,864	614,128	−0.4
Youngstown	115,510	95,706	−17.1	531,350	492,619	−7.3
Wisconsin						
Madison	170,616	191,262	12.1	323,545	367,085	13.5
Milwaukee	635,298	628,088	−1.1	1,397,020	1,432,149	2.5

Source: U.S. Census, 1980 and 1990.

Note: Cities included are East North Central Census District Metropolitan Areas with central cities
of 100,000 or more populations in 1980.

[1]Data for Chicago, Gary, Detroit, Cincinnati, Akron, Cleveland, and Milwaukee is for the Primary
Metropolitan Statistical Area. All other data is for the Metropolitan Statistical Area.

Chicago and Hammond are now affecting virtually the entire region. For
example, government repossessed homes, once confined to the three central cities, are now to be found throughout the region.[23] The problems of
crime, poverty, physical deterioration, homelessness, and AIDS, which up
to just a few years ago seemed to be limited to central cities, are now

regional in nature for northwest Indiana. What can Gary and northwest Indiana do by the twenty-first century to return the region to the level of functioning now experienced by other metropolises identified in chapter 3?

The critical first step toward that goal is for public and private sector leaders to reach an accommodation and sincerely work toward enhancing mutual interests. In the introduction, I indicated that a common myth perpetuated in the urban and political economy literature of the 1980s was that public and private elites will always find ways to reach an accommodation of mutual interests, and, as Stone and Sanders succinctly put it, "the only difference is how the accommodation is reached." During and after my time in Gary, I found, as evidenced by the case studies presented in this book, there was no effective effort to reach such an accommodation as the parties involved succumbed to jealousy and racism. They both refused to see the other side's point of view and to treat each other as equals. While this bickering has lessened in recent years—first with the overtures made by former Mayor Richard G. Hatcher after 1984 and then with efforts by Gary's present Mayor Thomas V. Barnes since he took office in 1988— much more needs to be done. In the Gary airport case, though the major problem was the infighting between the Hatcher and Barnes boards, total lack of support for the Gary airport on the part of suburban politicians, state government, and business leaders between 1978 and 1988, along with Governor Evan Bayh's less than solid support in 1990, simply gave credence to a statement in the *Indianapolis Star* article of July 28, 1987, which read, "Lastly there is an implication that Gary with its high unemployment and crime rate and its blue collar Rust Belt image doesn't have enough charm to serve as a major link in America's air service network."[24]

This article also quoted Richard Griebel, then head of the Northwest Indiana Forum, as saying, "That same opinion seemed appropriate for Newark, but that hasn't stopped that New Jersey city from using its proximity to New York to develop its airport." This second statement must be the prevailing thought if a true accommodation among Gary's elected officials, those of its suburbs and the state of Indiana, and private sector leaders is to be reached. Because, to an extent, all are now in the same boat.

Finally, the 1990 census shows that six additional Type II cities, all with populations between 50,000 and 100,000, are now majority black. They are Irvington, New Jersey; Mount Vernon, New York; Macon and Albany, Georgia; Pine Bluff, Arkansas; and Monroe, Louisiana. It is hoped that leaders in these cities and others learn from the example of Gary. In the immortal words of Santayana, "Those who cannot remember the past are condemned to repeat it." In the more recent words of Rodney King, "Can't we just get along?"

Notes

Introduction

1. Daniel L. Elazar, *American Federalism, A View from the States* (New York: Thomas and Crowell, 1972) 93-126.

2. Carl Abbott, *Portland: Planning, Politics and Growth in a Twentieth Century City* (Lincoln: Univ. of Nebraska Press, 1983).

3. York: Basil Blackwell, 1988).

4. *Post-Industrial Cities: Politics and Planning in New York, Paris, and London* (Princeton: Princeton Univ. Press, 1988).

5. (Chicago: Univ. of Chicago Press, 1981).

6. (Princeton: Princeton Univ. Press, 1983).

7. Clarence N. Stone and Heywood T. Sanders, eds., (Lawrence: Univ. Press of Kansas, 1987).

8. (New York: Paragon, 1989).

9. (New Brunswick, N.J.: Center for Urban Policy Research, 1986).

10. Susan S. Fainstein et al., *Restructuring the City: The Political Economy of Urban Redevelopment* (New York: Longman, 1986).

11. *Bum Rap on America's Cities: The Real Causes of Urban Decay* (Englewood Cliffs, N.J.: Prentice-Hall, 1980).

12. Paul R. Porter and David C. Sweet, eds., *Rebuilding America's Cities: Roads to Recovery* (New Brunswick, N.J.: Center for Urban Policy Research, 1984).

13. (Washington, D.C., Brookings Institution, 1982).

14. Richard Child Hill, "Crisis in the Motor City: The Politics of Economic Development in Detroit," in Fainstein, *Restructuring the City*.

15. (Philadelphia: Temple Univ. Press, 1987).

16. See, for example, William E. Nelson and Phillip Meranto, *Electing Black Mayors: Political Action in the Black Community* (Columbus: Ohio State Univ. Press, 1977); Huey Perry and Alfred Stokes, "Politics and Power in the Sunbelt Mayor Morial of New Orleans," in Lenneal Henderson, *The New Black Politics: The Search for Political Power* (New York: Longman, 1986); Robert T. Starks and Michael B. Preston, "Harold Washington and the Politics of Reform in Chicago, 1983-1987," in Rufus P. Browning, Dale Rogers Marshall, and David Tabb, eds., *Racial Politics in American*

Cities (New York: Longman, 1989); and Wilbur C. Rich, *Coleman Young and Detroit Politics: From Social Activist to Power Broker* (Detroit: Wayne State Univ. Press, 1989).

17. *Close to Power* (Chicago: Planners Press, 1988).

18. The political agenda of the U.S. District Attorney's Office was not lost on the Washington, D.C. jury who acquitted Marion Berry on all but one charge.

19. "Black Mayors and the Politics of Racial Economic Advancement," in Harlan Hahn and Charles Levine, eds., *Readings in Urban Politics: Past, Present, and Future* (London: Longman, 1984).

20. I choose to define racism as "the notion that because one's own race is superior, the inferior race deserves to be subordinated by any and all possible means."

Chapter 1. The Emergence of the Majority-Black/Black-Run City

1. Fifty thousand is the threshold figure used to define "large" cities. It is used because the U.S. Census Bureau's minimum population for the central city of a MSA is at that level. Also, cities of fifty thousand or more are eligible for direct entitlement monies from federal grant programs such as Community Development.

2. Political patronage was reduced considerably by the Shakman Decree in Chicago and "set asides" for the purpose of affirmative action were all but eliminated by the U.S. Supreme Court decision of *Richmond v. Croson* (1989).

3. In 1990, one of the hottest videos in the Washington, D.C. area was the tape made in secret by the federal government of Marion Barry in a hotel room with his mistress Rashita Moore, a tape made public in Barry's trial.

4. "A Ladder of Citizen Participation," *Journal of the American Institute of Planners* 35, (March 1969): 103-18.

5. For a concise review of black mayors in large cities, see Michael B. Preston, "Big City Black Mayors: Have They Made a Difference?" in Lucius J. Barker, ed., *Black Electoral Politics: National Political Science Review*, vol. 2, (New Brunswick, N.J.: Transaction Publishers, 1990), 129-135. Cities discussed include Atlanta, Washington, D.C., Birmingham, Chicago, Los Angeles, Detroit, and Philadelphia.

6. Bryan Jackson, "Black Political Power in the City of Angels: An Analysis of Mayor Tom Bradley's Electoral Success," in Barker, *Black Electoral Politics*, 169-75.

7. Barker, *Black Electoral Politics*, 138-44, 154-60 and 176-82.

8. "Black Political and Mayoral Leadership in Birmingham and New Orleans," in Barker, *Black Electoral Politics*, 154-60.

9. John J. Harrigan, *Political Change in the Metropolis* (Boston: Little, Brown, 1985), 86-116.

10. Dennis R. Judd, *The Politics of American Cities: Private Power and Public Policy,* (Boston: Little, Brown, 1979), 87-120.

11. Ibid., 112-16.

12. Starks and Preston, "Harold Washington."

13. Interview with Eva Mack and James Poole, May 14, 1990, West Palm Beach, Florida.

Chapter 2. The Evolution of Gary

1. See James Lane, *City of the Century* (Bloomington: Indiana Univ. Press, 1979), for a good overview of Gary's beginning development and history from 1900 to 1975.

2. Statement by E.J. Buffington, president of the Illinois Steel Company, who was responsible for development of the new site, in *Gary Tribune,* November 9, 1907.

3. *Gary Post-Tribune,* November 20, 1939.

4. Grahame R. Taylor, *Satellite Cities* (New York, 1915), 173-76, 229-30. Garden Press

5. Raymond A. Mohl and Neil Betten, "The Future of Industrial City Planning: Gary, Indiana, 1906-1910," *Journal of the American Institute of Planners* 38 (July 1972): 203-13.

6. Taylor, *Satellite Cities,* 173-76.

7. Mohl and Betten, "Future," 212.

8. U.S. Census of Population, 1910 and 1920.

9. Grahame R. Taylor, "Creating the Newest Steel City," Survey 23, No. 1 (April 1909): 24; Mohl and Betten, "Future," 204-12; John Appleton and H.B. Fuller, "Gary, Indiana: The Eighth Wonder of the Industrialized World," *Iron and Steel Industry Age Magazine* 7, 5 (May 1906): 9-13.

10. Ronald D. Cohen and Raymond A. Mohl, *The Paradox of Progressive Education: The Gary Plan and Urban Schooling* (New York: KenniKat, 1979), 11-22, 35-66, and 84-109.

11. *Gary Daily Tribune,* May 13, 1909.

12. *Gary Evening Post,* March 13 and 14, 1920.

13. *Gary Evening Post,* May 11, 1920; report from Bennett and Parsons, April 12, 1920.

14. *Gary Evening Post,* September 20, 1920.

15. Isaac James Quillen, "Industrial City: A History of Gary, Indiana to 1929" (Ph.D. diss., Yale, 1942), 392-93.

16. Robert Catlin, "Hillsborough County Backs Into Comprehensive Planning," in *Planning* (Feb. 1979): 35-42.

17. Quillen, "Industrial City," 394-96.

18. Annual Reports, Building Department of Gary, Indiana, 1923-1930.

19. Annual Reports, Gary Engineering Department, 1925-1929.

20. Edward Greer, *Big Steel: Black Politics and Corporate Power in Gary, Indiana* (New York: Monthly Review Press, 1979), 82.

21. Ibid., 82. Quillen, "Industrial City," 397.

22. Greer, *Big Steel,* 97.

23. Ibid., 98.

24. Ibid., 82-97.

25. U.S. Bureau of the Census, 1960, p. 13, Occupation and Industry Group of Employed.

26. Greer, *Big Steel,* 98.

27. Raymond Vernon, "The Changing Economic Function of the Central City," in James Q. Wilson, *Urban Renewal: The Record and The Controversy,* (Cambridge: M.I.T. Press, 1965), 3-11.

28. Some of these plans were the Minneapolis CBD Plan, 1960; Providence, Rhode Island, Downtown Revitalization, 1959; the Fresno Mall by Victor Gruen and Associates, 1959; the Los Angeles Centropolis Plan, 1964; and Hartford, Connecticut, Downtown Redevelopment Plan, 1961.

29. "Money is Still Flowing in the Steel City," *Chicago Magazine,* August 1980, p. 46.

30. *The Gary, Indiana Renewal Plan for Physical Development,* (Evanston: Tech-Search, Inc., 1964), 52.

31. Greer, *Big Steel,* 148.

32. Ibid., 145.

33. Ibid., 146.

34. Ibid., 98.

35. Gary Redevelopment Commission, *Community Renewal Program* (Mishawaka: Community Planning Associates, 1968); Greer, *Big Steel,* 98.

36. An example of this split between city government and the business community was Mayor George Chacharis, a Greek immigrant, who attempted to make the private Gary-Hobart Water Company a city-owned operation; another was Chacaris's use of the police force to assist steelworkers in the 1959 steel strike. Both actions were strongly resented by the business community. See Lane, *City of the Century,* and James Lane and Ronald D. Cohen, *A Pictorial History of Gary, Indiana* (Bloomington: Indiana Univ. Press, 1983).

37. Alex Poinsett *Black Power, Gary Style: The Making of Richard Hatcher* 80-81.

38. Ibid., 93-94.

39. Ibid., 105. For more details on the general election campaign, see Nelson and Meranto, *Electing Black Mayors,* 270-321.

40. In 1983, Harold Washington, after an intensive voter registration drive in the black community, ran against incumbent mayor Jane Byrne and Richard J. Daley, son of the legendary Chicago mayor, in the Democratic primary. Washington won with 35 percent of the vote as Byrne and Daley split the white vote. After the Chicago machine could not obtain Washington's consent to allow its leaders to choose the new administrators, they openly backed the Republican candidate Bernard Epton, who had won his party's primary with only three thousand votes total compared to 1.5 million who voted in the Democratic party. In the general election Washington was painted as a black power radical incapable of governing. As a result of massive black voter turnout, Washington won the April 1983 general election with 52 percent of the total vote. There was no transition, and, once in office, Washington had to fight against a city council majority of machine-aligned white ethnics. See Starks and Preston, "Harold Washington."

41. See Lane, *"City of the Century,"* 349-56; Poinsett, *Black Power, Gary Style,* 102-46.

42. See Lane, *"City of the Century,"* 345-61, Poinsett, *Black Power, Gary Style* 110-82.

43. *The National Commission on Civil Disorders,* G.P.P., 1968, pp. 70-82.

44. Gary Model Cities Agency, *Third Year Action Plan,* December 1, 1971, pp. III, 51-55. *Model Cities Closeout Evaluation,* July 1, 1975, pp. 92-96.

45. Greer, *Big Steel,* 149.

46. Dr. Alexander S. Williams with Hank Parkinson, *Which Way Gary?: A City at the Crossroads,* (New York Popular Library, 1971).

47. Gary Ashby, "Ten Years of Success—The Holiday Star Theatre and the White Family," *Post-Tribune,* Aug. 11, 1985, p. B 1, 3.

48. Interview with Dr. F.C. Richardson, Chairman of the Board, Methodist Hospitals of Gary, Oct. 17, 1982.

49. "The Negotiated Investment Strategy: A New Way to Co-ordinate Governmental Programs," *The American City,* Sept. 1978.

50. Interview with Taghi Arsharmi, Chief Planner, Gary Department of Planning and Development, April 18, 1985.

51. Interview with Joseph Shives, Deputy Director, Gary Housing Authority, September 30, 1984.

Chapter 3. External Constraints on Planning and Development

1. See J. Paul Freesma, "Black Central of Central Cities: The Hollow Prize," *Journal of the American Institute of Planner,* vol. 35, no. 2 (March 1969): 75-83; William G. Coleman, *Cities, Suburbs and States: Governing and Financing Urban America* (New York: Free Press, 1975); and John Walton and Donald E. Carnes, *Cities in Change: Studies on the Urban Condition,* (Boston: Allyn and Bacon, 1973).

2. William E. Nelson, Jr., "Black Mayoral Leadership: A Twenty Year Perspective," in Barker, 188-95.

3. Interview with Peter Shapiro, Stamford, Connecticut, Department of Economic Development, June 27, 1990.

4. Richard Julius Meister, "A History of Gary, Indiana, 1930-1940," (Ph.D. diss., Notre Dame University, 1967), 113-23.

5. *Post-Tribune,* January 17, 1986, Section B, p. 1.

6. *Post-Tribune,* December 6, 1985, p. 1. In November 1986, this facility was purchased by a developer who plans to subdivide it into industrial condominiums. A maximum of 800 jobs would be created and the wage scale would be much lower than that of the old Budd Company.

7. Indiana State Bureau of Employment Security, *Quarterly Report,* October-December 1986, pp. 3-5.

8. *Post-Tribune,* October 16, 1983.

9. *Post-Tribune,* October 15, 1985, pp. 1, 7.

10. *Post-Tribune,* January 16, 1986, pp. 1, 9.

11. Interview with Gail Pugh Harris, Gary's Planning Director, September 12, 1983. Interview with Attorney Arlene Colvin, Gary's zoning counsel from 1978 to 1984 and planning director since 1984, August 11, 1984.

12. Meister, "History of Gary," 284-89, 330-33.

13. Raymond A. Mohl and Neil Betten, "The Evolution of Racism in an Industrial City, 1906-1940; A Case Study of Gary, Indiana," *Journal of Negro History* 27 (August 1974): 54.

14. Cohen and Mohl, *Paradox of Progressive Education,* 110-14.

15. Ibid., 118-22.

16. Mohl and Betten, "Evolution," 54, 58-62.

17. *Post-Tribune,* August 26, 1984, pp. 1, 8. In this case a black hospital administrator moved into a previously all white neighborhood in Hobart, Indiana, a Gary suburb. The house that he purchased had been vacant, boarded up and an eyesore to the otherwise well-maintained block. The family unboarded the house, painted it, and replanted the lawn. Nearby citizens harassed the family, throwing trash on the lawn and burning their automobile parked in the driveway. The mayor, police chief, and leading clergymen all proclaimed that race was not a motive in these attacks.

Chapter 4. Getting Started

1. See Cohen and Mohl, *Paradox,* 11-12, 35-66, and 84-109. Also see Mohl and Betten, *Steel City,* (New York: Holmes and Meir, 1986), particularly Chapter 3, "Jim Crow in Gary."

2. Vernon Williams, "Gary Woman May Succeed Benjamin," *Post-Tribune,* Section A, p. 1, Sept. 13, 1982.

3. Joseph Conn, "A Profile of the Candidates," *Post-Tribune,* Section A, p. 1, Sept. 16, 1982.

4. Joseph Conn, "Judge OK's Hall Candidacy," *Post-Tribune*, Section A, p. 1 Sept. 28, 1982.

5. Joseph Conn, "Democrats Close Ranks for Hall," *Post-Tribune*, Section A, p. 1, Sept. 28, 1982.

6. Poinsett, *Black Power*, 28.

7. Ibid., 62-70.

8. It is general knowledge in Gary that after the downtown business and institutions left for Merrillville in the mid 1970s, Hatcher repeatedly made public statements urging Gary residents not to shop there but instead to patronize the River Oaks shopping district in Calumet City, Illinois, just across the Indiana line, for items they couldn't buy in town. Gary city employees knew that if they were caught shopping in Merrillville, they fared at best a dressing down by their supervisors and, at worst, termination.

9. Vernon Williams, "Jobless Rate Boosts Hall's Candidacy," *Post-Tribune*, Section A, p. 5, Oct. 16, 1982.

10. Thomas Sherberg, "Democrats Join Hands for Hall," *Post-Tribune*, Section A, p. 1, Oct. 19, 1983.

11. Editorial, "Our Choice for Congress," *Post-Tribune*, Oct. 23, 1982.

12. The Hatcher administration knew that workers employed in programs funded by federal monies could not participate in partisan activity. Therefore, the precinct workers were employees funded only by local dollars.

13. For example, between 1975 and 1985, the city of Lafayette, Indiana, one hundred miles south of Chicago and seventy-five miles south of Gary, added almost eleven hundred new jobs in diversified manufacturing. In 1983, Lafayette had a 3 percent unemployment rate compared to 18 percent for Gary. The city has a low crime rate and is next door to Purdue University.

14. Bernard Roundtree, "Gainer Officials Defend Removing Sign," *Post-Tribune*, Section B, p. 1, Oct. 27, 1982.

15. In 1986, I taught an urban planning studio course at IUN. The class surveyed a Gary neighborhood just south of the campus. The students were for the most part white suburbanites who traveled to school on the interstate and major arterials, never seeing the residential neighborhoods in the interior. As they conducted land use surveys on the interior residential blocks, many would remark, "I never knew Gary was this nice."

16. I had several Gary and suburban police officers in my urban studies courses at IUN. Many of the suburban officers were formerly with the Gary Police Force, and they would constantly remark that they wished they were still in Gary "because there you do real police work." Also, because of low pay, most Gary officers hold second full-time jobs, mainly in security work.

17. The 18-hole golf course is in what is known as South Gleason on the south bank of the Little Calumet River. On the north side of the river there is a waterlogged site that used to be the location of a 9-hole golf course reserved for blacks and known as North Gleason. The South Gleason course was reserved for whites only until the mid-1960s when it was integrated and the black course closed. In the 1940s and 1950s, Joe Louis was a frequent visitor to the North Gleason course, along with black golfers from Chicago who had no public course to play on at home.

18. This phenomena is well described by Wilbur Rich in "The Impact of Public Authorities on Urban Politics: Challenges for Black Politicians and Interest Groups," in *The New Black Politics* (New York: Longman, 1982), 209-20.

19. Of the fifteen cities surveyed in 1983, only Detroit and Gary had black mayors. Harold Washington had just been elected mayor of Chicago when my paper came out.

20. In Indiana, the Township Trustee has a great deal of power. This elected

official controls emergency relief and obtains monies to repair public rights of way. Dozier Allen was able to get federal anti-poverty monies channeled to his office for recreation and youth employment programs due to his friendship with Hatcher.

Chapter 5. The Comprehensive Plan of 1986

1. *Gary Evening Post,* Sept. 20, 1920.
2. Interview with William Staehle, former Gary planning director, Aug. 10, 1990.
3. I know about Staehle's basic fairness firsthand. He was one of my instructors at Illinois Tech, where I did my undergraduate work in planning. I was always the only black in my classes, and Staehle made extraordinary efforts to make certain that I felt comfortable and was graded in an equitable manner.
4. Gary did have considerable vacant land on its western border. The plan called for light industrial use in this area, a recommendation that was opposed by the business community, which favored residential development by small local contracts. The area had considerable residential zoning, and opposition to the plan's recommendations by small businessmen and property owners was one reason that it was never formally adopted by the city council.
5. *The Urban General Plan* (Berkeley: Univ. of California Press, 1964).
6. Melvin M. Webber, "Comprehensive Planning and Social Responsibility: Toward an AIP Consensus on the Profession's Roles and Purposes," *Journal of the American Institute of Planners* 29 (November 1963): 236.
7. Under the Community Development Black Grant Program (which in 1974 combined urban renewal, Model Cities, water and sewer grants, open space grants, and smaller social programs into a special revenue sharing package), all incorporated municipalities of fifty thousand or more population automatically qualified annually as grant recipients and did not have to compete with other political jurisdictions for monies.
8. See Frances Fox Piven and Richard A. Cloward, *Regulating the Poor: The Functions of Public Welfare* (New York: Vintage, 1972); James Wilson, "Citizen Participation in Urban Renewal," *Journal of the American Institute of Planners* 29, no. 3 (1963); and Edmund Burke, "Citizen Participation Strategies," *Journal of the American Planning Association* 34 (Sept. 1968): 287-94.
9. "Building the Middle Range Bridge for Comprehensive Planning," *Journal of the American Institute of Planners* 22, no. 2 (1956) pp. 56-64.
10. For a thorough examination of the planning process, see Frank So and Roth Getzels, *The Practice of Local Government Planning,* chapter 3 (Washington, D.C.: International City Managers Association, 1988); Melville Branch, *Comprehensive City Planning* (Chicago: American Planning Association Press); Arthur Gallion and Simon Eisner, *The Urban Pattern* (New York: Van Nostrand Reinhold, 1988); and Anthony Catanese and James Snyder, *Urban Planning* (New York: McGraw Hill, 1988).
11. It is rare for a freshman to receive a subcommittee chairmanship. Representative Hall was able to qualify because she came to Congress immediately upon election to serve the unexpired position of Adam Benjamin's term. Also, few freshmen sponsor legislation in Congress.
12. Greer, *Big Steel,* 39-40.
13. See June Manning Thomas, "Racial Crisis and the Failure of the Detroit Planning Commission," *Journal of the American Planning Association* 53, no. 2 (Spring 1988): and Rich, *Coleman Young.*
14. The AICP is official accreditation body for the planning profession. One gains

membership only by completing a planning program and passage of an examination after three to seven years of professional-level practice.

15. Rick James, "Hatcher Presents Development Strategies Plan," *Post-Tribune*, Aug. 31, 1985.

16. Only twenty-three of the twenty-six members of the planning committee attended the final meeting. Jack Bloom, the Miller representative who also strongly opposed the National Park Service West Beach access road, did not attend.

17. According to planning standards, a neighborhood shopping center serves about ten to twenty thousand people, and a supermarket is the major tenant. A community-level center serves twenty to forty thousand residents, and the major tenant is a junior department store such as K-Mart or Wal-Mart. See Urban Land Institute, *The Community Builders Handbook*, 2nd ed. (Washington, D.C., 1985), and Joseph De Chiaria and Fred Koppleman, *Urban Planning and Design Criteria* (New York: McGraw Hill, 1981).

18. Quillen, "Industrial City."

19. Mohl and Betten, *Steel City*, Lane and Cohen, *Pictorial History*.

20. "Buppies" stands for black urban professionals, the African-American counterpart to the white, middle-class yuppie group.

21. A "waste-to-energy" facility uses garbage as a fuel, and the resultant steam produces electricity that can be sold to a utility company. The model we used for the plan proposal was a facility recently constructed in San Bernardino, California.

22. *A History of Black Gary, 1906 1967* (New York: Vantage, 1973).

23. Edward Banfield, *The Unheavenly City* (Boston: MIT Press, 1970), and Charles Murray, *Losing Ground* (New York: Basic Books, 1986).

24. Thomas, "Racial Crisis"; Rich, *Coleman Young*; Robert J. Meir, et al. "Strategic Planning and the Pursuit of Reform, Economic Development and Equality," *Journal of the American Planning Association* 52, no. 3 (Autumn 1986): 299-309; Mack Jones, "Black Political Power in Atlanta" in Lucius J. Barker, ed., *Black Electoral Politics: National Political Science Review*, vol. 2 (New Brunswick, N.J.: Transaction Publishers, 1990), 101-18.

25. Catlin, "Hillsborough County."

26. Greer, *Big Steel*.

Chapter 6. Metrolake—Racism or Good Government?

1. See Steven Lawson, *Black Ballots: The Voting Rights Movement in the South Between 1946 and 1965*, (New York: Columbia University Press, 1978). Also see Robert Catlin, "Black Tampa," in Robert Bullard, ed., *Blacks in the New South* (Tuscaloosa: Univ. of Alabama Press, 1989).

2. Twiley W. Barker, Jr., and Lucius J. Barker, "The Courts, Section 5 of the Voting Rights Act, and the Future of Black Politics," in Michael B. Preston, Lenneal J. Henderson, Jr., and Paul Pureav, eds., *The New Black Politics: The Search for Political Power* (New York: Longman, 1982), 55-70.

3. John C. Bollens, and Henry J. Schmandt, *The Metropolis: Its People, Politics and Economic Life*, 4th ed. (New York: Harper and Row 1982), 309-11.

4. Ibid., 320.

5. Interview with George Chacharis, former Gary Indiana mayor, Oct. 20, 1982.

6. Nelson and Meranto, *Electing Black Mayors*, 204-307.

7. Ibid., 307.

8. Ibid., 366.

9. *Post-Tribune,* July 19, 1984.

10. *Post-Tribune,* July 28, 1984.

11. Bollens and Schmandt, *The Metropolis,* 307.

12. One of the better cases to illustrate this point was Chester A. Hartman's attack on the U.S. Housing and Home Finance Agency's Study on relocation by urban renewal agencies. Hartman complained that the study done by the U.S. General Accounting Office was simply an attempt by one federal agency to cover for another; the study should be done by an agency *outside* of government such as a university research institute *not* funded in full or in part, by federal monies. See Chester Hartman, "The Housing of Relocated Families," in James W. Wilson, ed., *Urban Renewal; The Record and the Controversy* (Cambridge: M.I.T. Press, 1972), 356.

13. Earl Harris represented most of the city of East Chicago and the western end of Gary. Senator Mosby and Representatives Charlie Brown and Earline Rogers serve constituencies that are within the boundaries of Gary.

14. By comparison, Gary's assessed value including the U.S. Steel properties was only $240 million, with 150,000 residents requiring services.

15. The three townships proposed for consolidation included North (Hammond, East Chicago, Whiting, Munster and Highland), Calumet (Gary, Griffith and an unincorporated area of Lake County), and Hobart (Hobart and Lake Station). See figure 4 showing the proposed consolidation.

16. This bias was first noted by Charles H. Levine in his book *Racial Conflict and the American Mayor* (New York: Heath, 1974), where he states on page 76 that during Hatcher's first term in office, he did not receive any support from the *Gary Post-Tribune.*

17. Arthur Bromage, *Political Representation in Metropolitan Areas* (Ann Arbor: Univ. of Michigan Press, 1969).

18. Bollens, and Schmandt, (1982), 343-44.

19. Eleanor Ostrum, John Tiebolt, and Daniel Warren, "In Defense of the Polycentric Metropolis," *American Political Science Review* 22 (1962).

20. U.S. Advisory Commission on Intergovernmental Relations, *Alternating Approaches to Governmental Reorganization in Metropolitan Areas* (1964).

21. Lane, *City of the Century.*

22. Nelson, and Meranto, *Electing Black Mayors*; Poinsett, *Black Power*; Greer, *Big Steel.*

23. Mohl and Betten, "Evolution of Racism."

24. Mohl and Betten, "Jim Crow in Gary," in *Steel City; Gary, Indiana, 1906-1950.*

25. *Big Steel,* 24.

26. *Regionalism and Minority Participation* (Washington, D.C.: Joint Center for Political Studies, 1974).

27. For example, Gary's 1,200 person city work force is 75 percent black. In 1986, blacks held three of five division director's positions and eleven of fifteen department head slots. The city's annual budget was $46 million, the sanitary district's was $48 million, and the school corporation's was $18 million. All three are black controlled.

28. U.S. Advisory Commission on Intergovernmental Relations, *Analysis of Special Districts: Their Role in the Metropolis* (1962).

29. U.S. Advisory Commission on Intergovernmental Relations, *The Problems with Special Districts in American Governments* (1963).

30. By 1989, ridership on the Chicago South Shore and South Bend Railroad had risen to 12,000 daily; by 1990, it had increased to 13,000. Source: Northwest Indiana Commuter Transit District.

31. James Owen and York Wilburn, *Governing Metropolitan Indianapolis* (Indianapolis: Bobbs-Merrill, 113, 196-99.

32. (Los Angeles: Univ. of California Press).

33. This literature included Council of State Governments, *State Legislature Program of the Advisory Commission on Intergovernmental Relations* (1961); American Municipal Association and National Association of Counties, *Program of Suggested State Legislation* (1962); W. Brooke Graves, "Volunteer City-County Regional Cooperation" in Gary Miller, ed., *American Intergovernmental Relations: Their Origins and Historical Development* (New York: Scribner, 1964); Gary Miller, *The History and Background of Intergovernmental Agreements* (Cambridge, Mass.: MIT Press, 1981); Gary Miller, "Cities by Contract: The Politics of Municipal Incorporation" in Jack Knott, ed., *Reforming Bureaucracy: The Politics of Institutional Choice* (Englewood Cliffs, N.J.: Prentice-Hall, 1987).

34. Richard Tolmach, "The Chicago South Shore and South Bend: America's Last Interurban Railroad" (unpublished paper, 1982).

35. Robert A. Catlin, "An Analysis of Metrolake: Brief Observation and a Review of the Literature Concerning Metropolitan Consolidation" in Knott, *Reforming Bureaucracy.* (Calumet Regional Archives, Indiana University Northwest, 1986).

36. Barry Saunders, "Metrolake Author Wins Respect, No Converts," *Post-Tribune*, Oct. 17, 1986.

37. By the end of November 1986, Gary's black community had been so well mobilized against Metrolake that Mayor Hatcher was quietly preparing for a march to Indianapolis if Metrolake ever reached the legislature's floor. Neighborhood Conservation had already lined up 500 marchers. If a march had taken place it would have drawn national attention to the issue of wiping out black political gains in cities like Gary through consolidation. There was no need for a march. No consolidation bills were introduced in the legislature's 1987 session. By 1990, no action on Metrolake had been taken.

38. This point was brought out by San Antonio Mayor Henry Cisneros, a Mexican-American, when he spoke at Indiana University Northwest on April 7, 1987. In a Latino Awareness Day Speech, Cisneros proudly exclaimed that Mexican-Americans were "a rich blend of Spanish adventurers and noble Indians."

39. Interview with State Senator Carolyn B. Mosby, Dec. 8, 1987.

40. interview with Richard C. Comer, Deputy Mayor, city of Gary, Feb. 11, 1989.

41. Interview with Dr. Manindra K. Mohapatra, Chairman of the Department of Political Science and the Center for Governmental Studies, Indiana State University, Oct. 12, 1990.

Chapter 7. Changing Pilots During Takeoff

1. Meyerson, "Building the Middle Range Bridge."

2. Interview with Dr. A. William Douglas, Director, Gary Regional Airport, Nov. 16, 1986.

3. See, for example, *National Air Traffic Demands Over the Period of 1960-1985*, Federal Aviation Authority, USGPO, 1958.

4. Gary Municipal Airport Authority District, *Gary Municipal Airport Development Program*, Nov. 1, 1978, pp. 1-23 and Table A.

5. Conversation with Richard G. Hatcher, Mayor of Gary, Nov. 16, 1983.

6. Nancy Winkley, "Hatcher Hosts Reception for Legislators," *Post-Tribune*, Jan. 18, 1985.

7. After returning to Gary from active military duty, Barnes served for twenty-seven years in the U.S. Army reserve, retiring in 1987 with the rank of colonel.

8. Calumet Township includes the city of Gary, towns of Lake Station and Griffith and some incorporated areas of Lake County. Its 1970 population was 225,515, 45 percent of which was black. In 1980, Calumet Township's population declined to only 185,467, 55 percent of which was black.

9. *Post-Tribune*, Feb. 11, 1984.

10. Moody's municipal bond rating service, 1983.

11. *Post-Tribune*, March 10, 1984.

12. Robert Catlin, "The Decline and Fall of Gary," *Planning* (June 1988): 8.

13. James Holley, "Residents Don't Seem to Care," *Gary Info*, p. 1, Jan. 23, 1987.

14. Charles Pierce, "Rockford Residents Shoot Down Airport," *Chicago Tribune*, Part B, p. 1, June 2, 1987.

15. *Post-Tribune*, June 2, 1987.

16. *Post-Tribune*, June 3, 1987.

17. Dan Wheat, "Airport Growth Plan Finds No Happy Landings," *Aurora Beacon-News*, June 4, 1987.

18. Memorandum from Dan G. Haney, Junior Manager to Peat, Marwick and Mitchell Headquarters, May 22, 1987.

19. S.P. Dinnen, "Destination Gary?" *Indianapolis Star*, July 28, 1987, p. 23A.

20. Ibid.

21. The person who reported this to me in an interview on November 16, 1987, is still a Gary city employee and wishes to remain unidentified.

22. Debra Gruszecki, "Gary Has Chance to Land Airport," *Hammond Times*, Oct. 11, 1987, p. A2.

23. Dan Wheat, "Barnes Says No to Regional Airport Control," *Hammond Times*, Oct. 11, 1987, p. A2.

24. Barry Saunders, "Airport Director: Stole Assurances Insulting," *Post-Tribune*, Oct. 13, 1987, p. B1.

25. Ibid.

26. Confidential interview with a Gary city employee, Jan. 12, 1988.

27. Barry Sanders, "Barnes Grounds Airport Board, Names New Board," *Post-Tribune*, Feb. 9, 1988.

28. Interview by author, Nov. 6, 1990.

29. Jim Proctor, "Airport to Seek Gary Feedback," *Post-Tribune*, Jan. 28, 1990.

30. Ibid.

31. At first, the U.S. District Court in Hammond ruled that the old board was illegally removed. Mayor Barnes then appealed to the U.S. Circuit Court, which stayed the District Court's order pending a review. On February 9, 1990, the Circuit Court of Appeals found that the issue was a state matter. Three of the four old board members' terms had expired since the action was filed, and the court gave the lone remaining old board member standing to sue in a state court.

32. *Chicago Wall*, a *Sun Times* publication, 1985, pp. 18-20, 33, 34.

33. Interview with Taghi Arsharmi, Dec. 11, 1990.

34. Jim Proctor, "Airport Needs Greater Than Anticipated," *Post-Tribune*, Jan. 26, 1990.

35. Jim Proctor, "Planners Weigh Airport's Cost," *Post-Tribune*, Jan. 23, 1990.

36. Jim Ashley, "Bayh Backs Gary Airport," *Post-Tribune*, May 24, 1990, pg. A1.

37. Nancy Winkley, "Luerssen is Chairman," *Post-Tribune*, Aug. 28, 1990.

38. "Bistate Trio Named: Daley Picks His Brother," *Post-Tribune*, Oct. 3, 1990.

39. Carmen Woodson, "Gary Airport $2.5 Million Richer," *Post-Tribune*, Sept. 27, 1990.

40. Mike Sante, "Tax a Lift to Chicago Airport," *Post-Tribune*, Oct. 27, 1990.

41. Jim Proctor, "Airport Sites Draw Objections," *Post-Tribune*, Jan. 20, 1990.

42. "Lake Calumet Airport Foes Voice Objections in Hearings," *Post-Tribune*, Sept. 19, 1990.

43. "Third Airport Doesn't Fly With the Voters In Illinois," *Post-Tribune*, Nov. 8, 1990.

44. Jim Proctor, "Consulting Firm Recommends Grant Application," *Post-Tribune*, Feb. 26, 1989, p. B1.

45. *Jet Magazine*, Nov. 1, 1989, p. 18.

46. Nancy Winkley, "Campaign an Attention Getter," *Post-Tribune*, Oct. 29, 1990.

47. Rich James, "Hatcher Rips Gary Casino Bill," *Post-Tribune*, Mar. 30, 1991.

48. Nancy Winkler, "Dobis: Casino Bill is Dead," *Post-Tribune*, Apr. 28, 1991.

49. Rick Pearson and Gary Washburn, "Key Airport Vote Opens Gift Giving Season," *Chicago Tribune*, Feb. 25, 1992, Section 1, p. 1.

50. "Lake Calumet—Barely," *Post-Tribune*, Feb. 25, 1992.

51. Ibid.

52. Ibid.

53. Ibid.

54. "Straight Answers Needed on Airport," *Post-Tribune*, Nov. 25, 1990.

55. Adolph Reed, Jr., "A Critique of New-Progressivism in Theorizing about Local Development Policy: A Case From Atlanta," in Stone and Sanders, *Politics of Urban Development*, 199-215.

Chapter 8. Implications of the Gary Experience

1. 1980 U.S. Census: Summary Characteristics of the Black Population for States and Selected Counties and Places Issued Jan. 1987.

2. For example, in HUD's Community Development Block Grant program, entitlement jurisdiction is given those cities with 50,000 or more population in 1970 or urban counties of 250,000 or more. Entitlement cities and counties automatically receive money from CDBG for program activities such as land acquisition, infrastructure provision, and economic development. All other cities/urban counties must compete for discretionary monies allocated by the states.

3. Camden, New Jersey is the headquarters for Campbell Soup Company, but for some reason that corporation has not taken the type of leadership in rebuilding Camden's downtown as, for example, Prudential Insurance did in Newark, New Jersey. Also, Whirlpool is still at least nominally headquartered in Benton Harbor, Michigan, although that city has been almost totally deserted by business and upscale residents. Interview with Camden city administrators and Alexandre Little, former city manager of Benton Harbor.

4. Compton is actually an extension of the Watts ghetto of Los Angeles, Inglewood is an extension of Los Angeles' middle class "Westside" ghetto, and East Orange is an extension of the Newark black community. All three were initially white working-class suburbs with upwardly mobile black middle-class types entering in the 1960s and 1970s. Present residents are for the most part lower-middle to middle-class families with a majority being homeowners.

5. June Manning Thomas, "Industrial Decline and the City of Detroit," *Journal of the American Planning Association* 52, no. 2 (June 1990).

6. Rich, *Coleman Young.*

7. Interview with Reverend Timothy Evans, Pastor of St. John's Baptist Church, Oct. 11, 1986.

8. Nelson and Meranto, *Electing Black Mayors.*

9. See Greer, *Big Steel,* 38-42: Nelson and Meranto, *Electing Black Mayors,* 367; and Levine, *Racial Conflict,* 76.

10. C. Sumner Stone, *Black Power in America* (New York: Bobbs-Merrill, 1968), 213-18.

11. Jan Wheat, "Barnes Says No to Regional Airport Control," *Post-Tribune,* Oct. 11, 1987.

12. Rich, *Coleman Young,* 206.

13. Eisinger, "Black Mayors."

14. *Guide to Graduate Education in Urban and Regional Planning* Fourth Edition, 1981, Fifth Edition, 1984, and Seventh Edition, 1990 (American Planning Association).

15. There was already a hospital in Crown Point and another in Dyer capable of serving the suburban Lake County population. The movement of Methodist to Merrillville and St. Mary's to Hobart was opposed by the local health planning agency because it would create duplication of facilities and a bed surplus. Interview with Dr. F.C. Richardson, board president, Methodist Hospital, Sept. 14, 1982. In 1980, the Gary-Hammond-East Chicago SMSA (Lake and Porter Counties) had a total of 632,000 residents; preliminary 1990 U.S. Census figures show a drop to only 620,000.

16. Interview with Dr. Otelia DuBose, city manager of Riviera Beach, Oct. 17, 1988.

17. See Meyerson, "Building the Middle Range Bridge," and John Friedman, "A Response to Altschuler," *Journal of the American Institute of Planners* (July 1965).

18. For example, in 1989, General Motors announced the closing of 19 plants in the United States with a loss of 30,000 jobs. Economists predicted that the loss of these 30,000 primary jobs would result in at least a 3-to-1 multiplier or the loss of an additional 90,000 jobs minimum in support activities such as retail trade, local finance, construction, real estate, and business and professional services.

19. See Robert D. Bullard and Beverly Hendrix Wright, "Environmentalism and the Politics of Equality: Emergent Trends in the Black Community," *Mid American Review of Sociology* 12, no. 2, (1987): 21-38; Robert D. Bullard, "Solid Wastes and the Black Houston Community," *Sociological Inquiry* 53, nos. 2/3 (Spring 1983); Robert D. Bullard and Beverly Hendrix Wright, "Blacks and the Environment," *Humboldt Journal of Social Relations* 14, nos. 1/2 (Summer 1986):165-84; and Robert Bullard, *Dumping in Dixie: Race, Class and Environmental Quality* (Boulder, Colo.: Westview, 1990).

20. Robert D. Bullard, "Environmental Blackmail in Minority Communities" Unpublished Paper presented Jan. 1990, Mid South Sociological Association meeting, pp. 7-8.

21. Center for Community Change, *America's Third Deficit: Too Little Investment in People and Infrastructures* (Washington, D.C., 1990).

22. Joseph Conn, "Census: Latin Growth Continues," *Post-Tribune,* Mar. 31, 1991.

23. For example, the Sunday, May 1991 edition of the *Post-Tribune* showed that, of HUD-VA homes advertised, *52* were in Gary, *19* in East Chicago or Hammond, and *14* in the suburbs of Lake and Porter counties. Another example of suburban decline in Northwest Indiana was the closing of Ditka's restaurant in Merrillville. Mike Ditka opened this restaurant in 1987 as part of the afterglow of the Chicago Bears 1986 Super Bowl championship. Its opening signaled to many the economic resurgence of south Lake County. However, because of little patronage, the restaurant filed for bankruptcy protection in 1990 and on May 18, 1991, it closed altogether.

24. S.P. Dineen, "Destination Gary?" *Indianapolis Star,* July 28, 1987, p. 23A.

Index

City of the Century (Lane), 44, 127
civil rights movement, 8, 23, 145
Civitan Club, 106
Cleveland, Ohio, 9, 13, 101
Cline Avenue Connector, 150, 151
Coates, Dan, 177, 181, 187, 190
cockroaches, 73
Cohen, Ronald, 44
College Park, Georgia, 206
Colvin, Arlene, 86, 99, 106, 176
Comer, Richard, 145, 184
Comer, Zeke, 99, 102
Committee of 100, 69
Community Development Block Grant
   Program, 28, 29, 30, 72, 152, 193
Community Redevelopment Program, 28
Comprehensive Employment and Training
   Administration (CETA), 56
Compton, James, 180
Compton, California, 10, 15, 195, 197
Congressional Black Caucus, 46
Congress of Industrial Organization (CIO),
   40
Conn, Joseph, 123
consolidation: and racial discrimination,
   110, 111, 122, 136-39, 141-43; for
   efficiency, 116, 136; vs.
   intergovernmental cooperation, 126-27,
   132, 137; literature on, 126-27, 132; and
   urban/regional planning, 143-44. *See
   also* Metrolake consolidation plan
Cooke, T., Jr., 15
Coote, Phillip, 157, 158, 159, 161
Cornell University School of Architecture,
   68
council manager governments, 13, 14, 16,
   193
Crawford, Jack, 82
Crowell, Charlene, 52, 134
Crown Point, Indiana, 65, 81, 94, 103, 119,
   122, 133, 136, 143, 203, 228 n 15
Crump, Thomas, 49, 63-64, 115, 141,
   162-63, 166
Cvitkovich, George W., 122

Dade County, Florida, 191
Daley, Richard J., 14, 197
Daley, Richard M., 148, 149, 178-81, 182,
   185, 186-87, 188, 190, 202, 219 n 40
Daley, William M., 180
Dallas, Texas, 111
Darden, Joe, 5
Davis, Danny K., 185
Davis, Isaac, 112

Dayton, Ohio, 28, 36, 37, 64
DeAngeles, Aldo, 185
Decatur, Georgia, 206
Delaware River Port Authority
   Headquarters, 213
Democratic National Committee, 150-51
Denver, Colorado, 5
Detroit, Michigan: black political
   leadership in, 2, 15, 32, 64, 84, 107;
   economic decline of, 5; black-majority
   population in, 10, 144, 193; retail sales
   in, 21; economy of, 32, 101, 197-98; tax
   rate in, 35; crime in, 53, 54
*Development Strategies for Gary's
   Neighborhoods* (draft), 85-86
Direct Air, 181
Ditka, Mike, 229 n 23
Dobis, Anthony, Jr., 112, 116
Dobis, Chester A., 114, 115-17, 121,
   123-24, 138, 141, 142, 143, 184
Douglas, Dr. A. William, 151, 156, 159,
   160-61, 169, 171, 175-77, 186
Douglass Aircraft, 149, 159
Downs, Anthony, 5
Downtown East (or Emerson)
   neighborhood (Gary), 90, 95-96
Downtown West neighborhood (Gary), 90,
   95-96, 101
Dunes Twin Cinema, 76
Durham, North Carolina, 127
Dyer, Indiana, 119, 228 n 15
Dzacky, Mary A., 112

East Chicago, Indiana, 39, 47, 51, 53, 70,
   71, 82, 83, 94, 102, 118, 119, 122, 123,
   128, 129, 130, 134, 136, 142, 144, 182,
   213
East Cleveland, Ohio, 197
East Gary, Indiana, 2, 40, 52
East Los Angeles, California, 111
East Orange, New Jersey, 10, 15, 195, 197
East Point, Georgia, 206
East St. Louis, Illinois, 6, 10, 15, 211
Economic Development Administration
   (EDA), 28, 29, 152
Edgar, Jim, 181
Eisenger, Peter, 7, 203-4
Eli Lilly and Company, 63
Elks Temple, 20
Emerson neighborhood (Gary). *See*
   Downtown East neighborhood (Gary)
enterprise zones, 3, 84, 91
entrepreneurship, 7
Epton, Bernard, 219 n 40

ethnic populations (white), 2, 13, 20, 23, 25, 44, 94, 95, 96-97, 103, 112
Eudora, Arkansas, 197
Evans, Timothy, 178
Evanseck, Marian, 112
Evanston, Illinois, 15

Fainstein, Susan, 5
Farag, Robert, 84, 156
Federal Aviation Administration (FAA), 39, 130, 148, 154, 156, 169, 172, 177, 179, 181, 182, 186
federal government: and aid to Gary, 2, 26, 27, 28-31, 46, 55, 64, 72, 77, 78, 80, 93, 102, 198; support for cities from, 4, 5, 8, 22, 26, 217 n 1.1; aid to Gary airport from, 39-40, 148, 150, 151, 152-54, 171, 181, 182
Ferree, Thurman, 122
Fifer, Jerome, 105
Fifth Avenue Houses (Gary), 28, 31
Fithian, Floyd, 50
Flint, Michigan, 15, 37, 64
Florida Growth Management Act of 1985, 209
Flossmoor, Illinois, 79, 149
Ford, Gerald, 198
Ford, Henry, II, 202, 208
Ft. Lauderdale, Florida, 54
Ft. Wayne, Indiana, 36, 60
Fox, Jeanne, 127
Fresno, California, 22
Friedmann, John, 209
Froebel High School, 95
Frontier's International, 106
Frost Belt, 4, 5
Fulton County, Georgia, 144

Gainer Bank, 2, 40, 54, 62, 73, 124, 165
Gainesville, Florida, 54, 105
Gainesville, Florida, Comprehensive Plan, 105
Galloway, Gary, 116
Gannett Newspapers, 40
Gantt, H., 15
Gardeau, Ortomease G., 112
Garden Grove, California, 191
Gardner, Richard, 157
Gary, Elbert, 17, 20
Gary, Indiana: economic decline of, 1-2, 22, 25, 33-34, 53; federal aid to, 2, 26, 27, 28-31, 46, 55, 64, 72, 77, 78, 80, 93, 102, 150, 198; housing in, 2, 17-20, 22, 23, 25, 26, 27, 30, 31, 38, 54, 57,

61, 63, 64, 76, 90, 94-95, 96, 97, 98, 101, 102, 108, 113-14, 214; positive attributes of, 2; black population of, 10, 20, 21, 23, 25, 32, 38-41, 70, 82, 83, 95, 96, 112, 127-28, 144, 182, 198-99; strong mayor government of, 14, 16, 75, 187; black political leadership of, 15, 112; land-use planning in, 17, 20, 21, 69, 92, 102; city planning in, 17-20, 67-72, 93; founding of, 17-20, 93; construction in, 17-21, 25-26, 27-31; school system of, 20, 35, 38, 45, 55, 74, 87, 91, 102, 107; state convention center in, 21, 28; suburbanization of, 21; tax rates in, 21, 35, 58, 76, 78-79, 115, 122, 133; retail sales in, 21-22, 25, 27, 36, 39, 68, 207; urban renewal in, 22, 25, 26, 54, 72, 102; conflict between local government and business elite in, 23, 25, 26-27, 62, 68; Jewish population of, 23, 45, 94; senior citizen housing in, 30, 63; transportation systems in, 30, 34, 42, 53, 91, 108, 118, 126, 129-30; unemployment in, 31, 34, 47, 49, 50, 53, 54, 65, 76, 90-91, 162; regional economy of, 33-34, 35-36; judicial system of, 35; academic infrastructures of, 36-38; tourism in, 40; police department of, 41, 42, 49, 55, 58, 63, 91, 103, 128, 164; fire department of, 42, 58, 91, 103, 133; books about, 44; infrastructures of, 49, 53, 55-56, 69, 76, 115, 118; public services in, 53, 55-56, 57, 58-59, 74; crime in, 53-54, 58, 73, 106, 113, 115, 164; appearance of entrances to, 54-55, 57, 62; private-sector investment in, 57, 61; public-private partnership fostered in, 57, 62-63, 65, 215; real estate loans in, 57, 61; refurbishment of business districts in, 57, 61-62, 76, 104; zoning in, 67, 68, 69; enterprise zone in, 84, 91; population projections for, 87-88, 91-92, 104, 182, 213, 214; neighborhood populations of, 89-90; as bedroom community for Chicago, 92-93, 98, 101, 108-9, 211; Hispanic population of, 96, 127, 128, 142; landfill site in, 97, 202; waste-to-energy facility for, 97, 103; air pollution in, 98, 108; proposed marina in, 102, 103, 147, 154, 173, 183, 202; consolidation in, 111, 118-46 passim; deannexation in, 111, 113, 141; library system in, 118, 129, 130; future of,

www.ingramcontent.com/pod-product-compliance
Lightning Source LLC
Chambersburg PA
CBHW030917150426
42812CB00045B/168

* 9 7 8 0 8 1 3 1 1 7 9 8 0 *